RICHARD A. ALIANO

# American Defense Policy
## *from*
# Eisenhower to Kennedy

*The Politics of Changing
Military Requirements, 1957-1961*

Ohio University Press: Athens, Ohio

THIS BOOK IS DEDICATED TO THE
DUKE AND DUCHESS

Their sacrifices for their sons
will be recorded here

# PREFACE

REVIEWING THIS STUDY FOR THE LAST TIME AS IT is readied for publication, I am reminded of Robert Burns' wise counsel concerning the best laid schemes of mice and men. Students of the political process are doubtlessly guilty of grasping too arrogantly at an understanding of the present through a heightened awareness of the recent past. Yet more importantly, perhaps, the political figures which they study are even more culpable of a haughty disdain for the lessons of history. Looking back upon the events of the last decade and a half, I cannot help but be struck by the unforeseen consequences of the intersection of men's ambitions as well as their hopes and dreams. John Kennedy's well-intended variation on the traditional American theme of making the world over in the benevolent image of the United States helped bring us the tragedy of Vietnam. The stubborn ego of Lyndon Johnson merely served to prolong that agony and precipitate a crisis of national identity. And then there is the strange case of Richard Nixon and the long quest for a unique place in history which, ironically, turned out to be quite different from the one he had envisioned. In 1960, all three struggled for the mantle of democratic leadership soon to be relinquished by Dwight Eisenhower. Eventually, each succeeded. And yet each failed.

Now other figures treated in this study have assumed national prominence. Nelson Rockefeller, who tenaciously coveted the Presidency, has finally settled for second place. His protege, Henry Kissinger, has become this country's most famous Secretary of State. And, finally, we find a rather minor actor, Gerald Ford, catapulted to the pinnacle of power.

Lest I leave the reader with a sense of undiluted pessimism, allow the author to add the following in way of introduction to this book. The United States may indeed be a troubled land plagued by both a spiralling inflation and a sense of rootlessness largely stemming from over-extension abroad and over-commitment to the efficacy of military power. And yet it was the most prosaic individual in our case study who proved to be the most prophetic concerning the consequences of abandoning prudent moderation in the art of government. Dwight Eisenhower, too, is gone. But he was the last of our Chief Executives to leave the political scene due to natural causes. Perhaps we have much to gain by taking another look at his Presidency. It is hoped that this work will contribute to that re-examination. Ultimately, as Francis Bacon wrote, "the mold of man's fortune is in his own hands."

I am indebted to a number of colleagues for their kind and patient comments on the several drafts of this manuscript. I must single out James R. O'Neill of Queens College of the City University of New York. The stimulating give-and-take which I experienced in his company over many a cup of coffee proved invaluable in crystallizing my thoughts and insights. Special gratitude, indeed, must be reserved for two scholars who have proven to be not only valued friends and distinguished colleagues, but above all else teachers—in the finest sense that the term is employed in the profession. It is extremely difficult to express one's gratitude to a man who demonstrated such early and unswerving faith in an untried graduate student. I hope this book will serve as partial vindication for the selfless devotion to my career on the part of Professor Harry J. Psomiades of Queens College. I find myself in an equal predicament in attempting to repay Professor Ronald M. Schneider, also of Queens College, for his aid in the preparation of this study. Without his continuous encouragement and benevolent oversight this book would not be going to press. To Elizabeth Martindale of Melbourne, Australia, who helped me through the most difficult chapter, there is little I can add here to what I have already said to her in the past. And, finally, I must thank the City University of New York for having given me the opportunity for both undergraduate and doctoral study. Despite all this assistance, of course, I assume full responsibility for all the errors, omissions, and faulty insights which may be found in this book.

R. A. A.
New York City

# TABLE OF CONTENTS

# 1

## INTRODUCTION

### I

IN OCTOBER OF 1957, TWO MONTHS AFTER ITS AN-
nouncement of the successful testing of the first intercontinental ballistic missile (ICBM), the Soviet Union successfully
launched the world's first artificial earth satellite. The near-hysteria which followed Sputnik among the nation's foreign policy
elite (outside the high counsels of the Eisenhower administration) manifested itself chiefly in the so-called "missile gap" controversy which served, in reality, as the focal point for a general
debate over the adequacy of American defense policy during the
Eisenhower-Dulles years.

This study will focus on the domestic forces behind the dramatic shift in American defense establishment policy which occurred during the transition years from the second Eisenhower
to the Kennedy administrations. Momentous decisions made
during that period (involving both strategic weapons deployment
and conventional war capabilities) had great influence on the
course of American security policy during the decade of the sixties. This fundamental shift in United States defense policy (that
is, from a strategy of "massive retaliation" to "flexible response"
and from strategic "sufficiency" to strategic "superiority"[1]) had
two ramifications. Firstly, it provided the Kennedy and Johnson

administrations with the means and rationale for massive intervention in Southeast Asia which the administration of Dwight Eisenhower had lacked. Secondly, it created a missile-gap-in-reverse (that is, a three to one American advantage over the Soviets by the Cuban missile crisis of 1962[2]) which provided the incentive for the vast Soviet effort of the late sixties to attain a position of parity.

## II

From the genesis of the Soviet-American struggle for world power following the Second World War until at least the middle of the last decade, American policy makers (whether the "moralists" of the John Foster Dulles type or the "pragmatists" of the John F. Kennedy variety) have approached what was essentially a traditional great power rivalry as a zero-sum game. From this perspective, the various confrontations of Soviet and American power and interests were transformed into an ideological crusade between a mythical monolithic Communist bloc emanating from the Kremlin and an equally mythical "free world" under the aegis of a benevolent American imperium. Thus, "any inroads Communism made anywhere were tantamount to an expansion of Soviet power hostile to the United States."[3] Yet, though this psychology was equally characteristic of both the Eisenhower and Kennedy administrations, it was only during the latter (as will be demonstrated in succeeding chapters) that American defense policy so shifted as to supply decision makers with readily available means for large-scale intervention in Southeast Asia "to stem the tide of Communism." Reflecting this rigid conception of an American role both ubiquitous and limitless, President Lyndon Johnson would declare (concerning Vietnam) in 1965: "To withdraw from one battlefield means only to prepare for the next. We must say in Southeast Asia—as we did in Europe—in the words of the Bible: 'hitherto shalt thou come, but no further.' "[4]

Therefore, the Kennedy administration, having buttressed itself with both the strategic and conventional capabilities which its predecessor had lacked, "transformed a policy of 'limited-risk gamble' [in Vietnam], which it inherited, into a 'broad commitment' that left President Johnson with a choice between more war and withdrawal."⁵ This is not to suggest that there is a necessary fatalism concerning the relationship between the means available to foreign policy makers and the ends to which they are eventually directed. Yet while defense policy may not *determine* the course of foreign policy, there can be little doubt that newly-acquired policy tools exert a powerful pressure for their utilization. As Reinhold Niebuhr cautioned nearly three decades ago, "it is the business of military strategists to prepare for all eventualities, and it is the fatal error of such strategists to create eventualities for which they must prepare."⁶ And as one recent observer has suggested, "some of the more ambitious Kennedy-McNamara foreign policy objectives may have derived from increased strategic capabilities as much as they dictated a need for those capabilities."⁷

Therefore, one need not embrace a *Weltanschauung* of technological determinism to note, for example, that the lack of American preparedness for limited war exerted a strong (if not decisive) pressure on President Kennedy not to intervene in Laos in March of 1961 and that, when his successor decided on such a course of action regarding Vietnam some four years later, the nearly 100 per cent increase in conventional war strength which had taken place in the interlude probably provided the opposite incentive.⁸ Thus, "when President Johnson decided to send large numbers of United States troops to South Vietnam, the forces were available and equipped."⁹ A careful comparison of the build-up of limited war forces (and the underlying assumptions of such a strategy) during the Kennedy years with the actual decisions on their commitment to the struggle raging in Indochina during the Johnson administration indicates much more than just a casual or coincidental relationship.¹⁰

## III

Defense policy is ultimately, at least in outward appearances, an almost reflexive response to a foreign threat—whether real or perceived. Indeed, given the anarchical (or decentralized) nature of the international system, the environment in which states are compelled to interact virtually ensures what John Herz has termed a "security dilemma"[11] and the never-ending quest for and fixation on self-preservation in a perpetually hostile world. In such an environment, adversaries, preoccupied as they are with their own safety and security, are bound to view the physical capabilities of one another (even if such capabilities were originally devised for purely defensive purposes) as an indication of hostile or aggressive intentions. Threat perceptions are, therefore, mutually reinforcing and, in fact, are an inevitable ramification of the nature of international politics. Security threats will be perceived whether or not there are objective grounds for such a determination.[12]

The existence of several states, all experiencing a sense of insecurity vis-a-vis one another, brings about what Kenneth Boulding has termed "reaction processes," what Morton Kaplan calls a "coupling" of domestic systems, what James N. Rosenau refers to as "reactive linkage," and what former Special Assistant to the President for National Security Affairs McGeorge Bundy has designated simply as "interlocking behavior."[13] Simply put, the phenomenon concerns the process whereby the decisions of one state tend to elicit a response by another state; or, put differently, it represents the situation where the outputs of one political system serve as inputs for another political system. According to this view, the spiralling arms race between the Soviet Union and its American rival is largely the result of the ambiguity of one actor's actions as perceived by the reacting party. The uncertainty of the nature of the threat posed (of one's adversary's intentions and capabilities) tends to bring about an overreaction geared to the worst possible contingencies of imperfect intelligence. This reaction, in turn, calls forth a response by the opponent and so on, until this mutually reinforcing behavior (anchored in a bed of suspicion and uncertainty) assumes runaway proportions.[14]

Regarding the analysis of alternative weapons systems, Thomas Schelling has written,

One of the many sources of uncertainty is the enemy himself; we do not know as much as we would like to know about how

4

he would perform in a war, how good his technology is, how rapid his research and development are progressing . . . and so forth. Among the uncertainties about the enemy there are some that are particularly intriguing because they involve the *decisions* that he is going to make. They involve what *he* knows or guesses about what *we* can do and about the decisions that *we* are going to make. There are, in other words, certain decisions that we and the enemy make in which we are trying to outguess each other and to avoid being outguessed, and trying to adapt to the decisions and choices that each of us is going to be led to.[15]

Similarly, elsewhere, Schelling notes that,

When the Secretary of Defense makes an announcement about the total number of missiles or submarines or long-range bombers this country plans to have on successive dates in the future, he is providing a guideline for the Soviet forces planning at the same time. . . .

Implicitly, then, if not explicitly, each of us in his own program must influence the other in some fashion.[16]

It should be apparent by this point, from our discussion thus far, that a simple "action-reaction syndrome" explanation would identify the build-up of United States strategic forces (that is, Minuteman ICBM's and Polaris Submarine Launched Ballistic Missiles—SLBM's) under the Kennedy administration as a "necessary" (given subjective reality) if "unnecessary" (given objective reality) result of the atmosphere of uncertainty concerning Russian intentions and capabilities following their Sputnik coup of late 1957. In fact, former Secretary of Defense Robert S. McNamara, at the end of his long tenure in office, justified the vast build-up of the early sixties in precisely those terms:

In 1961 when I became Secretary of Defense, the Soviet Union had a very small operational arsenal of intercontinental missiles. However, it did possess the technological and industrial *capacity* to enlarge that arsenal very substantially over the succeeding several years. We had *no evidence* that the Soviets

5

did plan, in fact, fully to use that capacity. But . . . a strategic planner must be conservative in his calculations; that is, *he must prepare for the worst possible case* and not be content to hope and prepare for the most probable.

Since we *could not be certain of Soviet intentions,* since we could not be sure that they would not undertake a massive build-up, we had to insure against such an eventuality by undertaking a major build-up of our own.

. . . Thus, in the course of hedging against what was then only a theoretically possible Soviet build-up, we took decisions which have resulted in our current superiority. . . . But the blunt fact remains that if *we had had more accurate information* about planned Soviet strategic forces, we simply would *not* have needed to build as large a nuclear arsenal as we have today.

. . .

Whatever their intentions or our intentions, actions—or even realistically potential actions—on either side relating to the build-up of nuclear forces *necessarily* trigger reactions on the other side. It is precisely this action-reaction phenomenon that fuels an arms race.[17]

Similarly, the subsequent Soviet effort of the *late* sixties may be viewed as the mere reaction to the initial American advantage caused by its strategic build-up of the *early* sixties (which, in turn, was the result of misperception itself).[18] As William C. Foster, former Deputy Secretary of Defense under President Eisenhower and Director of the U. S. Arms Control Agency under the two succeeding administrations, recalls:

In 1961, the Soviets had a small number of ICBM's. We in the United States did not know whether they would deploy a greater number. We undertook a very sizable build-up of Minuteman and Polaris forces. We thus ended up with a considerably larger arsenal than we actually required. But then the Soviets also began an extensive deployment—*probably in response to our efforts*—and so they have been catching up in ICBM's, and have begun to build-up their forces of Polaris-type missile submarines.[19]

*Introduction*

Though much of the uncertainty in defense planning stems from the highly sophisticated nature of the technology which it involves, and though it would therefore seem more attractive for policy makers to gauge an opponent's capabilities (which are more susceptible to intelligence analysis) rather than his intentions,[20] the simplistic "action-reaction syndrome" analysis is inadequate. It is inadequate because it assumes an automaticity of response which is overly deterministic. To embrace the "action-reaction" explanation would be to embrace what we had previously avoided in regard to conventional war capabilities—namely, technological determinism.

To be sure, this does not gainsay the fact that weapons technology does tend to generate its own imperatives. Yet though it is obviously the case that the two superpowers affect one another's defense planning, an apparent threat in no way fatalistically determines the exact degree of renewed emphasis on military allocations. The entire second Eisenhower administration was marked by vigorous debate over America's relative defense posture and the emerging Soviet missile threat. It was heralded in the halls and committee-rooms of the Congress, in the corridors of the Pentagon, in the debates and oratory of the Presidential election campaign of 1960, and in the nation's newspaper editorials and syndicated columns, that the United States was soon to be relegated to the status of a second-rate military power. And yet Dwight Eisenhower, himself a General of the Army, stood firm in the face of incessant demands for greater defense expenditures both for general and limited war capabilities. Indeed, he actually sought to reduce the military's share of the federal budget even after the near-hysteria following Sputnik and in the wake of the alarming revelations of both the official Gaither Committee Report and the independent Rockefeller Brothers Fund findings. It was during the last Eisenhower years that the Soviet missile threat seemed most ambiguous, but at the same time most ominous. And still the United States did not embark on a major build-up in either its strategic or conventional forces. Despite continuous Congressional pressure (and actual funding) to maintain the Army at a manpower level of 900,000 and the Marine Corps at

200,000, President Eisenhower simply refused to spend appropriated funds and actually cut both services to a post-Korean war low of 870,000 and 175,000, respectively. And despite incessant clamoring by the Congress, the press, the services, and academia for a substantial increase in the strategic missile program, the Commander in Chief stood fast and refused to program more than 200 ICBM's for deployment.[21]

It was only with the ascendance to the Presidency of John F. Kennedy, who as a candidate had politically exploited the widespread impression of America's declining power position vis-a-vis the Soviet Union, that rapid strategic and conventional expansion took place. (But perhaps the die had already been cast before election day 1960 inasmuch as virtually all serious contenders for either party's nomination—on the Democratic side, Senators Lyndon Johnson and Stuart Symington in addition to Kennedy, and on the Republican side, Vice President Richard Nixon and Governor Nelson Rockefeller of New York—had forcefully espoused programs of significant ICBM and limited war build-ups). Moreover, the shift in defense policy which occurred during the Kennedy-McNamara years was based less on the fear that a potential missile gap might develop in the future than on the implicit assumption that a missile-gap-in-reverse (that is, American superiority) was to be attained in order to implement a strategic counter-force umbrella under which a vigorous policy of counter-insurgency could operate.[22] (The "missile gap" rationale for an American build-up had been laid to rest by Defense Secretary McNamara himself less than a month after taking office in a background news briefing which, alas, was reported in the nation's newspapers the following day.[23])

Thus, the American strategic and conventional "reaction" to the Soviet threat was truly a *delayed* (by some three years) reaction which can in no way be simplistically explained away by the use of the "action-reaction syndrome" model or similar nuances. If changes in United States defense policy cannot be traced solely to this external linkage, then we must look to domestic linkages —a causal nexus within the internal political system.

8

*Introduction*

## IV

Thus far we have approached the shift in American defense establishment doctrines which occurred between 1957 and 1961 strictly in terms of its probable ramifications on the course of American foreign policy and the armaments race in which the Soviet Union and the United States have been engaged. Yet our study is concerned less with the realm of foreign policy per se than with the domestic forces which precipitated such a dramatic shift in military policy. We are confronted with what has been in all probability the most momentous shift in defense doctrines since the Korean war thrust rearmament upon the American people. And yet, for all it may have been, the Soviet Sputnik was hardly as disruptive as the Korean conflict. What it did, of course, was to serve as a catalyst for the mobilization of latent subterranean forces within the American polity. The formulation (or, more correctly, the re-formulation) of national security policy is to be found at the intersection of the international and domestic systems. Therefore, before elucidating the fundamental conceptual approach utilized in this study, we must first say something about the underlying framework of international politics adopted here as a way of affording the reader an adequate perspective on this particular case study.

It is tempting (perhaps because of its appealing simplicity and lucidity) to identify the determinants of state behavior in the international system wholly outside the structure of internal politics. Often, policy making is ascribed to some group in the executive branch (Locke's "federative" power, if you will[24])—usually referred to simply as "decision makers" or "policy makers"—a group which perceives a threat to the political system from its environment and, reacting to this stimulus, retorts with actions of its own intended to neutralize the intrusion or transform the conflict situation in its favor.[25] Such diverse schools of thought as realism, systems theory, and environmental simulation have reinforced this fallacious tendency.[26] The realist approach assumes that the national interest is given and thereby views the state as an actor with a single mind and will much like Machiavelli's prince; there-

9

fore, while correctly pointing to the paramount role of power and interest in inter-state relations, it presents an overly mechanistic model which all but neglects domestic determinants of the behavior of "national actors."[27] The realist model is thus a "closed system"—that is, "that which is under investigation is assumed to be separated from the outer environment, so that nothing new can enter or leave, and the outcome results from the initial conditions."[28]

In a similar manner, game and bargaining (as well as simulation) theories have contributed to this reification of the state by emphasizing cost/risk analyses and the calculation of values and objectives by "players" who, by analogy, are likened to individuals endowed with a singleness of will and purpose and a unity of the thought processes rather than resembling the complex intricacies of the domestic political system which, through a process of mutual adjustment of myriad claims and interests, eventually reaches composite or synthetic outcomes reflecting the quilt-like nature of the societal fabric.[29] And, finally, the Kaplanesque version of systems theory is also guilty (quite aside from its needlessly esoteric jargon) of neglecting internal sources of behavior and attempting to humanify the state system. Thus, because all of the above approaches identify merely the externally determined influences on governmental behavior (and because, in the real world, states seldom respond solely to outside stimuli), they force the observer to conclude that states frequently pursue "irrational" courses of action.

The "irrational" factor (that is, in actuality the deviation of real world behavior from that posited by restrictive frameworks) is, of course, easily accounted for by an "open systems" conceptualization. As opposed to the "closed system" approach, general systems theory emphasizes the wholeness and unity of process and organization. As McClelland states:

Its organismic conception begins with the empirically verified fact that living beings and their organizations are not collections of isolable units, the sum of which accounts for a total phenomenon. All the phenomena in the living world show the

characteristics of open systems in which the 'components' are
sets of organized actions which are maintained constantly by
exchanges in the environment. Thus components in the form
of open systems lower in the hierarchy of organization constantly enter and leave the general system in question.[30]

Therefore, the open systems model is able to account for the "irrational" influence of domestic variables by abandoning the
closed system assumption and in its stead assuming that "final outcomes are not determined by initial conditions, but rather by conditions of outflow and inflow over a period of time. A final outcome in a sequence of development may be reached by many
ways and from many types of beginning circumstances."[31]

Strategic policy formulation, then, may be viewed in much the
same manner as is domestic policy—that is, as a social rather than
an intellective process, involving myriad interests and opposing
values and their conciliation.[32] The distinction between the forces
affecting the making of internal and external political outcomes
(that is, the boundary separating the domestic and international
systems) has become progressively blurred with the process of
modernization and the transformation of the rather neatly divided
functions of traditional societies into those complex, overlapping
jurisdictions of the modern industrial or post-industrial society.[33]
With the vast growth of governmental authority and its rapidly
expanding sphere of involvement since the genesis of the nation-
state, with the concomitant dilatation of services and expenditures and the gradually preponderant influence of defense allocations on the economies of the world powers, with the revolutions
in commerce and communication which have made national au-
tarchy no longer tenable—with all these factors operative, it is
cause for little wonder that internal interests have projected themselves into the realm of traditionally isolated externally-oriented
processes.

Therefore, one must be careful to avoid both the Scylla of grand
cabinet-style diplomacy (the fallacy, for example, of realism) as
well as the Charybdis of manipulation by naked domestic pressures (the error of the neo-Marxist critique, for instance) in ana-

lyzing the foreign policy process of as complex a political system as that of the United States. For it is evident that a state's foreign policy (and, by implication, its defense policy[34]) represents a general reaction to external stimuli (that is, threat perceptions), but that at the same time the specific form which it eventually assumes is a result of a set of complex forces within the particular polity itself. Moreover, such an analytical framework applies not only to pluralist democratic systems of the American variety (where the manifestations of domestic influences are perhaps more visible), but to authoritarian systems as well. As one observer has noted of the evolving Soviet polity, for example:

> While it would be an oversimplification to think of Soviet foreign policy as purely and simply a dependent variable of domestic inputs, such an approach might well be a lesser error than to assume (as was done in the Stalin era and is often still an operative assumption) that Soviet leaders are immune to various constraints, diverse opinions, and political pressures arising out of their polity and society.[35]

In analyzing the factors involved in the present case study, one can neither view the expansion of the military during the early 1960's as a mere reaction to the Soviet threat (though, to be sure, a threat was indeed perceived) nor as the result of a single internal determinant (such as the machinations of industry or the military). Rather, a suitable framework must allow for a continuous flow-like process which deals with: (1) the entrance into the domestic political system of both facts and perceptions concerning the behavior of other states in the external environment; (2) the internal process by which these inputs from the international system are transformed into specific defense policies; and, (3) the manner in which these resulting policies serve, in turn, as new inputs for other domestic political systems. The present case study, concerned as it is primarily with the domestic aspects of the debate over the alleged missile gap and the adequacy of conventional forces, will focus for the most part on the middle phase (2) of this continual flow process. It will not, however, be arbitrarily divorced from its international setting.

*Introduction*

## V

The fundamental conceptual premise of the case study under examination is that the making of strategic policy takes place within a fundamentally political (as opposed to a bureaucratic-technical) environment. Thus, the policy process does not resemble a "rational-comprehensive method" of problem solving (that is, one which involves the ordering of values and the choice of one policy out of numerous alternatives to maximize those values), but one of partisan mutual adjustment (that is, where different versions of the public good are reconciled by means of a process of bargaining).[36]

Given the nature of the American political system, "military planning cannot be done, and it is not expected to be done, in a political vacuum."[37] The governmental process, premised as it is on a decentralization of power and the parcelling out of functions among several institutions, affords groups (both within and without government proper) myriad means of access to the decision-making process. This "multiple crack"[38] attribute of American government compels, in effect, the intervention of legislators into the affairs of bureaucracy and the cultivation of the Congress by administrators—a reciprocal relationship which blurs the distinction between the purely legislative and the purely executive roles. In regard to defense establishment policy the problem is particularly acute because the framers of the Constitution, in equating civilian control over the military with the dispersion of authority over military affairs, devised a system of government which purposefully fostered multiple dominion (and thus, multiple access). Therefore, at the same time, this delegation of overlapping functions has provided several means of access by the leaders of the uniformed services and the various civilian agency chiefs concerned with differing aspects of military-defense policy to the numerous levels of decision making.

Moreover, the intra-governmental tensions generated by the Madisonian system of checks and balances and the separation (or, more precisely, the sharing) of powers between the executive and legislative branches, has brought about a situation whereby either party (the President or the Congress) can actively enlist the support of the military chieftains (or their civilian counterparts in the Department of Defense) in their perpetual "cold war" with one another. The result has been that the tactics of organization normally associated with legislative politics (that is, temporary alliances, logrolling, bargaining, incessant and varied persuasive techniques) have pervaded the strategy-making process as well. This characteristic nature of strategic policy formulation (aptly termed an "executive legislation process" by Huntington) provides for the determination of military doctrine by competing groups within the executive with the Congress assuming the function of a lobbyist.[39]

In the bureaucratic process of legislating defense policy, therefore, strategy (much as is the case with, say, agricultural programs in the Congress) becomes a product of conflict, bargaining, and compromise among various competing interests within and between the armed services, the Department of Defense bureaucracy and the White House. And, as is the case with most policy formulation, much of the conflict over defense policy can be expected to be institutionally grounded: "Not sharing the same responsibilities (or, put the other way, not charged with the representation of the same values or skills), government organizations will necessarily bring divergent interests and approaches to the same problems."[40] Inasmuch as there is no objectively correct strategic mix, the allocation of the military budget becomes a struggle among quasi-independent agencies and departments, each seeking a larger share of the budgetary "pie" based upon arguments couched at all times in terms of the "national interest." To be sure, most of the propositions advanced in the debate over national needs are sincerely judged by their advocates as essential for the security requirements of the United States. Yet such notions are strongly reinforced by the internal requirements of vast bureaucracies, the vested interests of which soon develop their own momentum. Thus, as is often the case among competing sovereign states in international politics, particular parochial (that is, service or agency) interests soon become synonymous with the general (that is, national) interest.[41]

As we shall find in subsequent chapters, there is an inevitable tendency (given the division of responsibility between the executive and legislative branches) for conflicts within the bureaucracies to spill over into the sphere of Congressional competence. Those elements which (by their own standards) fare poorly at the hands of the administration in the allocation of funds will be tempted (given the Congress' ultimate and guarded "power of the purse strings" and the intimate relationship of many legislators with agency affairs) to appeal their cause to the legislature. By enlarging the scope of the conflict, the previously disadvantaged factions hope to enlist the support of influential members of the House and the Senate in order either to immediately redress their grievances through direct legislative intervention in the appropriation process or to serve notice on their executive superiors that, in regard to the future, funding had best be placed on a more "equitable" footing. As E. E. Schattschneider has observed on what he calls the "contagiousness" of conflict: "it is the weak, not the strong, who appeal . . . for relief. It is the weak who want to socialize conflict, that is, to involve more and more people in the conflict until the balance of forces is changed."[42] The Congress (or, in actuality, its respective committees), then, functions in effect as both a pressure group and as a court of last resort. This mode of behavior on the part of executive partisans is endemic because

> The average unit of the bureaucracy is far more deeply committed to its own particular program than to the program of the Administration as a whole. Accordingly, an agency whose pet project has been turned down by the Bureau of the Budget and the White House is seldom inclined to accept this verdict as final. If it has influential friends in Congress it may be in an excellent position to challenge the President's decision.[43]

In our particular study, though, we will find it imperative to go beyond the Huntingtonian model of the politics of national security doctrine; that is, we will adopt a framework which, while incorporating his essential components, goes further and expands the relevant area of policy making to include significant non-governmental actors as well.[44] Because a major factor in the outcome of the debate over defense posture during the late Eisenhower years was the change in administrations in 1961 (and because the new President came prepared for his new responsibilities with a rather well-articulated alternative doctrine), it will be necessary to examine the role of the communications media and academicians in both publicizing the new propositions and lending them credibility.

The dual faceted strategic debate of the late fifties and early sixties, and the resulting change in military policy fostered by a change in administration, was ultimately the function of the interaction of a broad coalition of forces, interests, and perspectives within and among: (1) the civilian and military bureaucracies of the Department of Defense; (2) the press (and communications media in general); (3) the academic world (specifically, strategic experts); (4) the arena of partisan politics; (5) the perennial tensions between the executive and legislative branches; (6) the nature of the electoral process (that is, the politics of Presidential election campaigns).

Using, then, what is basically an expanded and modified version of the Huntingtonian model, the following propositions will be suggested and examined in light of the available evidence:

1. The crucial difference between the Eisenhower and Kennedy administrations in the area of security policy was one of means (i.e., defense policy) rather than ends (i.e., foreign policy goals).

2. The shift in defense policy to "flexible response" and "nuclear superiority" (or the "damage limitation" doctrine) had significant ramifications for the future of the arms race and American intervention abroad.

3. The strategic policy-making arena for the missile gap/limited war controversy was truly broad, involving shifting alliances and coalitions among various groups in and out of government proper:
   a. the "innovators": those actors in both the civilian and military bureaucracies who initiated and sustained

16

the doctrinal controversy (e.g., Trevor Gardner, Generals Matthew B. Ridgway, Maxwell D. Taylor, Thomas Power, Lt. General James M. Gavin, Major Generals John B. Medaris and Bernard M. Schriever);

b. the "popularizers": that portion of the press (e.g., the Alsop brothers) and the academic world (e.g., Henry A. Kissinger, Robert E. Osgood, and Bernard Brodie) which lent credibility to the innovating arguments and afforded them an intellectual foundation;

c. the "capitalizers": those members of the opposition (i.e., Democratic) party, especially in the Senate (John F. Kennedy, Lyndon B. Johnson, Stuart Symington, Henry M. Jackson) who sought to embarrass the Republican administration of Dwight Eisenhower in order to contribute to their party's prospects in the elections of 1958 and 1960.

These propositions will be tested by means of the data obtained by a careful examination of the following: (1) Congressional hearings and testimony (especially that before the Senate Armed Services Committee's Preparedness Investigating Subcommittee, the Senate Committee on Aeronautical and Space Sciences, the Defense Appropriations Subcommittees of the Senate and House Committees on Appropriations); (2) public documents (such as the public papers of Presidents Dwight Eisenhower and John Kennedy and the complete record of the 1960 Presidential election campaign speeches as compiled by the Senate Commerce Committee's Subcommittee on Communications); (3) newspapers (especially the *New York Times*); (4) publications by participants (military, political, academic) in the strategic debate; (5) relevant materials at the Kennedy Library; (6) selected secondary sources for background data on American strategic doctrine, the Eisenhower and Kennedy administrations, the politics of the defense establishment, and theoretical insights.

Through such an examination, the roles of all three varieties of actors will be defined, analyzed, and weighed.

In the chapter which follows, we will examine the philosophical underpinnings and nature of the Eisenhower defense policy of the "long pull," as well as the three or four months which followed the orbiting of the Soviet Sputnik of October, 1957. We will be particularly interested in the forces which were at work within the American political system (in the wake of the space spectacular) which pressed for increased strategic and conventional expenditures as well as the response of the Eisenhower administration to such demands. The examination of the initial post-Sputnik period will afford the reader both an historical perspective and a microcosmic view of the debate which would follow and dominate the scene for the next several years.

In chapters three and four, we will be concerned with the role of the innovators. In the first part of the analysis, we will view the process whereby the dissenters within the elite nucleus of the military are moved to dissent from administration policy and ally themselves with the Chief Executive's opponents on Capitol Hill and elsewhere. Whether those in the military who become politically involved in active opposition to the administration differ from their colleagues who do not in educational and social backgrounds, degree of professionalism, or career experiences will also be considered. Finally, we can approach the actual process whereby the military dissenters are drawn into the political arena by both legislators and members of the executive branch alike and then suggest the instruments at the disposal of the politicized dissenters to influence the course of the strategic debate.

In the following two chapters we will study first the role of influential journalists, and the media in general, in publicizing the nature, extent, and ramifications of the alleged deficiencies in the Eisenhower defense program and the press' interaction with other actors (and especially their influence on the members of the Congress and the attentive public). Secondly, we look at the role of leading academicians and strategic experts in general in intellectually justifying the innovating views and attempt to weigh their overall effect on the course of the debate.

In chapters seven and eight both Congressional and Presidential politics will be considered. Chapter seven deals with the role of the Senate as a forum of criticism and as a pressure group for higher defense spending during the Eisenhower years and pays special attention to the pivotal role of those legislators at the vortex of power. Chapter eight focuses on the controversy over military policy as it comes to a head in the campaign strategy of John F. Kennedy; it views the shift of Richard Nixon from Eisenhower to Nelson Rockefeller on defense policy and the new consensus formed out of the areas of agreement between the Republican and Democratic candidates on national security policy. The second half of the chapter studies the "changing of the guard" as the incoming Kennedy administration begins a new era in defense establishment policy: how the new generation reacts to the now accepted mythical nature of the "missile gap"; the factors which prod the shift despite its having lost its original rationale; the role of counterinsurgency in the Kennedy defense posture and the reappearance of the Eisenhower dissenter, Maxwell Taylor.

In the concluding chapter the consequences of the setting of strategic policy formulation will be explored. After re-examining the roles of the innovators, popularizers, and capitalizers in the controversy, we will compare the Eisenhower and Kennedy defense programs. Specifically, we will note how the fiscal conservatism of the Republican years precluded massive United States intervention abroad while the world view of its successor provided the opposite incentive.

1. That the Eisenhower administration had accepted a position of strategic "sufficiency" vis-a-vis the Soviet Union during the late fifties as opposed to one of "superiority," see Samuel P. Huntington, *The Common Defense: Strategic Programs in National Politics* (Princeton: University Press, 1961), pp. 100-104.

2. Institute for Strategic Studies, *The Communist Bloc and the Western Alliances: The Military Balance, 1962-1963* (London: Institute for Strategic Studies, 1963), p. 26.

3. Hans J. Morgenthau, *A New Foreign Policy for the United States* (New York: Frederick A. Praeger, Publishers, 1969), pp. 8-9.

4. Cited in Seyom Brown, *The Faces of Power: Constancy and Change in United States Foreign Policy From Truman to Johnson* (New York: Columbia University Press, 1968), p. 335.

5. The New York Times, *The Pentagon Papers*, written by Neil Sheehan, et al. (New York: Quadrangle Books, 1972), p. xi.

6. Quoted in Sidney Lens, *The Military-Industrial Complex* (Philadelphia: Pilgrim Press and The National Catholic Reporter, 1970), p. 31.

7.   Stephen J. Cimbala, "New Myths and Old Realities: Defense and Its Critics," *World Politics*, vol. 24 (October, 1971), p. 151.

8.   Stewart Alsop, *The Center: People and Power in Political Washington* (New York: Harper & Row, Publishers, 1968), pp. 146-150. (It should be noted in passing that Alsop was an intimate friend of the late President.)

9.   Morton H. Halperin, *Defense Strategies for the Seventies* (Boston: Little, Brown and Company, 1971), p. 48.

10.   For example, compare Roger Hilsman's description of the Kennedy build-up of United States conventional and counterinsurgency capabilities (as well as its underlying rationale) in his *To Move A Nation: The Politics of Foreign Policy in the Administration of John F. Kennedy* (Garden City: Doubleday & Company, 1967) with Townshend Hoopes' analysis of the role of the doctrine of limited war in bringing about massive American involvement in Vietnam under Johnson in his *The Limits of Intervention* (New York: David McKay Company, 1970). Hilsman served as Director of the Bureau of Intelligence and Research in the State Department under President Kennedy and as Assistant Secretary of State for Far Eastern Affairs under President Johnson until 1964. Hoopes was Deputy Assistant Secretary of Defense for International Security Affairs and later Undersecretary of the Air Force during the Johnson years. Though both deal with different aspects of the case in hand, their cumulative analyses enforce the continuity suggested by the author.

11.   John H. Herz, *International Politics in the Atomic Age* (New York: Columbia University Press, 1959).

12.   On the role of perception in international relations, see: J. David Singer, "Threat Perception and the Armament-Tension Dilemma." *Journal of Conflict Resolution*, vol. 2 (1958), 90-105; Robert Jervis, "Hypotheses on Misperception," *World Politics*, vol. 20 (April, 1968), 454-479; John C. Farrell and Asa P. Smith, eds., *Image and Reality in World Politics* (New York: Columbia University Press, 1967); John G. Stoessinger, *Nations in Darkness: China, Russia and America* (New York: Random House, 1971).

13.   See, respectively, Kenneth E. Boulding, *Conflict and Defense: A General Theory* (New York: Harper & Row, Publishers, 1963), pp. 24-25; Morton A. Kaplan, *System and Process in International Politics* (New York: John Wiley & Sons, Inc., 1957), p. 5; James N. Rosenau, "Toward the Study of National-International Linkages," in Rosenau, ed., *Linkage Politics: Essays on the Convergence of National and International Systems* (New York: The Free Press, 1969), ch. 3; McGeorge Bundy, "To Cap the Volcano," *Foreign Affairs*, vol. 48 (October, 1969), 1-20.

14.   George Rathjens, *The Future of the Strategic Arms Race: Options for the 1970's* (New York: Carnegie Endowment for International Peace, 1969); Bundy, *op. cit.*

15.   Thomas C. Schelling, "Assumptions About Enemy Behavior," in E. S. Quade, ed., *Analysis for Military Decisions: The RAND Lectures on Systems Analysis* (Chicago: Rand McNally & Company, 1964), pp. 199-200. Emphasis in the original.

16.   Thomas C. Schelling, *Arms and Influence* (New Haven: Yale University Press, 1966), p. 271.

17. Robert S. McNamara, *The Essence of Security: Reflections in Office* (New York: Harper & Row, Publishers, 1968), pp. 57-59. Emphasis added.

18. The ratio of American strategic missile strength to that of the Soviets progressively decreased over the decade from 4 to 1 in 1964 to virtual equality in 1970. See *The Military Balance, 1969-1970* (London: Institute for Strategic Studies, 1969), p. 55.

19. William C. Foster, "Prospects for Arms Control," *Foreign Affairs,* vol. 47 (April, 1969), p. 68. Emphasis added.

20. It is interesting to note that McNamara's successor Melvin R. Laird also accepted the principle of judging capabilities rather than intentions: "As Secretary of Defense, I don't believe it is appropriate for me to try to assess the intentions of the Soviet Union. My responsibilities are to consider their real and potential capabilities, particularly in relation to our own policy of deterrence." "Dangers Confronting the U. S.: Interview with Defense Secretary Laird," *U. S. News & World Report* (11 May 1970), p. 68.

21. The estimate of an Eisenhower missile program of only 200 ICBM's has been made by Colin S. Gray, " 'Gap' Predictions and America's Defense: Arms Race Behavior in the Eisenhower Years," *Orbis*, vol. 16 (Spring, 1972), note p. 273. Congressional testimony by Eisenhower's Defense Secretary Thomas Gates would seem to substantiate this calculation. See his remarks before the Subcommittee of the Senate Committee on Appropriations, *Department of Defense Appropriations for 1961*, part 1, 86th Cong., 1st Sess. (Washington, D.C.: Government Printing Office, 1960), p. 8. Due to the "lead-lag" time factor (i.e., that the strategic force levels under one administration often reflect decisions on production and deployment made under the previous administration), future comparisons of the Eisenhower and Kennedy defense programs will rely for the most part on executive budgetary requests for the Department of Defense. These figures, which are less susceptible to the "lead-lag" complication factor than weapons and manpower levels, present a more accurate picture of the respective military priorities of the two administrations.

22. During his first appearance before the House Appropriations Committee's Subcommittee on Defense Appropriations, McNamara indicated that even a significant downgrading of the Soviet missile threat by the intelligence community would not really alter the Kennedy strategic build-up. See the exchange between Representative Gerald Ford, now House Minority Leader and the Defense Secretary: House Committee on Appropriations, Subcommittee on Department of Defense Appropriations, *Department of Defense Appropriations for 1962*, part 3, 87th Cong., 1st Sess. (Washington, D.C.: Government Printing Office, 1961), pp. 111-112.

23. See the *New York Times*, 7 February 1961, p. 1.

24. The English philosopher of the 17th century John Locke, it will be recalled, identified three varieties of political power in the commonwealth. That which he termed the "federative" (that is, the power of war and peace and the general conduct of foreign affairs) was of a distinct nature, but of necessity to be joined with the executive. See his *Second Treatise of Government* (New York: The New American Library, 1960), chapter 12.

25. For an example of this approach, see Charles O. Lerche and Abdul A. Said's brief introductory text *Concepts of International Politics* (Englewood Cliffs, N. J.: Prentice-Hall, 1963), ch. 2.

26. See, for example, respectively: Hans J. Morgenthau, *Politics Among Nations: The Struggle for Power and Peace*, 4th ed. (New York: Alfred A. Knopf, 1967); Morton A. Kaplan, *op. cit.*; Thomas Schelling, *The Strategy of Conflict* (New York: Oxford University Press, 1960); Harold Guetzkow, "Simulations in the Consolidations and Utilization of Knowledge About International Relations," in D. G. Pruitt and R. C. Snyder, eds., *Theory and Research in the Causes of War* (Englewood Cliffs, N. J.: Prentice-Hall, 1969).

27. Arnold Wolfers, "The Pole of Power and the Pole of Indifference," *World Politics*, vol. 4 (October, 1951), 39-63; Stanley Hoffman, "Contemporary Theories of International Relations," in Hoffman, ed., *Contemporary Theory in International Relations* (Englewood Cliffs, N. J.: Prentice-Hall, 1960), pp. 29-54.

28. Charles A. McClelland, "General Systems Theory in International Relations," *Main Currents in Modern Thought*, vol. 12 (November, 1955), p. 31. See also, by the same author, *Theory and The International System* (New York: The Macmillan Company, 1966).

29. See, for example, Thomas C. Schelling, "Experimental Games and Bargaining Theory," in Klaus Knorr and Sidney Verba, eds., *The International System: Theoretical Essays* (Princeton: Princeton University Press, 1961), pp. 47-68.

30. McClelland, "General Systems Theory in International Relations," *op. cit.*, p. 22.

31. *Ibid.*, pp. 29-30. It should be noted in passing, however, that the approach on the opposite extreme of the spectrum from the closed system model—that is, the viewpoint which seeks to explain all foreign policy in terms of one domestic variable (for example, economics)—is equally (if not more) erroneous. In fact, it represents but another variety of the closed system model; in this case, external determinants are neglected. For a neo-Leninist view of American foreign policy, see Harry Magdoff, *The Age of Imperialism* (New York: The Monthly Review Press, 1966).

32. For the social process view of policy making (and its contrast with the intellective), see Lester W. Milbrath, "Interest Groups and Foreign Policy," in James N. Rosenau, ed., *Domestic Sources of Foreign Policy* (New York: The Free Press, 1967), chapter 8. For the intellective approach, see Harold Lasswell, *The Decision Process: Seven Categories of Functional Analysis* (College Park, Md.: University of Maryland Press, 1956).

33. Edward L. Morse, "The Transformation of Foreign Policies: Modernization, Interdependence and Externalization," *World Politics*, vol. 22 (April, 1970), 371-392. See also, Adam Yarmolinsky, "Bureaucratic Structures and Political Outcomes," *Journal of International Affairs*, vol. 13 (Fall, 1969), 225-235.

34. Though highly interrelated, foreign policy and defense policy are not used synonymously in this study. Foreign policy is used here to signify a state's strategy in the international system for the attainment of those goals judged to be in its national interest by its government. Defense policy thus represents one of the tools (i.e., the military arm) of foreign policy. When

referring to defense as a goal rather than a means of foreign policy, the term "national security policy" would be more appropriate.

35. Alexander Dallin, "Soviet Foreign Policy and Domestic Politics: A Framework for Analysis," *Journal of International Affairs*, vol. 13, (Fall, 1969), 25-64; see also, Vernon V. Aspaturian, "Internal Politics and Foreign Policy in the Soviet System," in R. B. Farrell, ed., *Approaches to Comparative and International Politics* (Northwestern University: University Press, 1966), pp. 212-287.

36. Charles E. Lindbloom, "The Science of 'Muddling Through,'" *The Public Opinion Review*, vol. 19 (1959), 79-88; also, by the same author, *The Intelligence of Democracy: Decision Making Through Mutual Adjustment* (New York: The Free Press, 1965); David Braybrooke and Charles E. Lindbloom, *A Strategy of Decision: Policy Evaluation as a Social Process* (Glencoe, Ill.: The Free Press, 1963).

37. Paul Y. Hammond, *Organizing for Defense* (Princeton University Press, 1961), p. 346.

38. This apt term has been suggested by Morton Grodzins, "American Political Parties and the American System," *The Western Political Quarterly*, vol. 13 (Fall, 1960), 974-998. Others have simply employed the word "access" to describe the same peculiar aspect of the American system; see, in this regard, David B. Truman, *The Governmental Process: Political Interests and Public Opinion* (New York: Alfred A. Knopf, 1951).

39. *Op. cit.*, chapters 3-6; also, by the same author, *The Soldier and the State: The Theory and Politics of Civil-Military Relations* (New York: Vintage Books, 1957), part 3. The "legislative environment" has been usefully described as one in which there exists a disparity of goals and a rough equality of resources among competing parties. See Roger H. Davidson, *The Role of the Congressman* (New York: Pegasus, 1969), chapter 1.

40. Warner R. Schilling, et al., *Strategy, Politics, and Defense Budgets* (New York: Columbia University Press, 1962), p. 21.

41. As Henry A. Kissinger remarks: "The internal requirements of the bureaucracy may come to predominate over the purposes which it was intended to serve." See his "Domestic Structure and Foreign Policy," *Daedalus*, vol. 95 (Spring, 1966), 503-529.

42. E. E. Schattschneider, *The Semi-Sovereign People: A Realist's View of Democracy in America* (New York: Holt, Rinehart and Winston, 1960), p. 40.

43. Bertram M. Gross, *The Legislative Struggle* (New York: McGraw-Hill, 1953), p. 80.

44. Roger Hilsman's "concentric rings of policy making," by incorporating attentive publics as well as executive and legislative participants, is a useful expansion of the conceptual scheme. Hilsman, however, apparently applies it only to foreign policy making processes. See his *The Politics of Policy Making in Defense and Foreign Affairs* (New York: Harper & Row, Publishers, 1971), especially chapter 7.

# 2

## AMERICAN DEFENSE POLICY IN THE 1950's

### I

FEW AMERICAN PRESIDENTS HAVE BEEN AT FIRST so maligned and then so revered in so short a period of time (and by the same people) as has Dwight D. Eisenhower. Perhaps much of this is due to the natural rhythmic tides of historiography, where tradition (or the orthodoxy of the moment) must constantly be subjected to rigorous confrontation with revisionist claims. (In good liberal form, then, it is hoped that out of this clash of opinions and facts, a new approximation of the truth will arise which incorporates the best offerings of both antithetical arguments.) Or perhaps the reconsideration of the Eisenhower years may be attributed to the changing times and differing perspectives afforded by a rather jealous history which, as it unfolds, appears to go off in directions unforeseen by even its most astute observers. Thus, for those dissatisfied with the placidness and lack of movement of the fifties, the Eisenhower stewardship symbolized the stagnation of the times; and the Russian Sputnik of 1957 would be seen as "our generation's stock market crash" or "today's scientific Pearl Harbor"[1] which, hopefully, would shake America loose from the prosaic complacency which had gripped it since the Korean War and turn the nation toward a leadership dedicated to movement and progress. Paradoxically, after having lived through the tumultuous sixties—a decade where the fruition of dynamic leadership seemed to be the tragedy of Vietnam—students of history once again turn back to the Eisenhower regency, this time to discover the elements of that salutary neglect which brought the United States both peace abroad and stability at home. Whatever the reasons for this dramatic re-evaluation of Eisenhower as Chief Executive, it took a mere ten years for scholars to do a *volte face*—from America's leading students of the Presidency rating him next to the bottom of the "average" category (three steps below Herbert Hoover, sandwiched in by Chester A. Arthur and Andrew Johnson)[2] to the recent lavish and extravagent claims that he was, in reality, a Machiavellian political genius.[3] As one observer has noted:

Many of those who judged him most harshly until only a few years ago are now having second and third thoughts about the man and his Presidency—thoughts that ring most agreeably in the ears of those whose faith had never never wavered. Such nay–sayers on the left as Murray Kempton and I. F. Stone are finding virtues in him they failed to detect while he served, and others are making claims for him that not even his partisans made when he sought office or held it.[4]

Perhaps the early dearth of appreciation to be found in academic circles for Eisenhower owes its origin to that conception of democratic leadership which has placed a premium on action rather than inaction (which itself may be, in fact, a conscious decision), and movement rather than inertia (even when the times may call for stasis). Pundits of liberal credentials (but perhaps tinged with a slight admixture of the Burkeian theory of representation), in pondering over the necessary elements of prudent government in mass democratic societies, have often arrived at the conclusion that the primordial ingredient is of necessity energetic and aggressive leadership. Thus, the spiritual father of the realist school Reinhold Niebuhr wrote: "The defects of democracy in foreign policy can be overcome only by leadership which is willing to risk its prestige by words and actions which anticipate the perils to which the State is exposed and which defy the common lethargy of the moment in order to ward off ultimate peril."[5]

From such a perspective, the bland and inarticulate Eisenhower interregnum could only be disparaged (even if unduly and unfairly so). But it may be that the times called for such a moderate and often negative brand of executive guidance—that in the America of the fifties, "already burgeoning with the problems and tensions which were to erupt so tragically in the sixties, it was the President's outward serenity and counsel of moderation which did so much to contain the trouble and preserve the national cohesion."[6] As we shall discover as we enquire into Eisenhower's role in the post-Sputnik onslaught against his conservative defense policy, it was his social and political philosophy of balance and proportion which counselled against demands for a radical upward revision of military expenditures. It was, indeed, his particular version of the general good which caused him to eschew the academically-tailored mode of active and positive leadership and, in its stead, to embrace the role of the stalwart negativist and defender of the existing precarious balance of values. As one former advisor to the late President recalls:

> The man—and the President—was never more decisive than when he held to a steely resolve *not* to do something that he sincerely believed wrong in itself or alien to his office. . . .
>
> . . .
>
> Ultimately, all that Eisenhower did, or refused to do, as a democratic leader was rigorously faithful to his understanding of democracy itself. When the record of his Presidency was written and done, he could look back upon it and soberly reflect: "One definition of democracy that I like is merely the opportunity for self-discipline." He lived by this definition. And by all acts of eight years of his Presidency, he urged its acceptance by the people of his nation.[7]

## II

Though the rather unimaginative and inarticulate reign of Dwight Eisenhower failed to elicit the intense attachment of the

intellectual community (some of whom, perhaps, occasionally react more to rhetoric and form than substance), there was, to be
sure, a definite philosophical underpinning to the President's programs. In Presidential style, Eisenhower combined the benign
monarchical temperament of Washington and the consistent devotion to moderation of Madison with the burdening sense of
pathos of Lincoln and the firm commitment to the free enterprise
system of Herbert Hoover. Unlike his successor who relished the
role of Chief Executive and carried Rudyard Kipling's sense of
mission and Theodore Roosevelt's quest for national glory to the
White House, Eisenhower simply did not like politics.[8] For Eisenhower, the Presidency was a great trust, as well as a necessary
burden, and though he might have seriously considered stepping
down after his first term, his sense of duty precluded his sacrificing the national interest (as he interpreted it) to his own personal desire for a less taxing existence.[9]

For Eisenhower the sacred trust of his Presidency was to conduct American foreign relations in a manner which would provide simultaneously for the external security of the United States
(which he identified with the containment of international Communism) and the preservation of the core values of American
society (which he saw as inseparable from the free enterprise
economic system). Thus, the supreme task was to strike a work-
able long-run balance between the needs of defense and those
inherently tied to the healthy functioning of the domestic system.
In the first few months of his first administration, the President
would caution the Congress that "[i]n providing the kind of military security that our country needs, we must keep our people
free and our economy solvent. We must not create a nation
mighty in arms that is lacking in liberty and bankrupt in resources."[10] And in the closing years of his second term he would
reaffirm that the basic purpose of his defense policies had been
and would continue to be: "To promote strength and security
side by side with liberty and opportunity."[11]

In classically laissez-faire liberal form, Eisenhower identified
individual liberty and freedom with the initiative afforded by the
free economic system. The spontaneity and creativity of the in-

27

dividual as channelled into the free marketplace would (as Adam Smith's "invisible hand" theory had taught) result in the greatest good for the greatest number. "The mainspring of our economy," the President informed the Congress, "is to be formed in the qualities of the American people. Given free institutions, and a favorable physical environment, an expanding economy is the natural fruit of the enterprise of such a people."[12] Given this unbounding faith in both individual initiative and the free economy, the role of government was to be relegated to that of underwriting the smooth operation of such a system. Eisenhower would often fondly quote Lincoln's definition of the role of government in a free society: "The legitimate object of Government is to do for a community of people whatever they need to have done, but cannot do at all, or cannot so well do for themselves—in their separate and individual capacities. In all that the people can individually do themselves, Government ought not to interfere."[13] The domestic role of the federal government was thus defined purely in terms of the free economy and, because of the imperatives of the free market, its role was to be severely circumscribed. Inasmuch as prosperity and economic growth were resultants of forces operating in the private sector of the economy, anything which government might do to hamper the free interaction of supply and demand (at least as long as the interaction was beneficial, which was assumed to be the normal arrangement) was dysfunctional. Therefore, it would be the consistent goal of the Eisenhower administration to cut governmental spending in order to lower individual and corporate taxes, for the laws of supply and demand were such that an increase in disposable income (brought about by tax cuts) would inevitably be reflected in greater consumer demand and, thus, greater capital investment.[14] Conversely, every dollar appropriated from the pocketbooks of the people and spent in the public sector represented, as his close advisor Treasury Secretary George Humphrey would counsel, an impoverishment of the private sector (and its job generating capability) and the possibility of inflation resulting from a long series of deficit budgets.[15] From the General's perspective, all this had an appealing simplicity and, in any case, probably reinforced his imperturbable faith in individual self-reliance and autonomy fostered by his Kansas boyhood and military experience.

The fundamental role of government, then, was to "create an environment in which individual enterprise can work constructively to serve the ends of economic progress," to "build a floor over the point of personal disaster" (that is, a minimal welfare state), and "to encourage thrift" (that is, stem the tide of inflation).[16] This last element (the prevention of inflation) was of particular concern to Eisenhower the fiscal conservative. Firstly, inflation undermined confidence in the free economy and hindered the high degree of calculability necessary in the capitalist system for sustained expansion. Presenting the Economic Report of 1959 to the Congress, he cautioned that: "Our objective must be to establish a firm foundation for extending economic growth with the stable prices into the months and years ahead. . . . To attain our goal, we must safeguard and improve the institutions of our free competitive economy. These are basic to America's unassailable strength."[17] Thus, the long-run effect of inflation would be to jeopardize the continuation of the system itself—unfettered by bureaucratic controls—and its role as the material benefactor of all citizens. Secondly, unstable prices would destroy the inherent dynamism of the capitalist system by reducing job opportunities, pricing the United States out of the world market, and shrinking the value of savings, thus penalizing the thrift so essential to finance a growing economy.[18] Finally, for Eisenhower the fight against inflation was "a public trust," for rather than inflation acting as a Robin Hood which takes from the rich to give to the poor, "it deals most cruelly with those who can least protect themselves"—those on fixed incomes such as pensioners and widows, and those blue- and white-collar workers who see their savings melt away.[19]

From the fiscal point of view (as well as the human), Eisenhower dreaded the inflationary repercussions of increased government spending (and huge deficits largely caused by heavy defense expenditures). The overriding domestic problem, as ar-

29

ticulated by Arthur F. Burns (Chairman of the Council of Economic Advisors in the first Eisenhower administration) was that of "creeping inflation":

> It is highly important that we try to manage our economic affairs so as to stop the upward drift of the price level. True, a gradual inflation does not carry the horrors of runaway inflation. But even a price trend that rises no more than 1 percent a year will cut the purchasing power of the dollar by over a fifth in twenty-five years, while an average rise of 2 percent will cut the purchasing power of the dollar by nearly two-fifths. Such a slow but persistent rise in the price level, to say nothing of stronger doses of inflation, is bound to deal harshly with the plans and hopes of millions of people in the course of a generation.[20]

Other conservative economic advisors reinforced Burns' views. Raymond J. Saulnier (Burns' successor as Chairman of the Council of Economic Advisors) strongly attacked the liberal notion that a succession of budgetary deficits could be beneficial for economic expansion. Quite the contrary, Saulnier viewed with great apprehension the rise of the consumer price index in mid-1956 after four years of comparative stability as a propagator of a dangerous inflation psychology which could only wreak ruin on the American system.[21] And Henry C. Wallich (another member of the Council) was even more forthright in his consideration of the problem:

> Deliberate inflation, if not a crime, is at least of very debatable morality, because it involves an attempt to deceive people, and works hardships on those least able to defend themselves: the unorganized, the dependent, the old. . . . The economy, working under full steam with the safety valve tied down, would expand more rapidly. But eventually, these force draft measures would exact their penalty. The lid may blow off, control of inflation may be lost altogether, the economy may spiral off into chaos.[22]

To prevent the horror of inflation, the President's advisors counselled, not only for the elimination of budgetary deficits and the presentation to the Congress of balanced budgets, but for significant surpluses. In order to counteract the likely trend toward an overstimulated economy, conservative economists argued that balanced budgets alone were insufficient, that because governmental expenditures normally have a greater impact on the free economy than equivalent sums spent in the private sector, surpluses must be sought.[23]

Thus, when Eisenhower first assumed office he revised downward significantly the Truman budget for fiscal year (FY) 1954, cutting the projected deficit from 9.9 billion dollars to 5.5 billion. Beyond this, however, he refused to go, not wanting to sacrifice the nation's security abroad to economic stability at home. (Eisenhower's sense of balance between defense spending and the economic necessities of the type of system he sought to defend was a paramount element in his programs throughout his eight years in office.) And though he highly valued the goal of cutting taxes in order to stimulate private initiative, he refused to do so until deficit spending could be eliminated: the "essential first measure" would be to check inflation by balancing the budget—only then could taxes be reduced.[24] This immediately brought him into conflict with the conservative wing of the Republican party which valued tax cuts more highly than defense spending. In fact Eisenhower's attempt to balance the two brought him a heated confrontation with Senate Majority Leader and chief conservative spokesman Robert A. Taft. At a White House meeting soon after the new administration took office, Senator Taft declared that the budget would have to be re-formulated and balanced so that a tax cut could go into effect immediately, and further declared "that he had no confidence in the Joint Chiefs of Staff and that Eisenhower in maintaining a high level of defense spending was being badly taken in by these professional military men."[25] But the President was unmoved by the arguments of the conservatives (as he would remain unmoved some five years later when liberal Democrats presented opposite pressures) for both he and his staff believed firmly that the American people had elected him to office with complete confidence, given his military background, in his judgment concerning the needs of national security.[26]

## III

Eisenhower saw his twin roles as Commander in Chief (and, therefore, defender of United States security interests abroad) and that of Chief Executive (that is, protector of liberty—defined in terms of the free enterprise system—at home) as highly interrelated. In fact, he viewed international security and the well-being of the American economy as being inseparable. Quite early in his Presidency he declared that "our military strength and our economic strength are truly one—neither can sensibly be purchased at the price of destroying the other."[27] The interdependence of the two was quite apparent: the highly productive American economic system provided the wherewithal for the expensive armaments necessary to deter attack on the United States and to prevent the absorption of the vital noncommunist areas of the world by the Soviet camp; the ultimate *raison d'être* of this vast military machine was to protect the integrity of that same system which also provided for the liberty of the nation's citizens. Therefore, neither could one cut defense spending below a certain threshold in the hope of stimulating the capitalist economy without simultaneously subjecting it to dangers from abroad,[28] nor could one significantly increase defense allocations with the aim of providing the system with more relative security from external threats without at the same time endangering those core values which the defense establishment was created to protect.[29] The dilemma was particularly acute because the Russo-American rivalry promised to be of indeterminate duration, and the Communist menace would confront the United States with successive crises in unforeseen places and according to an unknown time schedule devised by the Soviet rulers in the Kremlin. Upon taking office (and in the wake of the Korean War and the economic controls which accompanied it), Eisenhower sought to devise a defense policy able to reconcile external security with internal liberty well into the future.

Having defined the nation's defense establishment in terms of its service in protecting individual liberty (that is, that precious freedom of initiative and spontaneity which was seen as an inalienable by-product of the unplanned free enterprise system), and in turn having identified the highly productive American economy as the chief pillar of military strength, Eisenhower fell back upon a policy of vigilant balance which he termed the "long pull." Defense planning for the "long pull" assumed that the cold war would be of indeterminate duration and that the "free world cannot indefinitely remain in a posture of paralyzed tension, leaving forever to the aggressor the time and place and means to cause greatest hurt to us at least cost to himself."[30] The United States, by planning as it had under the administration of Harry S. Truman to repel the calculated assaults of "Communist imperialism" on the terms which the Soviet aggressor dictated (namely, conventional ground forces as in Korea), was dangerously threatening the functioning of its economic system. As former Special Assistant to the President Sherman Adams recalled:

When he took office Eisenhower was irritated to find that the Defense Department under the Truman administration had been trying to prepare the armed forces for a confusing variety of strategic plans to meet various kinds of war. There was no clear-cut policy about whether or not nuclear weapons would be used in an outbreak of hostilities with Russia, for example. This meant that budget allowances were still being made for enough Army ground troops and Naval sea forces to fight a nonatomic world war, the theory being that atomic weapons might be excluded in such a general conflict unless the Soviets began the use of them first. At the same time the Air Force was planning for a nuclear war. There were also plans for short wars, for police actions like the Korean War, for peripheral wars, for infantry wars, for air war and for completely destructive atomic attacks. As the nonmilitary minded but sensible [Treasury Secretary] George Humphrey remarked after his first look at the Defense Department budget, the military planners seemed to be following six plans of strategy simultaneously, two for each service.

Eisenhower cleared away some of the underbrush by ordering the Pentagon to assume that if we got into war it would be fought with nuclear weapons. The decision instantly diminished the importance of ground troops, to the chagrin of the Army, and of large aircraft carriers, to the discomfort of the Navy, and it gave priority in budgetary funds to the Air Force, to the intense anguish of both the Army and the Navy. The basic defense strategy, advocated by [Secretary of State John Foster] Dulles, was the build-up of a strong deterrent force of atomic and thermonuclear striking power. . . .[31]

With America's grim experience with the frustrations and indecisiveness of limited war in Korea firmly noted, and with a wary appreciation of the economic controls and deficit spending which it had entailed, the new administration vowed never again to fight the enemy on its own terms. Massive limited engagements in response to frequent and simultaneous Soviet probes at myriad points along the periphery of the free world could only gnaw away at the fiber of the United States' economic potential. Forced into a state of constant mobilization, the country would experience a progressive dilatation of military expenditures which would choke the American policy to death and accomplish from within what Communist arms could not bring about from without. "There is no defense for any country," the President said to Republican Congressional leaders in March of 1957, "that busts its own economy."[32] And even if the economic chaos of inflation and dislocation could be checked initially by governmental controls, the long-run effect of postponing the inevitable would be the regimentation of American society and the correlative loss of liberty. In either case, that which was to be preserved by defense preparedness would be sacrificed to the voracious appetite of the military machine—the instruments originally designed to serve the ends of the society would serve instead to end the society. Thus, the regimentation of society which would be the necessary concomitant of perpetual mobilization for war and the quest for absolute security abroad would bring with it all "the grim paraphernalia of the garrison state." Therefore, anything which would contribute to the realization of Eisenhower's paramount fear would be rejected:

We can't be an armed camp. We are not going to transform ourselves into militarists. We are not going to be in uniform, going around yelling 'Heil' anything. We are simply going to do our job, but do it intelligently.

We do not intend to become a garrison state. We do not intend to impose rigid controls on everything that the American people do—their going into uniform, their living, their thinking, their talking—not at all. We expect to live as a free state, which means that we must develop a program that can, under the general practice of a free economy, carry the security burden for a long, long time if that is necessary. . . .

· · ·

Now we have a free enterprise; we place above all other values our own individual freedoms and rights; and we believe, moreover, that the operation of such a system in the long-run produces more, not only more happiness, more satisfaction, and pride in our people, but also more goods, more wealth.

Let's remember that dictatorships have been very efficient. . . .

If you take our country and make it an armed camp and regiment it, why, for a while you might do it with great morale, too, if you could get people steamed up like you did in wars; you might do this thing in very greater [*sic*] tempo than we are now doing it.

Democracy, we hope, is an enduring form of government. We are, therefore, trying to do these things [i.e., build our armed might] at the same time we keep these values.

· · ·

In the counsels of government, we must guard against the acquisition of unwarranted influence, whether sought or unsought, by the military-industrial complex. The potential for the rise of misplaced power exists and will persist.

We must never let the weight of this combination endanger our liberties or democratic processes. We should take nothing for granted. Only an alert and knowledgeable citizenry can compel the proper meshing of the huge industrial and military machinery of defense with our peaceful methods and goals, so that security and liberty may prosper together.

· · ·

. . . some of this misuse of influence and power could come about unwittingly but just by the very nature of the thing.

When you see almost every one of your magazines, no matter what they are advertising, has a picture of the Titan missile or the Atlas or solid fuel or other things, there is becoming [*sic*] a great influence, almost an insidious penetration of our minds that the only thing this country is engaged in is weaponry and missiles. And, I'll tell you we just can't afford to do that. The reason we have them is to protect the great values in which we believe, and they are far deeper. . . .[33]

(As can be seen by placing the last two passages from 1961 in juxtaposition with the first two of 1953, between his first year in office and his last, Eisenhower's frustrations in checking the growth of the military establishment would lead him to believe that there were latent forces within the American polity—within the Congress, the Pentagon, the press, academia, and industry—which might tend to push the United States in the direction of the garrison state despite the best efforts of a vigilant and beneficent protector. Thus, while in his early years he saw the dilemma being solved quite simply by a program of meticulous and almost mechanistic balance and moderation on the part of the President, he would soon come to appreciate that even a less-than-totally-mobilized cold war oriented system would spawn its own pressures for self-perpetuation and, indeed, aggrandizement. The threat which he initially assumed to be the external menace of Communism was being gradually transformed into an equally dangerous but much more difficult to combat internalization of the foreign threat in the form of a nation-under-siege psychology.)

## IV

The notion of the necessity for a "long pull" in defense was not new with the Eisenhower administration. Yet those (like General of the Army Omar N. Bradley, first chairman of the Joint Chiefs of Staff) who had previously advocated such a course of action, did so largely to escape from the historic "feast or famine" pattern of American defense spending.[34] Under Harry Truman, military planning proceeded under the assumption that American military strength had to be directed to successive "periods of maximum danger," of which the years 1954-1955 were to be one. Eisenhower rejected such a basis for military planning and sought instead to insulate the defense budget from both crises in foreign affairs and likely discontent at home. This was to be done not only to terminate the alternating peaks and valleys in defense allocations which had plagued American preparedness in the past, but at the same time to immunize the domestic economic system against the vagaries of international politics.

Thus, the New Look[35] was born as an attempt to allow planning for the long haul and to provide a viable structure for the indispensable balance of external defense and internal liberty. Having decided on a budgetary ceiling of 38 to 40 billion dollars a year for the military establishment as being compatible with the healthy functioning of the American economy (that is, one which would produce neither inflation nor the government controls necessary to combat it, nor a false prosperity dependent upon arms spending[36]), the Eisenhower administration, then, set out to obtain "the maximum military strength within economic capacities."[37] As has been indicated above in the passage quoted from Sherman Adams, the primary element in the New Look was a re-allocation of existing military resources away from conventional ground forces and toward the buttressing of airpower and nuclear capabilities. The revolution in weapons technology following the Second World War which had produced the nuclear and thermonuclear bombs and the means for their long-range delivery (at first the manned bomber and later the strategic missile), had provided the United States with the means to persist in the worldwide struggle between freedom and slavery without impairing the vitality of its economic system. Thus, the Commander in Chief could now rely upon less costly (but equally effective) means to combat the Soviet menace. By serving notice on our adversaries that the United States would simply refuse to engage in numerous debilitating engagements of the Korean variety but would, quite possibly, respond swiftly and selectively to major assaults on the non-Communist world with nuclear airpower, the Eisenhower administration believed it could successfully deter

Soviet-inspired aggression and simultaneously prevent the mobilization of the American system.

The new strategy, then, would do what the more costly Truman doctrine had done (that is, check Soviet advances), but would also, regarding the free economy, make abnormal times which otherwise would have required governmental interference and controls, ostensibly normal. In short, Eisenhower believed he had arrived at the golden mean—a middle way that perhaps lacked the drama and sensation, but which made sense by preserving the strength of the nation at home and abroad.[38]

Mr. Eisenhower, himself a General of the Army, saw no need for inordinately large conventional forces. A series of small wars would merely drain the resources and manpower of the United States and play into the hands of the Sino-Soviet bloc which placed so little emphasis on the value of human life. America simply did not have the resources to intervene in all possible trouble spots across the globe and therefore "would not try to maintain the conventional power to police the whole world."[39] Requirements for ground forces were limited to the overseas deployment of a "trip-wire" contingent in Western Europe which would politically demonstrate the determination of the United States to come to the defense of its allies with the Strategic Air Command, and which would, militarily, serve as a "burglar alarm" by giving early and indisputable evidence of a major Russian attack. Secondarily, reserves of sufficient strength as would be necessary to meet limited and isolated "brush-fire" conflicts in other areas would be needed. Beyond this, larger forces were not only superfluous but dysfunctional. In regard to the most vital theater, Europe, forces large enough to match the Warsaw Pact armies were not needed because the United States had no intention of waging a conventional war to stem a Soviet advance. Moreover, the creation of such a Western capability might give the Russians the impression that they could attack with nuclear impunity and would thereby precipitate atomic Armeggedon through miscalculation. Thus, when the Soviet Union provoked a severe crisis in 1959 by demanding the evacuation of Western forces from Berlin and threatening to sign a separate peace with East Germany (thus jeopardizing Western access to the defenseless enclave), Eisenhower refused to embark on the course of action which his successor did under similar circumstances in 1961—the build-up of American troops in Europe. As the President explained at a news conference in March of 1959 amid the clamor of critics for mobilization:

> Now, you make out a plan and you follow that plan. You do not want, and, as a matter of fact, it would be ruinous to be pushed off this plan time and again by something suddenly described as a crisis.
>
> I have argued and urged for years that we are living and we are going to live in a tense period because of the actions and attitudes of Communist imperialism.
>
> Now every time one of these incidents, one of these, you might say, these foci of tension occur, we have something that's called a crisis, and everybody has an answer.
>
> Whether it's Sputnik or it's Quemoy or it's Korea or whatever it is, what we have to do is to stand steadily. . . .
>
> What I am trying to point out is this: the adequacy of our defenses is not going to be especially increased or strengthened by any particular sudden action in response to one of these moments of increased tension.
>
> We are certainly not going to fight a ground war in Europe. What good would it do to send a few more thousands or indeed even a few divisions of troops to Europe?[40]

And in regard to less vital areas on the periphery, a conflagration inspired by Communist collusion (whether due to internal subversion or invasion) would have to be met by indigenous forces with limited United States assistance whether in materiel or manpower. If the aggression were so great as to be incapable of containment by the forces available on the ground, or if "conflicts started in a number of places simultaneously, then we would automatically be in a major war, which was a different problem entirely," and which would require the nuclear capabilities of the free world.[41] And because "no single country, even one so powerful as ours, can alone defend the liberty of all nations threatened by Communist aggression from without or subversion within," the

United States was forced to rely primarily on its mutual security program to reinforce the capacity for self-defense of the multitude of small powers on the rimland of Soviet Eurasia.[42] For Eisenhower, the country's foreign aid program (in which military aid originally dominated economic and technical by a ratio of 10 to 1) was "one of our most effective, most practical, least costly methods of achieving our international objectives in this age of peril" because it was a much less expensive proposition (in terms of American blood and treasure) than direct United States intervention.[43] (Nor would the United Nations be totally neglected in the Eisenhower scheme, for in cases such as Suez in 1956 and the Congo in 1960 it could be utilized as a substitute action to thwart Soviet designs of expansion.[44])

## V

The logic of the policy of the "long pull" led most dramatically to the enunciation of the much-maligned and misunderstood doctrine of "massive retaliation" by Secretary of State John Foster Dulles. Even prior to assuming office, Dulles had decided that, after the American experience in Korea, the United States would in the future have to respond to aggression by the Communist bloc "at times and places of our own choosing."[45] To rely on conventional land forces to meet Soviet aggression was illogical inasmuch as it would prove impossible to match the potential enemy at all points on a man-for-man basis. "If we try to do that," he declared, "we are going to bust."[46] In May of 1952, while still a private citizen (if, indeed, Dulles were ever really such) he defined for the first time the doctrine of massive retaliation as "the will . . . and means to retaliate instantly against open aggression by Red armies so that, if it occurred anywhere, we could strike back where it hurts, by means of our own choosing."[47] But relatively little note was taken of this proposition until he delivered, as Secretary of State, his speech before the Council of Foreign Relations in New York in January of 1954 in which he warned the potential aggressor that he "cannot always prescribe battle conditions that suit him" and that, in the event of such attacks, the United States intended "to respond vigorously at places and with means of our own choosing." For it was evident to Dulles (as it was with Eisenhower) that if Soviet Russia could pick its time and place and method of warfare—and if it were the continued policy of the United States to meet this aggression with traditional means and by local opposition—"then we had to be ready to fight in the Arctic and in the tropics, in Asia, in the Middle East, and in Europe; by land and by air; by old weapons and by new weapons."[48]

The uproar by critics who tainted the administration with, as one favorable Dulles biographer terms it,[49] "an aura of adventurism," quickly brought about attempts by the Secretary of State at clarification of a strategy which, in regard to Europe at any rate,[50] was hardly so radical a departure. At first he qualified his previous remarks (or, in any case, changed his emphasis) in a press conference in March in which he reminded his audience that he had merely advocated the *capacity* for such retaliation and not a blanket policy of automatic and instant response.[51] In April, he published a further clarification in which he stated that a policy of massive retaliation did not mean the dropping of atomic bombs on Moscow or Peking in response to limited aggression. Rather, what the doctrine sought to do was to make Communist adventures unprofitable (and thereby unattractive) by means of *selective* retaliation, not against great population centers, but on "specific targets reasonably related to the area." The most important element, though, was the sheer deterrent power of such a policy. Wars being caused largely due to miscalculation, in Dulles' view, the stated intention of the United States to make the costs of aggression to the Communist world greater than any possible gains they could receive would preclude the need for such retaliation because the aggression which would trigger it would simply not occur.[52]

Contrary to the limited war critics of the late fifties, there was nothing illogical about the massive retaliation doctrine even after the Soviet Union itself acquired the means for nuclear retaliation.[53] As a threat of selective and limited retaliation (if the aggression occurred outside of the European theater), the doctrine conveyed to America's rivals that the United States would not necessarily meet ground attacks where they took place, but might conceivably respond with attacks (conventional or nuclear) by air on strategic targets elsewhere. And as a threat of general war if Europe itself were attacked, massive retaliation was indeed a viable policy, for even if the Soviets placed less than 100 per cent faith in the credibility of such a suicidal American response, the mere possibility of such a course of action (discounted by its probability) would have been sufficient to make aggression appear disadvantageous.[54]

Nor did the concept of the "long pull" (and its concomitant massive retaliation) indicate the administration's reliance upon military means in foreign policy. Dulles himself had long appreciated the fact that the ultimate nature of the Soviet challenge was not military at all, but fundamentally an indirect challenge of a diplomatic-political and psychological character. Though if it were thought to be expedient, the Red army might be employed (as it had been in Finland and Poland in the early days of the Second World War), he never felt that the Soviet leaders were overawed by military advice or that their strategy and tactics were dominated by military considerations. On the contrary, with the exception of the two cases just mentioned, the expansion of Soviet power had been accomplished without any direct use of the Russian army. As an observer who readily appreciated that the menace of Communism was of a long-term nature, he believed that, ultimately, the morale of the United States for the long haul would determine the outcome of the conflict between the two moral systems. "I suppose that most of the American people feel that our foreign policy should try to give the military whatever they think will help them defend the United States most effectively in case of war," he observed in 1950. "It is, however, dangerous to let military factors determine foreign policy."[55] In the epochal struggle of the cold war, the primary function of military power was defensive (that is, to prevent attack), while the course of the struggle itself would be determined by the persistence of one of the contrasting ideologies:

The hope of America and the hope of the world does not lie in our economic and military might. We have a duty to be materially strong and share that strength with others who are in peril. But that is only a defensive holding operation. The role of material power . . . is to give moral ideas the opportunity to take root. Our basic strength is in our capacity to propagate these moral ideas which must prevail if there is to be peace and justice in the world.[56]

## VI

Though both Eisenhower and Dulles may have forcefully and consistently seized upon the policy of the "long pull" as the best possible alternative in an imperfect world, the President did so only with a sense of tragedy reminiscent of the pathos of Abraham Lincoln. Like Lincoln, Eisenhower saw his world divided and at war with itself, with men forced to bear the burdens of arms and inordinate taxation while the rest of humanity suffered a life of privation, and with what was to give it all the essential elements of a Greek tragedy—no viable alternative existence. Perhaps the essence of the Eisenhower approach to international politics can best be summed up in two passages from his many addresses on the matter—two rather eloquent and revealing passages from a man who has too often been dismissed as both shallow and inarticulate:

We maintain the formations of war and all the modern weapons. Why? Because we must. As long as this spirit that has prevailed up to now continues to prevail in the world, we cannot expose our rights, our privileges, our homes, our wives, our children to the risk which would come to an unarmed country. But we want to make it perfectly clear that these armaments do not reflect the way we *want* to live. They merely reflect the way, under present conditions, we *have* to live.[57]

. . .

Every gun made, every warship launched, every rocket fired signifies, in the final sense, a theft from those who hunger and are not fed, those who are cold and are not clothed. . . .

This is not a way of life at all, in any true sense. Under the cloud of threatening war, it is humanity hanging from a cross of iron.[58]

43

In the cold war, Eisenhower saw the culmination of the historical clash of good against evil, freedom against slavery, lightness against the dark. And all that stood between the godless and immoral tyranny of Communist totalitarianism and free men everywhere was the strength of a single nation. The United States was, indeed, for Eisenhower, the hope of the world and its great power (moral as well as military) was a sacred trust granted by Providence.[59] For Americans the ultimate values were liberty and peace, and, left to themselves in a world free from Communist machinations, they would prefer to play the role of the benign and generous shopkeeper—laboring hard in order to attain the good life for themselves and a charitable relationship with the less fortunate and the less worthy. In Eisenhower's eyes, he led a nation of Cincinnatuses—peaceful men who periodically were called from their ploughs to take up swords against foreign aggressors. And, like the patriot of ancient Rome, when their tasks were completed they would return to their farms to concentrate on the new harvest rather than on the spoils of war. America was not a nation in arms, but a people in the shops, in the factories, in the schools, in the homes. But after having subdued the fascist terror in the great crusade of the early forties, Americans were not to remain at peace for long, and the new threat of subjugation by the barbarous hordes of the Marxist creed would summon them once more—this time not as transient warriors in one great decisive battle, but as sentinels for the long watch. And the task of leadership at home was to see to it that the ploughs did not rust nor the fields lie fallow.

The United States was thus to pursue a balanced middle way for the long haul, avoiding both the garrison state at home and retreat or surrender abroad.[60] The burden of arms having been thrust upon it by Soviet Russia, America could do no other. But Eisenhower wanted the American people and the world to realize the nature of the dilemma and the country's commitment to peace and prosperity for all peoples.[61]

## VII

If Eisenhower saw the United States as a Cincinnatus who could not return to his farm, he also reviewed its plight as a resultant of the ambiguous but total nature of the Soviet threat. Unlike the crusades of America's past, the Communist design appeared to be one of protracted conflict, with no decisive confrontations and with victory always evasive. Moreover, the bizarre nature of this twilight existence—a world of no-war, no-peace, a nation armed but not fully mobilized—owed much to the state of military technology. Eisenhower, the Soldier-President, was quick to grasp the realities of nuclear stalemate. Despite his espousal of the doctrine of massive retaliation and emphasis on air-atomic power, his apt phrase "there is no alternative to peace" nicely summed up his appreciation of the revolution in international relations wrought by the secret of the atom.

Upon assuming the duties of Commander in Chief, he recognized that America's brief atomic monopoly had ended, and that, though the United States retained a quantitative lead, "even a vast superiority in numbers of weapons, and a consequent capability of devastating retaliation, is no prevention, of itself, against the fearful material damage and toll of human lives that would be reflected" in a nuclear exchange.[62] He warned the nation quite early that the Soviet Union would soon have an arsenal of hydrogen bombs and the capability to drop them on American cities —a capability which he pointed out could be expected to increase over the years. Yet he announced that there would be no plans for an increase in defense spending inasmuch as it could have little if any effect on that capability, thus implying an acceptance of nuclear stalemate as early as 1953.[63] Indeed, with all the current discussion over the change in U. S. strategy from one of "superiority" to one of "sufficiency" under President Nixon,[64] one is inclined to forget that a conscious policy of nuclear superiority was an aberration of the Kennedy-McNamara years.

As early as 1955, when the first rumblings about a potential missile lag were felt by the administration, Eisenhower explicitly rejected the notion that superiority in all nuclear weaponry should be the goal of American defense policy: "there comes a time, possibly, when a lead is not significant in the defense arrangements of a country. If you get enough of a particular type of weapon, I doubt that it is particularly important to have a lot more of it."[65] To Eisenhower, "enough" meant simply a capacity to destroy the viability of a foe's society even after absorbing the first blow and, given the horrors of thermonuclear bombs, it was apparent to him that it would not take much to remove the incentive for surprise attack. Deterrent power was absolute and not relative. It depended not on the ratio of one country's arsenal of bombs to that of another, but simply on the capability to knock out major industrial and population centers. In any event, the atomic bomb had made general war in our time "an anachronism" which would no longer serve a useful purpose: major war was no longer a rational instrument of foreign policy. The Soviet Union and the United States had reached the point where warfare now represented, not a contest of wills as in the past, but "race suicide."[66] Therefore, long before the outcries which followed Sputnik and its "missile gap" of the late fifties, Eisenhower decided upon a course of action which would give the United States just enough intercontinental ballistic missiles and manned bombers to preserve the deterrent power of SAC and no more. In response to a reporter's query in May of 1956 on whether the President agreed that it was vital for this country to stay ahead in long-range bombers, Eisenhower replied forcefully: "No! I say it is vital to get what we believe we need. That does not necessarily mean more than anybody else does. We have to get what we need." And at his next confrontation with a similar question a week later, he refused to play what he called "the numbers racket" and reiterated that, "There comes a time . . . when the destructiveness of weapons is so great as to be beyond imagination, when enough is certainly plenty, and you do no good, as I see it, by increasing these numbers."[67] And when apprehensions over the ephemeral "bomber gap" turned into those over the "missile gap," his response was always of the same nature: the United States had an absolute capability to destroy the Soviet Union by means of strategic bombers in the event of an attack, and missiles would merely reinforce this ability.[68] Thus would the President defend his delicate and intricate philosophy of the "long pull" against those who, failing to comprehend the interrelationship of domestic liberty and international security as he had, would seek much greater

46

defense spending in response to a potential threat which never materialized.

## VIII

The Eisenhower administration was hardly shocked by the Sputnik launching in early October of 1957. The President had been informed of such a Soviet capability a year before and advised, at the same time, about the likelihood of such a time schedule.[69] Yet Eisenhower had been careful in handling the various missile efforts to keep the military implications apart from the purely scientific; he had simply committed the United States to the launching of an earth satellite during the International Geophysical Year (I. G. Y., June, 1957, to December, 1958) for academic purposes and maintained later that the "American space effort . . . in no way began as a race or contest with any other nation." Based upon the criterion of national defense, he saw "no obvious requirement for a crash satellite program,"[70] and until the uproar in the press and the Congress over Sputnik (as Sherman Adams later recalled) "nobody in Washington had really given much consideration to the possible importance of an invasion of space as psychological propaganda or even as a scientific achievement."[71]

If the Soviet space achievement did not surprise the administration, the resulting outcry in the media and on Capitol Hill certainly did catch Dwight Eisenhower off guard. (It seems it never occurred to him that such a scientific success would dramatize the ICBM potential of the Russians.[72]) Rockets and earth satellites were the furthest things from the minds of the American people at the beginning of October, 1957. The news was dominated by the race friction at Little Rock, the World Series in baseball, and the Asian flu epidemic which was spreading in the East. The outgoing Defense Secretary "Engine Charlie" Wilson, whom columnist Jack Raymond charged with cutting American forces to a "dangerous minimum" in his latest economy drive, was praised in the editorials of such prestigious papers as the *New York Times*.[73] Then, out of the blue, the story broke in banner

47

headlines all across the country: SOVIET FIRES EARTH SAT-
ELLITE INTO SPACE; IT IS CIRCLING THE GLOBE AT
18,000 M. P. H.; SPHERE TRACKED IN 4 CROSSINGS OVER
U. S. The American people were told that the 184-pound device
was eight times heavier than the one planned by the United States.
Tass, the Soviet news agency, claimed in its announcement of the
launch that the world could now see how "the new socialist society had turned the boldest dreams of mankind into reality."
The *Times'* Robert K. Plumb declared that the "Soviet has taken
a great step into space, a step beyond that contemplated by science in this country," and the chairman of the U. S. committee
for I. G. Y. termed it "fantastic" and warned that "if they can
launch that they can launch much heavier ones."[74] *Times* columnists Jack Raymond and Harry Schwartz were preoccupied
with the military and political implications abroad; John W. Finney was analyzing the economy drives in the Defense Department and suggesting that the United States might be losing the
ICBM race because of them; Arthur Krock saw the Eisenhower
magic tarnished and the stock of the Democrats rising; and James
Reston was in Moscow reporting on his interview with Nikita
Khrushchev where the confident Russian leader warned that due
to Communist advances in rocketry, though the capitalist world
would be destroyed in a war, "socialism will live on."[75] In the
*New Statesman and Nation,* British science writer Ritchie Calder
warned that "no one can have any doubts about the reality and
range of a Russian ICBM, and that, of course, has military implications which are now immediate. . . ."[76]

In its editorial column, the *New York Times* admonished:

> [T]he Soviet satellite now revolving in the skies obviously
> raises questions of the gravest character regarding the correct-
> ness of our present and past national policies. Those questions
> must be faced unblinkingly.
> . . . [I]t is part of wisdom to assume that the Soviet Union
> does have such a missile capability [to hit the United States],
> and that it is now engaged in a major effort to provide itself as
> soon as possible with large numbers of such weapons. It is clear

we do not have such missiles now, and the time when we may
have them is uncertain.

. . .

Is the world faced with a radical change in the military balance of power at that time, presumably to be measured in
months or a small number of years, when the Soviet Union
has enough such missiles to place every major United States
city and base under threat of annihilation?

Is the policy of putting domestic budgetary and political
considerations ahead of security considerations in allocating
funds for defense still a tenable policy in the present situation?

Are we making a maximum effort at the present time . . . to
assure that we too have intercontinental ballistic missiles at the
earliest possible time?

If not, should we not increase our effort so that it is the maximum possible, utilizing all the rich resources of our science,
technology, and industry?[77]

Even the television newscasts carried the grim forebodings of respected commentators such as Eric Sevareid:

If the intercontinental missile is, indeed, the ultimate, final
weapon of warfare, then at the present rate Russia will soon
come to a period during which she can stand astride the world,
its military master. If she refrains from *acting* the role, the period should be short and we will equal and neutralize her mas-
tery. If she does not refrain, then the freer, the more tolerant
parts of the world will be confronted with the ultimate choice
that Patrick Henry once expressed. . . .[78]

Meanwhile, the nation's crisis of self-confidence and the mis-
sile-mania sent the stock market plummeting to its lowest point
since May of 1955, and in one day the economy would experience
the sharpest drop in stock prices in two years in a record volume
of trading.[79]

While shock and uncertainty gripped the nation, President
Eisenhower retained his perennial sense of balance and proclivity
for moderation. He was not particularly troubled by the evidence

of Soviet rocket technology, because to launch a satellite the size of the "traveling companion" a booster was required of far greater thrust than that necessary for our own missiles given the efficiency we had attained in yield per pound of warhead. Thus, the whole affair would have no effect on American security. In Eisenhower's view of Sputnik, the "most harmful effects were to cause those people who had manifold reasons to be proud to be temporarily fearful, and to add fuel to the fire of demands for larger appropriations as the answer to everything"; thus, he sought "to find ways of affording perspective to our people and so relieve the current wave of near-hysteria."[80] It did not take the President long to appreciate the real danger of Sputnik—namely, the upsetting in one rash stroke of the careful balance of priorities which he had meticulously nurtured for some five years. The immediate reaction of Senators Stuart Symington and Henry M. Jackson[81] (and, a few days later, Senate Majority Leader Lyndon Johnson's call for an investigation by his Preparedness Investigating Subcommittee) convinced Eisenhower that his fears of new pressures for larger defense allocations were real.

Therefore, he instructed his top echelon of advisors that, in the words of Governor Adams, "he preferred to play down the whole thing."[82] Accordingly, the administration began the counterattack on its critics to preserve the policy of the "long pull." On the day after Sputnik, Rear Admiral Rawson Bennett, Chief of Naval Operations, referred to the satellite as a "hunk of iron almost anybody could launch." On the same day, Press Secretary James Hagerty dismissed the event as one which "did not come as a surprise," and reiterated the President's view that, "we never thought of our program as one which was a race with the Soviets." On 15 October Sherman Adams declared rather cavalierly: "The Administration is not interested in serving a high score in an outer space basketball game." In a similar manner, Defense Secretary Wilson (who had just stepped down from office) termed the satellite "a neat scientific trick," and reminded reporters that, "Nobody is going to drop anything on you from a satellite while you are asleep, so don't worry about it." And Secretary of the Treasury George M. Humphrey cautioned in a more serious tone: "The real danger of the Sputnik is that some too eager people may demand hasty and sensational action regardless of cost and relative merit in an attempt to surpass what they have done. Americans must never lose their sense of balance and proportion."[83]

And while Khrushchev was already beginning to rattle his rockets over the Middle East crisis between Turkey and Syria, Eisenhower himself set about to dispel the fears of peril abroad and ineptitude at home. In his first post-Sputnik news conference, he immediately separated the issues of the satellite and missile programs, reassuring his audience that they were entirely distinct programs. He emphasized that the country's missile (but not space) programs had had top priority for several years, discounted the value of satellites in national defense, declared that Khrushchev's claims that manned aircraft (that is, SAC) was obsolescent was nonsensical, and finally, said that the Soviet launching had not raised his apprehensions, "not one iota." The President also moved to the offensive and voiced thoughtful concern over the cost overruns of the satellite program, which had progressively bulged from a 22 million dollar budget to 66 million and then 110 million.[84]

In addition to the barrage of verbal pronouncements (many of which, through "an overemphasis on the de-emphasis," had backfired by inciting myriad charges of complacency in the Congress and in the press[85]), the administration countered with tangible efforts of movement in the missile field. Soon after his press conference, Eisenhower made public his directive to the Defense Department to speed up the missile program (but *within* the budget previously allocated), and the new Secretary of Defense Neil H. McElroy briefed the news media on his plans to expedite the programs (which again, it was emphasized, would *not* involve more expenditures) by assuming personal direction over missile development. The Pentagon began its carefully orchestrated counteroffensive and proceeded to announce a multitude of advances in the missile field and in other strategic weaponry: the Air Force successfully fired its Thor intermediate range ballistic missile (IRBM) four days after Sputnik, the Army tested its Jupiter IRBM and the Navy its Vanguard two weeks later. Simultaneously, Eisenhower met with British Prime Minister Harold Macmillan and agreed that the two powers would henceforth pool their scientific know-how and promised to deliver a series of talks to the nation the following month. Prematurely convinced that he had succeeded in extinguishing the needless panic, the President concurrently announced his plans to reduce the federal budget in 1958 by some two billion dollars while leaving DOD expenditures at their current level. And in order to underscore the continued validity of the policy of the "long pull," Secretary of State Dulles threatened the Russians with massive retaliation if they should be foolish enough to attack Turkey (as Khrushchev had indicated they might).[86]

But Eisenhower had seriously miscalculated. He had correctly perceived the gravity of Sputnik as a threat to his program of the "long pull," but failed to appreciate how deeply the shock waves had penetrated the American polity. The humiliation of the Soviet space spectacular had incited movement among the latent forces of discontent within the country—interests within the Congress, the military, industry, labor, and academia which had long bridled under the tight reins of the parsimonious Eisenhower years. Moreover, the President simply had no control over unfortunate events which would serve merely to exacerbate the crisis and further impugn the veracity of his reassurances and bring into question the propriety of his policies. As soon as the initial trauma of Sputnik appeared to be subsiding, Eisenhower announced on 1 November that he would begin his series of a half-dozen nationwide addresses on the thirteenth to "stimulate the faith and confidence" of the American people in their defense preparations. The following day the Russians launched a new satellite (six times heavier than Sputnik I) carrying a canine cosmonaut. The lid blew off once more as journalists wondered whether the next Soviet feat would be a flight to the moon, as Khrushchev claimed that his rockets had negated the value of the United States' overseas bases, and as Democrats in the Congress attacked the obvious "complacency" of the administration.

Hastily moving up his planned first radio and television speech to the nation by a week, President Eisenhower assured the people that the country's security posture was sound, that, with forward bases in Europe, our IRBMs would serve the same function as longer-range missiles, and that the earth satellites "have no direct present effect upon the nation's security." He further announced that James R. Killian of the Massachusetts Institute of Technology would be appointed his personal advisor on science and technology and that inter-service rivalry would be eliminated, thus enhancing the efficiency of the missile and satellite programs. And in conclusion, he, as usual, counselled for moderation: "We must apply our resources at that point as fully as the need demands. This means selectivity in national expenditures of all kinds. We cannot on an unlimited scale have both what we must have and what we would like to have."[87]

The consistent and prudent equilibrium of the popular Eisenhower began once again to take effect. Then, two weeks later, the General suffered a stroke. Within a fortnight, America's Vanguard rocket, scheduled to carry the first Explorer satellite into orbit, blew up in flames before a worldwide audience on its launch pad at Cape Canaveral. The nation, which previously had looked to the wise guidance of its Soldier-President, seemed for the moment to founder, rudderless, on a sea of Sputniks, rockets, and Khrushchevs.

## IX

If Sputnik served as a focal point for a fundamental onslaught against the defense policies and tutelage of Dwight Eisenhower, the controversy also may be viewed heuristically as a microcosm of the debate which would last until the Presidential election of 1960. The last three years of the Eisenhower administration were marked by contentious arguments concerning the adequacy of America's defenses and the validity of its underlying doctrines. The long controversy would culminate in the rejection of the policy of the "long pull" by the Kennedy administration and the substitution of the "flexible response" doctrine for that of "massive retaliation." The Soviet Sputnik of the fall of 1957 had opened the floodgates of criticism, and the three or four months which would follow, preoccupied as they were with military matters, served as a portent of things to come.

The autumn and winter of 1957-1958 witnessed the rise of a coalition of forces, each (for its own reasons and in its own interest) seeking to modify or overturn the Eisenhower program of defense. Not only military men, but scientists and educators as well, saw in the wake of the satellite launching the vindication of their parochial views on the neglect or starvation of the programs which each group considered in the national interest. Democrats (and some liberal Republicans) in the national legislature, who had long taken issue with the conservative administration over its if-not-today-then-tomorrow attitude toward domestic and/or defense funding, seized upon the country's temporary disorientation in order to move it in new directions which, from their perspective, better served the general welfare. And industry and labor union leaders saw greater defense expenditures not only as the cure for America's security dilemma, but also perhaps as a means of breaking out of the stagnating recession which had set in in late 1957 and had continued through the following year.

The Army, the military service which had fared worst under the philosophy of the "long pull" and its emphasis on strategic rather than conventional forces, naturally was the first military interest to be heard. Within days after Sputnik, Generals Holgar Nelson Toftay (commander of the Redstone Arsenal) and John A. Barclay (deputy commander of the Army Ballistic Missile Agency)—both involved in the Army's satellite program—claimed that they could have launched a United States satellite in 1955 but had been interfered with by the Navy, which had been allotted the task by the administration. The Soviets were winning the race to the moon, they further suggested, because the President refused to accept the challenge. (This was soon followed by an administration attempt to stifle comments on satellite policy in a memorandum issued by Army Secretary Wilber M. Bruckner.)[88] Later in the month, Chief of Staff Maxwell D. Taylor (later to resign in frustration over administration military policy and then to re-appear as Kennedy's military advisor and chairman of his Joint Chiefs of Staff) intimated that Sputnik signalled the end of America's nuclear superiority and that, in the era of stalemate which was to follow, greater emphasis would have to be placed on conventional limited war capabilities.

I see the picture as being composed of two great power blocs: the Communist bloc and the free Western world aligned against one another; the evidence of the great effort on the part of the Communist bloc to improve their power position; the evidence that both sides have an atomic destructive possibility which, if employed without restriction, would probably result in mutual destruction.

Under this situation of relative parity of destructive capability, it would appear that the most probable threat to us is the small aggression, the limited war, subversion, coup d'etat and that sort of thing. So, in my opinion, having made adequate provision for a strong atomic retaliatory force, as we have, the free world should concern itself very seriously about its ability to resist the situations short of general war.[89]

And if funds were to be directed toward strategic weaponry, Taylor maintained that they should be expended for an active anti-ballistic missile defense, such as the Army's Nike-Zeus system.[90]

At a series of meetings of the Association of the U. S. Army, service partisans heard a deluge of attacks upon the doctrine of massive retaliation and were presented with the case for limited war by academicians like Henry A. Kissinger and military men like Vice Chief of Staff Lyman L. Lemnitzer. The Association itself, in its resolution of 30 October, urged the maintenance of an Army of one million as opposed to that of 900,000 proposed by the administration.[91] At the same time, those within the service concerned with strategic weapons (such as Major General John B. Medaris, chief of the Army Ballistic Missile Agency) charged that the United States was far behind the Soviet Union in the missile field and that the Russians had apparently solved the reentry problem for warheads and thus were well on their way to ICBM superiority.[92] By the close of the year, Army frustration with its apparent share of the Sputnik budgetary dividend was revealed most dramatically in the retirement of James M. Gavin, who had been the service's chief of research and development. Gavin, who had severely criticized the lack of money being spent by the administration for limited war forces before the Congress the month before, saw in the steady deterioration of the Army the makings of disaster. "I'll not be party to another Korea," he declared in an interview with the *New York Times*' Hanson Baldwin, "and this is what the country is facing up to."[93]

Meanwhile, the Air Force and Navy were not to remain idle. Those elements of the former concerned primarily with airpower (as opposed to missile power) were forced to defend the future of the manned bomber against charges of obsolescence and called for more expenditures on long-range aircraft, not less, in the face of the Soviet threat.[94] Others, the Air Force missile faction, who had waged a long battle within the service against the bomber men, emphasized the need for greater appropriations for strategic missiles.[95] And, finally, those like Chief of Staff Thomas D. White and Secretary James H. Douglas, concerned as they were with the needs of the Air Force as a whole, concentrated on balancing these two divergent interests and, at the same time, asserting the role of the service against infringements by either the Army or the Navy.[96] The Navy, for its part, was also plagued by contending factions. The Project Vanguard people hoped the shock of Sputnik would pry loose funds from the administration for their satellite program and provide the Navy with a major space role, especially in the race to the moon.[97] And similar to the role of their Air Force counterparts, Admiral Arleigh A. Burke (Chief of Naval Operations) and Navy Secretary Thomas S. Gates sought to preserve the role of the service as a whole, which meant infringing on the primary spheres of both the Army (limited war) and the Air Force (general war).[98]

## X

It is, of course, more fashionable to focus on the American military's unquenchable thirst for greater expenditures. And it is, indeed, true that pressures for more and more defense spending came, not only from each service, but from numerous rival factions within each service. (To a large extent, of course, given the administration's firm desire to hold down the lid on military appropriations, much of the contending pressures cancelled one another out inasmuch as all were, for the most part, fighting over a fixed piece of the Eisenhower budgetary pie). However, the gentlemen in uniform were hardly the only ones seeking something they believed necessary for the well-being of the nation out of what was hoped would be the fiscal grab-bag of Sputnik. Business and labor, as well as scientists and educators (not to mention the Democrats on Capitol Hill) were eager to get in on the Sputnik dividend in order to further their respective versions of the common good.

The pages of the country's prestigious newspapers for several months following the momentous events of October were virtually inundated with articles on the conferences, conventions, and reports of science and education organizations decrying the meager funding for their fields by federal, state, and local governments. Some were concerned with the poor state of science education in the country, others with protecting the humanities against an overemphasis on the physical sciences. Still others called for more government student scholarships and loans, larger grants to universities, and higher teacher salaries. The chronicle of demands was virtually endless—and sometimes contradictory. But the message to the administration was the same: more money! A listing of the groups which voiced their criticisms and dissatisfactions would include: the American Council of Education, the National Science Foundation, the Conference of Science and Engineering, the American Association of Graduate Schools, the New York City Board of Education, the National Association of Teachers, the Office of Science and Education, the National Advisory Committee on Aeronautics, the American Council of Education, the National Education Association, the New York State Board of Regents, the New York City Board of Higher Education. (The list, of course, is in no way intended to be exhaustive, merely suggestive.)[99] In addition to organizations, many of the country's leading educators took up the cause, in one form or the other.[100]

Both organized labor and business got on the Sputnik band-wagon. The news of the satellite launching was but a few days old when the United Automobile Workers (UAW) union attacked the defense cutbacks of the Eisenhower administration for alleg-edly endangering the security of the United States. Layoffs as-sociated with the cutbacks were termed "socially irresponsible and economically questionable." One week later, in a televised interview, UAW president Walter P. Reuther (who, of course, was also vice president of the AFL-CIO) called Sputnik a "blood-less Pearl Harbor," and asked for the mobilization of American resources in an emergency program to catch up with the Sovi-ets.[101] By the beginning of the new year, AFL-CIO president George Meany resolved that the main job for the country in 1958 was to strengthen its defenses. And he added that, "American workers are prepared to shoulder their just share of that cost"[102] —presumably in more overtime and new jobs as well as higher taxes and inflation. The National Association of Manufacturers sent a message to the President after Sputnik II pledging its co-operation "to prevent this country from being outdistanced by the Soviet Union in any category of scientific or economic achieve-ment." By February of the following year, even the fiscally con-servative U. S. Chamber of Commerce had announced its sup-port for greater defense spending, only the year before having refused to endorse the Eisenhower budget because it had claimed it was too high.[103] As could be expected, the aviation in-dustry was only too willing to speed up its programs and assume new responsibilities.[104]

To be sure, then, there was a good deal of pressure from vari-ous quarters for a shift in administration policy. However, much of this would not have come to fruition without the active inter-vention of the Congress. It was here in the legislative branch—and especially in the Senate—that the rumblings of discontent in the press, academia, the military, business, and labor would be transformed from an inchoate disgruntlement into a political force with which the administration would have to come to terms, especially in an election year. A good part, if not most, of the Congressional activity during these several months was probably precipitated less by partisan desire for political gain than by genuine apprehension over the future of American security. And this was generally true of all the interests discussed above. One need only read summaries of the alarming Gaither Committee Report leaked to the press in November, 1957, and the private Rockefeller Brothers Fund study published in January of the following year to realize the nature of the threat to the country as it was then perceived.[105] But party loyalties still remained operative (and would become more evident as 1960 approached) as can readily be seen by comparing the reactions of Republican as opposed to Democratic legislators to President Eisenhower's first reassurance speech of 7 November.[106]

## XI

The coalition of forces mounted against the Eisenhower defense policy of the "long pull," thus reflected and abetted by the Congress, was eventually to have its effect. But, for the most part, it would have to await Dwight Eisenhower's retirement from the Presidency. Though the Sputnik controversy was partly reflected in the supplemental budget of 1.26 billion dollars in new funds (for SAC dispersal and the satellite and missile programs) requested of Congress by the President for FY 1958, and though succeeding budgets registered nominal gains for DOD expenditures, Eisenhower proved to be rather successful in preserving the nation's outward sense of moderation and balance for the remainder of his term. Measured in constant dollars (that is, adjusted for inflation), the budgets for FY 1959 through FY 1961 were really no greater than those before. And though, perhaps, more land-based and submarine-launched ballistic missiles were eventually programmed (due to Congressional insistence) than the President had really planned, the increase was negligible when compared with the vast build-up which proceeded under his successor. Finally, he succeeded in further cutting the manpower and budget for the Army. Major increases, here as well, would have to await the Kennedy administration.

All in all, this writer is inclined to support the observation of Sherman Adams, who maintained that Dwight Eisenhower's greatest service as President was his "relentless effort during the cold war with Russia to keep America from draining its economy by plunging into a frantic build-up of military strength."[107] Those who engage in the polemics of gauging his "Machiavellian genius" miss the point. For that is conjecture. Yet his accomplishments were real. And the question of whether they owed their origin to an incisively realistic analysis of the needs of mid-twentieth century America or stemmed from a rather simple and anachronistic model of an America that was no more, is dwarfed by the stature of the values which his policies defended.

1. These two characterizations of the Soviet space spectacular were made by newspaper columnists William V. Shannon (the *New York Post*) and Marguerite Higgins (the *New York Herald Tribune*), respectively, during the fateful days which followed the news of the satellite launching. Cited in Richard Witkin, ed., *The Challenge of Sputnik* (Garden City: Doubleday & Company, 1958), pp. 44, 49.

2. Arthur M. Schlesinger, "Our Presidents: A Rating by 75 Historians," *The New York Times Magazine*, 29 July 1962, pp. 12 ff.

3. The new extreme in judging Eisenhower's performance as President is aptly illustrated in the analyses of Garry Wills and Herbert S. Parmet. In Wills' *Nixon Agonistes: The Crisis of the Self-Made Man* (Boston: Houghton Mifflin Company, 1969), a glowing account of Eisenhower suggests that the General possessed a genius for politics which has generally been neglected. In Parmet's *Eisenhower and the American Crusades* (New York: The Macmillan Company, 1972), the amiable and fatherly Ike becomes nothing less than the incarnation of Machiavelli's lion and the fox.

4. Richard H. Rovere, "Eisenhower Revisited—A Political Genius? A Brilliant Man?," *The New York Times Magazine*, 7 February 1971, p. 14. For those desiring to go beyond the analysis of the Eisenhower years presented in this study, the following works should be consulted: Arthur Larson, *Eisenhower: The President Nobody Knew* (New York: Charles Scribner's Sons, 1968); Marquis William Childs, *Eisenhower: Captive Hero* (New York: Harcourt, Brace and World, 1958); Dean Albertson, *Eisenhower as President* (New York: Hill and Wang, 1963); Robert J. Donovan, *Eisenhower: The Inside Story* (New York: Harper Brothers, 1956).

5. Reinhold Niebuhr, *Christianity and Power Politics* (New York: Charles Scribner's Sons, 1940), p. 71. Similarly, see Walter Lippman's analysis of the challenges facing leadership in democratic societies through the inordinate influence of a public opinion which counsels dangerous inaction in times of peril in his *The Public Philosophy* (New York: The New American Library, 1955).

6. Adam B. Ulam, *The Rivals: America and Russia Since World War II* (New York: The Viking Press, 1971), p. 233.

7. Emmet John Hughes, *The Ordeal of Power: A Political Memoir of the Eisenhower Years* (New York: Atheneum, 1963), pp. 349-350. Eisenhower's preference for that description of democracy which emphasizes the need for self-discipline would appear to vaunt its descent from (among others) Edmund Burke, England's classical conservative of the 18th century. (There seems to be a good deal of classical conservatism evident in Eisenhower's political philosophy, especially his emphasis on balance, moderation, and gradualism.) For Burke, individual liberty necessitated the exercise of self-restraint on the part of the citizenry so as to prevent the intervention of the state as arbiter in human affairs. Compare the Eisenhower definition of democracy with the Burkeian conception of liberty:

> Men are qualified for civil liberty in exact proportion to their disposition to put moral chains upon their own appetites—in proportion as their love of justice is above their rapacity,—in proportion as their soundness and sobriety of understanding is above their vanity and presumption,—in proportion as they are more disposed to listen to the counsels of the wise and the good, in preference to the flattery of knaves. Society cannot exist unless a controlling power upon will and appetite be placed somewhere; and the less of it there is within, the more there must be without. It is ordained in the external constitution of things, that men of intemperate minds cannot be free.

See Burke's "A Letter to a Member of the National Assembly, 1790," in Robert A. Smith, ed., *Edmund Burke on Revolution* (New York: Harper & Row, Publishers, 1968), pp. 149-150.

8. See John F. Kennedy's speech of 14 January 1960 to the National Press Club where he quoted Eisenhower on the latter's dislike for politics; the *New York Times*, 15 January 1960, p. 15.

9. Sherman Adams, *First-Hand Report: The Story of the Eisenhower Administration* (New York: Harper & Brothers, 1961), p. 220.

10. U. S. Presidents, *Public Papers of the Presidents of the United States: Dwight D. Eisenhower, 1953-1961*, 8 vols. (Washington, D.C.: Government Printing Office, 1960-1); vol. I, p. 227, "Special Message to the Congress on Department of Defense Reorganization, 19 April 1953." (Hereafter cited as *Public Papers: Eisenhower*).

11. "Annual Message to the Congress on the State of the Union, 9 January 1959," *ibid.*, vol. VII, p. 5.

12. "Annual Message Transmitting the Economic Report to the Congress, 24 January 1956," *ibid.*, vol. IV, p. 177.

13. "Address to the National Security Industrial Association, 25 October 1954," *ibid.*, vol. II, p. 956; also, "News Conference, 30 January 1957," vol. V, pp. 99-100, and "Remarks at the National Press Club, 14 January 1959," vol. VII, p. 20.

14. See, for example, "Budget Message to the Congress: Fiscal Year 1955, 21 January 1954," *ibid.*, vol. II, pp. 72-192.

15. Dwight D. Eisenhower, *Waging Peace: The White House Years, 1956-1961* (Garden City: Doubleday & Company, 1965), chapter 5.

16. "Annual Message Transmitting the Economic Report to the Congress, 20 January 1959," *Public Papers: Eisenhower*, vol. II, p. 215.

17. "Annual Message Presenting the Economic Report to the Congress, 20 January 1959," *ibid.*, vol. VII, p. 117.

18. "Annual Message to the Congress on the State of the Union, 9 January 1959," *ibid.*, p. 6.

19. "Annual Message to the Congress on the State of the Union, 5 January 1956," *ibid.*, vol. IV, pp. 11-12; "Annual Message to the Congress on the State of the Union, 9 January 1959," vol. VII, p. 6.

20. Arthur F. Burns, *Prosperity Without Inflation* (Garden City: Doubleday & Company, 1958), p. 201.

21. See Raymond J. Saulnier, "Do Deficits Matter?," in Ralph de Toledano and Karl Kess, eds., *The Conservative Papers* (Garden City: Doubleday & Company, 1964), pp. 145-161.

22. Henry C. Wallich, "Conservative Economic Policy," *Yale Review* (Autumn, 1956). Reprinted in Paul A. Samuelson, et al., eds., *Readings in Economics*, 3rd ed. (New York: McGraw-Hill Book Company, 1958), p. 441. See also Wallich's *The Cost of Freedom: Conservatism and Modern Capitalism* (New York: Collier Books, 1962). This latter work is an excellent exposition of the underlying assumption of conservative economics; that is, that the cost of freedom (defined largely in terms of those liberties consonant with the free enterprise system) is a lower rate of economic growth than would be attainable under a socialist or planned economy.

23. Burns, *op. cit.*, pp. 74-75; Wallich, *The Cost of Freedom*, p. 147.

24. "Annual Message to the Congress on the State of the Union, 2 February 1953," *Public Papers: Eisenhower*, vol. I, pp. 19-20.

25. Adams, *op. cit.*, p. 21. It is interesting to note that Eisenhower, who would be assailed in later years by liberal Democrats for spending too little on defense and for allegedly sacrificing national security on the altar of the sacred cow of the balanced budget, was constantly at odds (especially in his first administration) with conservative Republicans for overspending, particularly on defense. In neither case was the President moved by his critics to embrace programs which he considered imprudent. He constantly defended the middle way—balancing defense spending against the needs of a free economy as he saw them so as to attain the golden mean and further both values.

26. *Ibid.*, p. 397; "Televised Panel Discussion, 21 October 1958," *Public Papers: Eisenhower*, vol. IV, p. 765; "News Conference, 13 January 1960," vol. VIII, p. 7. Not until January of 1955 would Eisenhower be able to announce a 7.4 billion dollar cut in taxes made possible by reductions in the Defense Department budget.

27. "Address to the Annual Convention of the National Junior Chamber of Commerce, 10 June 1953," *ibid.*, vol. I, p. 386.

28. As Eisenhower counselled during the 1956 Presidential election campaign on the proposal to abolish the military draft:

> For 20 years or more our government alternated between costly peaks [in defense spending] in years of military crisis and starving valleys in years of apparent calm. Twice in this generation relaxations of America's military strength have been followed by costly wars.
>
> Now, since 1953, we have once more gained freedom from armed conflict. We must not let down our guard again. We must not by weakness invite another war.

("Statement on the Need for Maintaining the Draft, 7 October 1956," *ibid.*, vol. IV, p. 867).

29.  In his first State of the Union address, Eisenhower declared: "Our problem is to achieve adequate military strength within the limits of endurable strain upon our economy. To amass military power without regard to our economic capacity would be to defend ourselves against one kind of disaster by inviting another." ("Annual Message to the Congress on the State of the Union, 2 February," *ibid.*, vol. I, p. 17.)

30.  *Ibid.*, p. 13.

31.  Adams, *op. cit.*, p. 398.

32.  *Ibid.*, p. 371.

33.  "Address to the Annual Convention of the National Junior Chamber of Commerce, 10 June 1953," *Public Papers: Eisenhower*, vol. I, p. 9; "Remarks at the Opening of the White House Conference of Mayors, 14 October 1953," vol. I, p. 827; "Recorded Summary of an Address to the American People on National Security, 19 May 1953," vol. I, p. 317; "News Conference, 3 February 1960," vol. VIII, pp. 152-153; "Farewell Radio and Television Address to the American People, 17 January 1961," vol. VIII, p. 1038; "Last News Conference, 18 January 1961," vol. VIII, p. 1045.

34.  Omar N. Bradley, "This Way Lies Peace," *Saturday Evening Post*, 15 October 1949, p. 33; Walter Millis, ed., *The Forrestal Diaries* (New York: Viking Press, 1951), p. 508; Warner R. Schilling, et al., *Strategy Politics and Defense Budgets* (New York: Columbia University Press, 1962), pp. 8-10.

35.  For detailed analyses of the Eisenhower "New Look," see: Glen H. Snyder, "The 'New Look' of 1953," in Schilling, *op. cit.*, pp. 379-524; Samuel P. Huntington, *The Common Defense: Strategic Programs in National Politics* (New York: Columbia University Press, 1961), pp. 64-88; Dwight D. Eisenhower, *Mandate for Change: The White House Years, 1953-1956* (Garden City: Doubleday & Company, 1963), chapter 18.

36.  See, for example: "Address at the 'Salute to Eisenhower' Dinner, 20 January 1956," *Public Papers: Eisenhower*, vol. IV, pp. 173-176; "Letter to the Defense Secretary on National Security Requirements, 15 January 1955," vol. III, pp. 2-6. Also, see the testimony of Defense Secretary Charles E. Wilson before the House Defense Appropriations Subcommittee in January of 1957: House of Representatives, Committee on Appropriations, Subcommittee on Department of Defense Appropriations, *Department of Defense Appropriations for 1958*, part I, 85th Congress, 1st Session (Washington, D.C.: Government Printing Office, 1957), pp. 3-9.

37.  "News Conference, 30 April 1953," *Public Papers: Eisenhower*, vol. VII, pp. 243-244.

38.  "Radio and Television Address to the American People on the National Security and Its Costs, 19 May 1953," *ibid.*, pp. 306-316.

39.  Eisenhower, *Waging Peace*, p. 454.

40.  "News Conference, 4 March 1959," *Public Papers: Eisenhower*, vol. VII, pp. 243-244.

41.  Eisenhower, *Waging Peace*, p. 452.

42.  "Annual Message to the Congress on the State of the Union, 2 February 1958," *Public Papers: Eisenhower*, Vol. VI, p. 14.

43.  "Special Message to the Congress on the Mutual Security Program of 1955, 23 June 1954," *ibid.*, vol. II, p. 590; see also: "Special Message to the

Congress on the Mutual Security Program of 1954, 5 May 1953," vol. I, pp. 256-259; "Special Message to the Congress on the Mutual Security Program of 1957, 19 March 1956," vol. IV, pp. 314-319. As the Soviet threat seemed to change in later years from one of a military nature to a primarily economic attempt at domination, the economic aspect of the foreign aid program would be given greater emphasis. See Eisenhower's "Remarks at the Fourteenth Annual Conference of the Advertising Council, 6 May 1958," vol. IV, pp. 372-386; "Address at the Annual Dinner of the American Society of Newspaper Editors, 21 April 1956," vol. IV, pp. 411-417.

44. See, for example, "Address to the Nation on the Middle East Crisis, 20 February 1957," *Department of State Bulletin*, vol. 39, (11 March 1957), pp. 123-127; "Address Before the Fifteenth Session of the United Nations General Assembly, 4 October 1960," *ibid.*, vol. 42 (10 October 1960), pp. 551-555.

45. Address to the French National Political Science Institute in Paris, 5 May 1952; cited in John Robinson Beal, *John Foster Dulles, 1888-1959* (New York: Harper & Row, 1959), p. 129.

46. Quoted in William W. Kaufmann, "The Requirements of Deterrence," in Kaufmann, ed., *Military Policy and National Security* (Princeton: University Press, 1956).

47. John Foster Dulles, "A Policy of Boldness," *Life*, vol. 32 (19 May 1952), p. 151.

48. *New York Times*, 13 January 1954, pp. 19-20.

49. Eleanor Lansing Dulles, *John Foster Dulles: The Last Year* (New York: Harcourt, Brace & World, 1963), p. 151.

50. The Truman administration had previously adopted a strategy of nuclear retaliation to massive conventional attack upon Western Europe. What Dulles added was the possibility that such weapons might be used in response to lesser attacks in other parts of the world. For further discussion, see Huntington, *op. cit.*, pp. 73-89.

51. *New York Times*, 17 March 1954, p. 1.

52. John Foster Dulles, "Policy for Security and Peace," *Foreign Affairs*, vol. 32 (April, 1954), pp. 353-364. See also: James Shepley, "How Dulles Averted War," *Life*, vol. 40 (16 January 1956), pp. 70 ff.; Roscoe Drummond and Gaston Coblentz, *Duel at the Brink: John Foster Dulles' Command of American Power* (Garden City: Doubleday & Company, 1960), pp. 65-70.

53. When it became apparent that the Soviet Union had acquired the capability to strike at the continental United States with nuclear weapons, thus bringing the credibility of the American doctrine into question, Dulles simply rephrased it to include the possibility of employing tactical nuclear weapons rather than airpower. The substance of the policy remained unchanged, inasmuch as "massive retaliation" had meant in reality "selective" retaliation from the beginning. See John Foster Dulles, "Challenge and Response in U. S. Foreign Policy," *Foreign Affairs*, vol. 36 (October, 1957), pp. 29-42.

54. On the effectiveness of the doctrine of selective retaliation for non-European aggression and actual massive retaliation for an attack upon Western Europe, see: Morton H. Halperin, *Defense Strategies for the Seventies*

(Boston: Little, Brown and Company, 1971), pp. 43-44; Thomas C. Schelling, *Arms and Influence* (New Haven: Yale University Press, 1966), pp. 107-109; Richard Goold-Adams. *John Foster Dulles: A Reappraisal* (New York: Appleton-Century-Crofts, Inc., 1962), pp. 109 ff.

55.  John Foster Dulles, *War or Peace* (New York: The Macmillan Company, 1950), pp. 113-114, 235-240.

56.  "Address at the First Presbyterian Church, Watertown, New York (28 August 1949)," in Harry P. Van Dusen, ed., *The Spiritual Legacy of John Foster Dulles: Selections from his Articles and Addresses* (Philadelphia: Westminster Press, 1960), pp. 910. Though Dulles did possess an intensely moral sense of mission, this did not necessarily impart a rigid moralistic or idealistic tinge to the means which he employed in conducting the foreign relations of the United States. For an interpretation of Dulles as a realist rather than a dogmatist, see: Michael A. Guhin, "Dulles' Thoughts on International Politics: Myth and Reality," *Orbis*, vol. XIII (Fall, 1969), pp. 865-889; and, by the same author, *John Foster Dulles: A Statesman and His Times* (New York: Columbia University Press, 1972).

57.  "Radio and Television Address to the American People on Departure for the Big Four Conference in Geneva, 15 July 1955," *Public Papers: Eisenhower*, vol. III, pp. 704-705. (Emphasis added.)

58.  " 'The Chance for Peace': An Address to the American Society of Newspaper Editors, 16 April 1953," *ibid.*, vol. I, pp. 216-220.

59.  "Inaugural Address, 20 January 1953," *ibid.*, pp. 1-7.

60.  The discussion thus far may have unfortunately stressed the one half of the Eisenhower formula for the "long pull"—namely, the avoidance of spending too much for defense. Because the present study focuses on the effects of the Soviet Sputnik in upsetting the careful balance by pressuring for greater military allocation, this may have been unavoidable. However, it should be emphasized that the Eisenhower administration was as adamant against those who would spend too much on national defense as against those who would spend too little. Having provided a defense posture which he believed to be minimal, he constantly fought off pressures for further cuts which he believed would jeopardize security. True, armaments were a burden. But they were a necessary burden in a world of adversity, and he would not preside over any version of unilateral disarmament. In this regard, see the following: "News Conference, 16 March 1955," *ibid.*, vol. III, pp. 338-339; "Radio and Television Address Opening the Campaign for Re-election, 19 September 1956," vol. IV, pp. 785-787; "Acceptance Speech at the Republican National Convention, 23 August 1956," vol. IV, p. 711; "Statement of the Need for Maintaining the Draft, 7 October 1956," vol. IV, p. 867; "Address at Seattle, Washington, 17 October 1956," vol. IV, p. 947; "Address at Beverly Hills, California, 19 October 1956," vol. IV, pp. 971-978; "Statement by the President Reviewing the Government's Policies with respect to the Developing and Testing of Nuclear Weapons," vol. IV, pp. 997-1002; "Address at Madison Square Garden, New York City, 25 October 1956," vol. IV, pp. 1020-1023; "Radio and Television Address to the American People, 14 May 1957," vol. V. pp. 341-352. (Note that these sources are all before Sputnik. The events of October, 1957, would cause him to exert countervail-

ing pressures on the other side of the scale, thus making him appear to be the defender of the economy rather than the guardian of national security. His program, of course, sought to perform both functions.)

61.  For examples of his frequent lamentations on the burden of armaments made necessary by the intransigence of Communist Russia, see: "Address at the Dinner of the National Conference on the Foreign Aspects of National Security, 25 February 1958," *ibid.*, vol. VI, pp. 77-78; "Address to the American Society of Newspaper Editors, 17 April 1958," vol. VI, pp. 325-334.

62.  "Address Before the General Assembly of the United Nations on the Peaceful Uses of Atomic Energy, 8 December 1953," *ibid.*, vol. I, p. 818.

63.  "News Conference, 8 October 1953," *ibid.*, pp. 644-652.

64.  The defense policies of the Nixon administration represented, to a larger extent than currently appreciated, a return to the wisdom of the President under whom Richard Nixon served. The "Nixon Doctrine," as enunciated on Guam in 1969, eschews the world-policeman role embraced by John Kennedy and previously rejected by Dwight Eisenhower. As stated by President Nixon, the central thesis of this program of retrenchment is "that the United States will participate in the defense and development of allies and friends, but America cannot—and will not—conceive *all* the plans, design *all* the programs, execute *all* the decisions and undertake *all* the defense of the free nations of the world." And the policy of "realistic deterrence," unveiled by Defense Secretary Melvin Laird in March of 1971, is a fundamental shift back to the Eisenhower policy of nuclear "sufficiency." See the publication of the President's report to the Congress of 18 February 1970: Richard M. Nixon, *United States Foreign Policy for the 1970's: A New Strategy for Peace* (New York: Bantam Books, 1970); for a discussion of the Laird plan of "realistic deterrence," see the *New York Times*, 10 March 1971, pp. 1 ff.

65.  "News Conference, 2 March 1955," *Public Papers: Eisenhower*, vol. III, p. 303.

66.  "Address at the Annual Dinner of the American Society of Newspaper Editors, 21 April 1956," *ibid.*, vol. IV, p. 418; "News Conference, 6 February 1956," vol. IV, p. 236.

67.  "News Conference, 4 May 1956," *ibid.*, p. 463; "News Conference, 9 May 1956," p. 74.

68.  "News Conference, 25 April 1956," *ibid.*, p. 433; "News Conference, 27 August 1958," vol. VI, p. 628.

69.  Eisenhower, *Waging Peace*, p. 206; also, see John B. Medaris, *Countdown for Decision* (New York: G. P. Putnam's Sons, 1960). In fact, had it so desired, the United States could have launched an earth satellite by the end of 1956, a full year before Sputnik.

70.  Eisenhower, *Waging Peace*, pp. 208-209.

71.  Adams, *op. cit.*, p. 415.

72.  It is interesting to note that since Sputnik we have become quite aware of the relationship between space and weapons development. As the *New York Times* noted in regard to a Chinese satellite of over a decade later: "Specialists here point out that technologists who can make a rocket that can propel a 380-pound vehicle into space can also make a missile for deliv-

ering the nuclear weapons that China is now producing." (26 April 1970, pp. 1 ff.)

73. *New York Times*, 3 October 1957 (p. 1), 4 October 1957) p. 22.
74. *Ibid.*, 5 October 1957, pp. 1, 3.
75. *Ibid.*, 6 October (p. 43), 7 October (pp. 1 and 16), 8 October p. 1, 9 October (p. 13), 10 October p. 10, 11 October p. 1, 13 October 1957 (sec. 4, pp. 3, 5).
76. Reprinted in Witkin, *op. cit.*, p. 12.
77. *New York Times*, 7 October 1957, p. 26.
78. CBS news broadcast of 7 October 1957, reprinted in Witkin, *op. cit.*, p. 10 (Emphasis in the original.)
79. *New York Times*, 9 October p. 31 and 11 October 1957 p. 39.
80. Eisenhower, *Waging Peace*, pp. 226, 211.
81. *New York Times*, 5 October p. 2 and 6 October 1957 p. 11.
82. Adams, *op. cit.*, p. 415.
83. *New York Times*, 5 October p. 2, 6 October p. 1, 9 October p. 1, 16 October 1957 (p. 1); also, Witkin, *op. cit.*, p. 6.
84. "News Conference, 9 October 1957," *Public Papers: Eisenhower*, vol. V, pp. 719-732. Mr. Eisenhower was particularly irked by the cost overruns of the space program. As he remarked to *Life* editor Emmet John Hughes some three weeks after Sputnik:

Sure, we had a large satellite program and could have pushed it. But first these science boys come to me and want twenty-two million dollars—and I say, 'Sure.' After a while, they want sixty-odd million, and I say, 'Fine.' So they pack some trickier instruments into the thing—and want eighty million and more. And I say, 'Okay.' But—finally—when they need another 150 million dollars, I *have* to say: 'Just a minute, fellows, where does this end?'

See Hughes, *op. cit.*, p. 250. (Emphasis in the original.)

85. Adams, *op. cit.*, p. 415.
86. *New York Times*, 12 October (pp. 1 ff.), 13 October (pp. 1 ff.), 17 October (pp. 1 ff.), 19 October (pp. 1 ff.), 23 October (pp. 1, 18), 24 October (pp. 1 ff.), 25 October (pp. 1 ff.), 27 October 1957 (pp. 1 ff.).
87. "Radio and Television Address to the American People on Science and National Security, 7 November 1957," *Public Papers: Eisenhower*, vol. V, pp. 789-799; also, the *New York Times*, 2 November (pp. 1 ff.), 3 November (pp. 1 ff.), 4 November (pp. 1, 7, 10), 5 November 1957 (pp. 1, 10).
88. *New York Times*, 9 October (p. 12), 10 October 1957 (p. 18).
89. *Ibid.*, 27 October 1957, p. 27.
90. *Ibid.*, 29 October (pp. 1, 10), 14 November p. 12, 20 November 1957 pp. 1, 15.
91. *Ibid.*, 30 October (p. 13), and 31 October 1957 p. 14.
92. *Ibid.*, 15 November (p. 7), and 24 November 1957 sec. 4, p. 5.
93. *Ibid.*, 12 January 1958, p. 14. See his testimony before the Johnson subcommittee: U. S. Senate, Preparedness Investigating Subcommittee of the Committee on Armed Services, *Inquiry into Satellite and Missile Programs*, 8th Congress, 1st-2nd Sessions, parts 1-3, 25 November 1957 to 24 July 1958 (Washington, D.C.: Government Printing Office, 1958); part 1, pp. 485 ff. (Hereafter cited as Senate: *Inquiry*.)

94. See the remarks by the head of the Continental Air Command at Mitchell Air Force base, New York, and those by the former chief of the Strategic Air Command in the *New York Times*, 13 October (p. 11), and 12 November 1957 (p. 33), respectively. See also the testimony of Vice Chief of Staff (and former SAC commander) Curtis E. LeMay, Senate: *Inquiry*, part 1, pp. 900 ff.

95. See the *New York Times*, 19 November 1957 (p. 16), in regard to the struggle between missile chief Bernard A. Schriever and bomber advocate LeMay going back to 1952. Also, see Schriever's testimony, Senate: *Inquiry*, part 1, pp. 1607 ff. (9 January 1958).

96. *New York Times*, 16 November (p. 2), 21 November (pp. 1 ff.), 30 November 1957 (pp. 1 ff.), 9 January 1958 (pp. 1 ff.). Also Senate: *Inquiry*, part 1, pp. 837 ff. (17 December 1957); part 2, pp. 1550 ff. (8 January 1958).

97. See the comments by Dr. John P. Hagen, Project Vanguard director, in the *New York Times*, 12 November pp. 1 ff., 27 November 1957 pp. 1 ff., 1 February 1958 (p. 7).

98. *Ibid.*, 17 November 1957, p. 40. Also, see their Congressional testimony, Senate: *Inquiry*, part 1, pp. 638 ff. (14 December 1957).

99. This list has been compiled from the *New York Times* on the following days: October 11 and 28; November 2, 10, 11, 13, 17, 21; December 1, 22, 23, 28 (1957); January 3 and 23 (1958).

100. Another partial listing would include: Dr. Elmer Hutchinson, director of the American Institute of Physics in New York (*New York Times*, 8 October 1957, p. 14); Dr. John R. Dunnings, dean of the Columbia School of Engineering (10 October, p. 19); Dr. Donald J. Hugher, senior scientist at the Brookhaven National Laboratory in New York (22 October, p. 22); Dr. Nathan M. Pusey, president of Harvard University (25 October, p. 5, and 14 November, p. 10); Dr. Nicholas De Witt of the Russian Institute at Harvard (1 November, p. 3); Dr. Howard L. Bevis, chairman of the Presidents Committee and Scientists and Engineers (14 November, p. 10); Dr. Eugene Raknowitch, editor of the *Bulletin of the Atomic Scientists* (25 November, p. 11); Dr. Isidor I. Rabi, chairman of the President's Science Advisory Committee (4 February 1958, p. 12).

101. *Ibid.*, 13 October p. 61, and 21 October 1957 p. 13. The cutbacks in spending for defense in late 1957 had created a serious problem for areas highly dependent upon defense contracts. The New York State Department of Labor estimated that of the 11,000 New Yorkers who lost their jobs due to that cutback, half lived in the Long Island counties of Nassau and Suffolk. (*Ibid.*, 25 October 1957, p. 16).

102. *Ibid.*, 1 January 1958, p. 22.

103. *Ibid.*, 8 November 1957 (p. 2), and 5 February 1958 p. 12.

104. See the testimony of the spokesmen for R. C. A., Lockheed Aircraft Corporation, Aerojet General Corporation, Hughes Aircraft Corporation, Curtiss-Wright Corporation, the Convair Division of General Dynamics, Douglas Aircraft, Boeing, North American Aviation: Senate: *Inquiry*, part 1, pp. 1070 ff. (13 to 17 January 1958).

105. For summaries of the secret Gaither Committee Report, see: Huntington, *op. cit.*, pp. 106-113; Eisenhower, *Waging Peace*, pp. 220-224; the *New York Times*, 23 November pp. 1 ff., 21 December p. 8 and 29 De-

cember 1957 (p. 10); the *New York Herald Tribune*, 25 November (p. 18), 22 December pp. 1 ff., 27 December 1957 (p. 10). For the text of the Rockefeller Report, see: *Rockefeller Brothers Fund, Prospects for America: The Rockefeller Panel Reports, Report II: International Security: The Military Aspect* (Garden City: Doubleday & Company, 1958), pp. 95-155; also, see the testimony of Nelson A. Rockefeller, Senate: *Inquiry,* part 1, pp. 1005 ff. (10 January 1958).

106. *New York Times,* 8 November (p. 11), 9 November 1957 pp. 1, 3, 12. For example, two of the first reactions to the Eisenhower speech were from Senators Jacob Javits (Republican, New York) and John L. McClelland (Democrat, Arkansas). The former remarked: "This is the Eisenhower of the Crusade in Europe." McClelland: "The speech was intended to be reassuring, but in my view it was not altogether convincing."

107. Adams, *op. cit.,* p. 396.

# 3

## THE INNOVATORS I:
## THE SOURCES OF MILITARY DISSENSION

### I[1]

RECENTLY ADDRESSING THE WEST POINT SOCIETY of Western Pennsylvania, former Army Chief of Staff Mathew B. Ridgway remarked: "Not before in my lifetime—and I was born into the Army in the nineteenth century—has the Army's public image suffered so many grievous blows and fallen to such low esteem in such wide areas of our society."[2] Both indicative of and reinforcing this trend have been certain schools of thought which have sought to define the role of the military in American society strictly in terms of such nuances as the "Warfare state," the "military-industrial complex," "American militarism." Given the present vogue of these terms in many circles, the student of the American governmental process (and of defense establishment policymaking in particular) is intellectually compelled to consider the validity of these analytical frameworks. Though much of the terminology is, I fear, rapidly degenerating into rather meaningless cliches—or, worse still, is in the hands of some imprudent enthusiasts reflective of cabalist thinking and fear of the paranoid "they"[3]—the critical arguments which are presented by thoughtful analysts cannot be so easily gainsaid.

This popular line of thinking probably stems, in large part, from the general disillusionment over the Vietnam war and from a significant impatience with the Cold War itself. To a great extent, it represents the correlative of the intellectual movement of historical revisionism evident in academia even before the intensification of the Southeast Asian conflict. The revisionist historians,[4] through a re-examination of the events of the later years of the Second World War in particular and the entire postwar era in general, have sought to recast the traditionally accepted antagonism and hostility of the Soviet Union into a defensive reaction much more amenable to detente and accommodation rather than conflict and confrontation. Placing the foreign policy of the United States in a much less favorable light, one is bound to view its military establishment as either an integral element of the malaise of aggression which is said to pervade the American character, or (worse yet) as a partner in a sinister conspiracy for power. Moreover, much of the new criticism of the military owes its origins to a resentment against the siphoning away of federal expenditures from domestic areas. (Though the emphasis on domestic expenditures is a rather recent phenomenon, it is not altogether lacking in comparison to the protests of an earlier era when business interests claimed that governmental revenues allocated the military were a threat to the economic prosperity of a free enterprise system.[5]) Given the fact that even before America's large-scale commitment to South Vietnam a full three-quarters of the federal budget was being directed toward the expense of military involvement in wars past, present, and future, the debate over the alleged distortion of national priorities was bound to arise sooner or later. The domestic reaction to the trauma of Vietnam determined that it would be sooner. And the military was obviously to be the primary target.

The central problem with this line of thinking, from the perspective of the present investigation, is that it tends to becloud the true nature and role of the military establishment. Failing to instruct us in the actual functioning of the military in the American decision-making process, it too frequently reduces itself to an emotion-laden indictment rather than a sober investigation. As

71

Tocqueville prophetically noted about American society over a century and a third ago: "When a military spirit foresakes a people, the profession of arms immediately ceases to be held in honor and military men fall to the lowest ranks of the public servants; they are little esteemed and no longer understood."[6] And as a much more recent student has observed; "The military is often hidden from public scrutiny, leaving students without adequate information and popular commentators with few alternatives between panegyrics and paranoid suspicion."[7]

The contemporary critical frameworks view the American military from one of three fundamental perspectives. The first, which is primarily a resurrection and renovation of the late C. Wright Mills' "power elite" thesis, suggests that the military establishment can be best understood as a force in alliance with an industrial sector dependent upon military procurement contracts. This agglomeration of power and interests (the "military-industrial complex"), the proponents of this thesis maintain, is in the process of enveloping the elected civilian institutions of government in order to mold public policy to fit its own parochial ends. Though this school has its roots deep in America's past,[8] recent representatives include such writers as Fred J. Cook, John M. Swomley, Richard J. Barnet, Sidney Lens, and C. Merton Tyrrell.[9] Alternatively, we have those who speak in terms of a "new American militarism." Though apparently concerned less with the growth of militarism among the nation's officer corps than with what they claim has been a gradual pervading of the American culture in general with a universal aggressive predisposition, this approach too must be examined inasmuch as it implies a certain symbiotic relationship between the professional soldier and the civilian society which has spawned him. Indicative of this mode of thought are General David M. Shoup (Commandant of the Marine Corps from 1956 to 1963) and Colonel James A. Donovan (USMC, Retired).[10] And, finally, if the first school approaches the military as a rather mysterious partner elite of power, the third reduces the leadership of the armed services to the role of mere wards of the corporate rich. No longer to be considered active partners of the industrial sector, military officers are now viewed as pawns which

lend themselves to manipulation by those who supposedly dominate the American economy. Studies which advance this argument
include those of G. William Domhoff and Gabriel Kolko.[11] (Many
of the more than seven hundred books and articles written as critiques of the American military since 1961 do not necessarily fit
neatly into one of the three above categories. This is naturally to
be expected when one deals with such a rich variety of mono-
graphs on so controversial a subject. Nevertheless, the threefold
classification suggested here applies to many, if not most, of the
most important works, and those which do not seem to fit tend to
either overlap two of the categories or are only tangentially related to the present study.[12])

It is the object of this chapter (given its primary purpose and
necessary brevity) neither to completely refute the various arguments nor to dismiss certain valid contributions. For example, the
military-industrial complex premise defined not as a cabal but as
"a deliberate and symbiotic sharing of interests on the part of the
military establishment, industry, and high ranking political figures," can be an extremely useful analytical construct which can
be applied to non-capitalist systems as well.[13] Yet, paradoxically,
the limits to the utility of the concept are set by its virtually
boundless nature. Logically applied, the military-industrial complex "includes all those elements of American society—economic,
political, professional—that have a material or philosophical stake
in a large defense establishment."[14] It thus includes not only the
military and large corporations dependent on the production of
war materiel, but government officials at the federal, state, and
local levels, labor union leaders and workers, teachers and academicians. The list is in reality endless and to attempt to complete
it would present an unworkable definition for the purposes of the
present study. For what we are saying is that the military-industrial complex *is* American society. Moreover, one must be aware
of the confusion generated by many of the scholars cited above
and the erroneous conclusions to which they are led.

In his study of the locus of power in American society, for example, Domhoff attempts to account for the newly acquired influence of the military in American government since World War

II in terms of their relation to what he terms the "business aristocracy."[15] Domhoff has attempted to empirically substantiate a modified version of Mills' "power elite" thesis[16] by seeking to demonstrate that the upper classes of America's social structure do indeed constitute a governing class. Mills, of course, had maintained that the nuclear military elite comprised one side of a triangle of power (the other two being occupied by the directors of large corporations and the political elite) which successfully monopolized influence over all socially relevant decisions of the first magnitude—questions of war and peace and control over the economic system. (Congress, lesser officials, and the group process in general were relegated to the "middle levels of power"—that is, decisions of only marginal importance.) Much of Mills' discussion of the expanding military role stemmed from accounts of the War Department's paramount importance in domestic economic decisions during the Second World War and from the evidence that military men had occupied key governmental posts during the early postwar years.[17] Yet given certain subsequent findings (especially those by Janowitz which indicate that not only was the incidence of military men in civilian governmental posts merely a transient postwar phenomenon, but that civilians thoroughly dominated the military during the war years themselves[18]), Domhoff is led to the erroneous conclusion that the military elite, while not members of the upper class themselves, are ultimately controlled by the upper class. (The only real proof he offers is data which suggest that the leading civilian personnel of the Defense Department have been either members of the upper class or former businessmen who have been co-opted by the upper class.[19] He apparently never doubts that the upper class civilians control the military at the Pentagon, but nor does he ever tell us what this control is supposed to consist of.[20])

Thus, if in Mills the military chieftains are viewed mysteriously and ominously as partner elites of power, in Domhoff's scheme they are reduced to being wards of the business aristocracy. In neither, however, do we get an accurate notion of how the military actually fits into the decision-making process—that is, how strategic alternatives are sorted out, argued upon, and how the conflicts are ultimately resolved. Only by means of analyzing concretely the process by which relevant defense policies are arrived at (decisions which, in Mills' terms, involve the "upper levels" of power) can we adequately resolve the problem as to where the locus of power resides in American society.

Another major problem with regard to the new critics of the military is their unfortunate—unfortunate because it inexorably leads to needless distortion—tendency to identify the military with some sinister conspiracy for power. Indicative of this view is Swomley's contention that the professional officer corps is aided in its conscious "drive for power" by industrialists who are dependent upon defense contracts. As Swomley writes of the American military elite:

> the professional officer group in the American military establishment has been steadily expanding its influence and control over civilian institutions and government. This group has been aided in its *drive for power* by civilians closely associated with the military—industrialists whose profits depend upon military contracts, and scientists and technicians whose careers depend upon the construction of military weapons.[21]

At least two simplifying assumptions are implicit here, both of which lead to erroneous premises. Firstly, it is assumed as almost axiomatic that there exists a monolithic military clique which consciously plans for power. However, as has been noted by Janowitz, for example:

> The military profession is not a monolithic power group. A deep split pervades its ranks in respect to its doctrines and viewpoints on foreign affairs, a split which mirrors civilian disagreements. Instead, the military profession and the military establishment conform more to the pattern of an administrative pressure group, but one with a strong internal conflict of interest. It is a very special pressure group because of its immense resources, and because of its grave problems of national security. The military have accumulated considerable power, and power protrudes into the political fabric of contemporary society. It could not be otherwise.[22]

Secondly, it is further assumed that, in alliance with this military clique, there exists a monolithic technical and industrial establishment. But as has been frequently pointed out (by Barnet, for instance, from the very ranks of the critics themselves[23]), by no means do all corporations benefit equally (or even at all) from the allocations of the military budget. As Huntington has noted in regard to the Eisenhower years, defense contractors played a rather peripheral role being primarily concerned with (and often competing among themselves over) those programs which directly affected their particular interests: "No one group or even coalition of groups existed to mobilize support for the defense program as a whole."[24]

Similarly, there has been a dysfunctional confusion generated by the use of the term "militarism" by certain commentators on the American military establishment. General Shoup's contention is that a spirit of militarism has engulfed American society and has unavoidably spilled over into foreign policy. In the course of one enlightening observation, he notes that: "For years up to 1964 the chiefs of the armed services, of whom the author was one, deemed it unnecessary and unwise for U. S. forces to become involved in any ground war in Southeast Asia."[25] Inasmuch as Shoup attributes much of the subsequent escalation of the war to changes in the composition of the Joint Chiefs of Staff (and given the fact that such changes have traditionally been the result of political decisions made in the White House[26]), then ultimate responsibility is to be laid with the civilian leadership of the executive branch and not with the officer corps. In quite the same manner, Shoup's confidant James Donovan again leaves us with the perplexing problem of the utility of the term "militarism" in understanding the American military. As with Shoup, he too fails to explicitly define the term and uses it quite ambiguously, equating the professional military man with the militarist: "I consider myself a professional militarist," he writes at the outset of his study.[27] Moreover, citing whom he considers to have been the top militarists of the sixties, he names Dean Rusk, McGeorge Bundy, W. W. Rostow, Robert S. McNamara, and but one military man, General Maxwell Taylor.[28] (And as will be discussed below, Taylor's credentials as a true military professional may be called into question.) Obviously, this beclouding of the issue will not do; if such a term is to be used efficaciously, it must answer more questions than it poses. A much more functional (and less polemical) delineation is presented by Alfred Vagts, who distinguishes between "the military way" and militarism:

> The military way is marked by a primary concentration of men and materials on winning specific objectives of power with utmost efficiency, that is with the least expenditure of blood and treasure. It is limited in scope, confined to one function, and scientific in its essential qualities. Militarism, on the other hand, presents a vast array of customs, interests, prestige, actions, and thought associated with armies and wars and yet transcends true military purposes. Indeed, militarism is so constituted that it may hamper and defeat the purposes of the military way. Its influence is unlimited in scope. It may permeate all society and become dominant over industry and arts. Rejecting the scientific character of the military way, militarism displays the qualities of caste and cult, authority and belief.[29]

## II

The American military has traditionally been, and is still, subject to the domination of the civilian elements of government rather than vice versa. The rearmament of the United States during the postwar years has been accomplished only with the utmost reluctance. Indeed, it took the Korean war to impress upon policy-makers the necessity of such a course of action so repugnant to the national character and liberal tradition.[30] Yet given the ascendancy of foreign and national security policy during the Cold War era and the underlying American resistance to the military establishment, it is cause for little wonder that cries are now heard (as exaggerated as they sometimes may be) protesting the protrusion of the military man into the public domain. Ultimately, the protests result from the exigencies of the strategy of nuclear deterrence. As *New York Times* Pentagon correspondent Jack Raymond has noted: "For the military to serve as a deterrent, it must be credible; to be credible, it must be visible. The process of making it visible calls for reaffirmations and demonstrations of strength that have been alien to us in the past."[31] Moreover, because the nature of the American system of government is such that it not only authorizes but encourages the military elite to join in the frequent debate on security posture, it simultaneously makes the military fair game for criticism and a visible object of contempt and scorn in that debate.[32] In short, the precarious position of the military is truly not an enviable one. In fulfilling its security role it is confronted by a people who have been nurtured and conditioned by the fortunes of history and geography to look upon security as the natural concomitant of sovereignty. Among an impatient people who are used to waging crusades for total ends rather than fighting wars for limited goals or maintaining a sustained level of armed strength during interludes of peace, the military man is bound to find public opinion oscillating between short periods of idolizing gratitude and long eras of disregard at best or active hostility at worst. And the history of American civil-military relations indicates that the latter represents normal times and the former aberrations.

Despite the many contributions made by the new critics of the American military in identifying the perennial dangers of misplaced influence or irresponsible power, a common error committed is simply a matter of poor historiography; that is, they have resurrected the benevolent image of Dwight Eisenhower and transformed him into a prophet warning of the coming of militarism in the United States—and this has been accomplished to an unfortunate degree by taking his admonitions out of their original context.[33] (It is interesting to note in passing that Senator J. William Fulbright—who had very few kind words to say about Eisenhower while he lived—upon being informed of the death of the former President, respectfully adjourned his Foreign Relations Committee meeting noting that the General's greatest contribution had been his early identification of the military-industrial complex—a strangely brief and selective eulogy for a man who had served his country in so many significant ways in both war and peace[34]). It is quite true that Eisenhower, throughout his administrations, was concerned with the entire picture of balancing defense needs against the exigencies of keeping military spending in check. As was dealt with at length in the preceding chapter, though, as a fiscal conservative and classical liberal, he was concerned not so much with the drain-off effect of military programs from domestic programs as with the necessity of budgetary surpluses and minimal government spending so as to check the inflationary trend which he believed plagued the fifties and preserve the spontaneous nature of the unplanned economy. It was Dwight Eisenhower who sought, above all else, a "balanced" program of defense geared to the "long haul"—an indefinite future of crises and tensions necessitating sustained preparedness. And the balance of values involved removing the question of military expenditures from the influences of the traditional "feast or famine" psychology; that is, neither rapidly increasing the defense budget because of short-range fears (e.g., Sputnik and the alleged missile/limited war gap), nor drastically reducing military allocations either out of illusory hopes of detente or because of the pressures of domestic priorities. It is, of course, true that Eisenhower believed that imprudent and inordinately huge defense budgets had to be checked inasmuch as deficit spending could lead only to the economic ills of inflation or government controls and, in either case, the undermining of the nation's economic might (the principle pillar of its overall strength) and its liberty.

Yet, taken out of their original context, his admonitions are used by the new critics of American defense policy to support policies which would upset the precarious balance which Eisenhower sought from the opposite pole and accomplish what, as both General of the Army and later Commander in Chief, he feared at least as much as too great an emphasis on arms—that is, severely cutting back on the defense effort. Thus, selective quotations from the President's statements give the erroneous impression that he favored some sort of unilateral disarmament.[35] For example, two passages are cited most frequently to give this distorted view. The first (cited in chapter two) is from his address before the American Society of Newspaper Editors. Speaking in April of 1953, a mere three months after assuming the office of President, he lamented that the Russo-American rivalry could offer mankind at worst nuclear holocaust and at best,

> a life of perpetual fear and tension; a burden of arms draining the wealth and the labor of all peoples; a wasting of strength that defies the American system. . . .
>
> Every gun made, every warship launched, every rocket fired signifies, in the final sense, a theft from those who hunger and are not fed, those who are cold and are not clothed.
>
> This world in arms is not spending money alone.
>
> It is spending the sweat of its laborers, the genius of its scientists, the hopes of its children.
>
> The cost of a modern heavy bomber is this: a modern brick school in more than thirty cities.
>
> It is two electric power plants, each servicing a town of 60,000 population.
>
> It is two fine, fully equipped hospitals.
>
> It is some fifty miles of concrete highway.
>
> We pay for a single fighter with one-half million bushels of wheat.
>
> We pay for a single destroyer with new homes that could house more than 8,000 people.
>
> This is not a life at all, in any true sense. Under the cloud of threatening war, it is humanity hanging from a cross of iron.[36]

This, naturally, is the passage selected by the new critics for emphasis. Yet if we examine carefully the full text of his remarks, we are struck by the fact that he viewed this "cross of iron" as the (and herein lies the Eisenhower sense of tragedy) *inevitable* result of Soviet hostility and that he had an even greater fear of doing what many of our present critics suggest—i.e., excessively cutting back on defense spending out of a fear of a mammoth military establishment. While hopeful that a meaningful accommodation could one day be reached with the Soviets which would allow a mutual reduction in armaments, he maintained (in the same address) an "unshakable conviction that, as long as there is a threat to freedom, they [the free nations] must, *at any price*, remain armed, strong, and ready for the risk of war."[37] And the second oft-quoted admonition (also cited in chapter two) in his

Farewell Address about the "conjunction of an immense military establishment and a large arms industry" is even more popularly recited—so much so that one often wonders if he ever wrote or said anything else of consequence. But it must not go unnoticed that just preceding his famed warning about the potential threat of a military-industrial complex, he cautioned that,

> Any failure traceable to arrogance, or our lack of comprehension or readiness, to sacrifice, would inflict upon us grievous hurt both home and abroad. . . .
> A vital element in keeping the peace is our military establishment. Our arms must be mighty, ready for instant action, so that no potential aggressor may be tempted to risk his own destruction.[38]

## III

The role of the military in the governmental process of the United States is, in the broadest sense, analogous to military intervention in developing areas except that it functions solidly within the "rules of the game" of a pluralist liberal democratic system. As Wilson McWilliams puts it, the

> political intervention of the military may be part of the rules of a system of institutions. War is too important to be left to generals, as Clemenceau remarked. So, similarly, war is too important a thing to be left entirely to civilians. . . . Much military intervention is 'concealed' by the fact that it is so institutional that citizens do not recognize it as military intervention at all.[39]

Involvement by the military in the political budgetary process is rooted in professional and institutional interests and groupings within the military which strive in competition with each other and non-military interests for their respective shares of the federal budget. In an environment where the rewards to be allocated are finite, where the final decision on allocation is allotted to different (and often antagonistic) institutions, and where there exist multiple means of access to influence that decision, the process of allocation is bound to involve pervasive and insistent bargaining among the potential beneficiaries. As was suggested in the first chapter of this study, the strategic debate of the late fifties and early sixties (over the alleged missile gap and adequacy of conventional forces) was a complex process involving numerous interests and forces within the political system, the most important of which we have designated the innovators, the popularizers, and the capitalizers. Those who seek to explain the controversy solely in terms of the military's "thirst for power" are grossly oversimplifying a highly intricate intersection of interests and demands, forcing it to fit into a predesigned framework. Fred J. Cook, for example, presents the missile gap as the brainstorm of General Thomas S. Power of the Strategic Air Command, initiated in January of 1960 in order to "scare up" more funds for SAC.[40] This obviously overlooks the fact that the origins of the controversy go back several years (at least to Sputnik in 1957) and that the groundwork for the debate had already been laid by the end of the decade, being perpetuated by many diverse forces representing different interests and institutional perspectives.

The schematic model of the behavior of the relevant groups in the present case study can be presented as follows: (1) dissenters within the military elite nucleus, failing to gain a favorable response to their particular innovations within the Eisenhower administration, seek allies elsewhere; (2) various members of the press corps popularize the dissension that has developed within the defense establishment; (3) academicians, and strategic experts in particular, provide the intellectual arguments for innovation; (4) administration opponents in the Congress (and especially in the upper chamber) bring pressure to bear upon the responsible executive authorities by means of investigations, hearings, statements, publications, and the power of appropriations; (5) a change in administrations brings to power a major proponent of the innovating military policy (John Kennedy), who has committed himself to strategic build-up (i.e., intercontinental ballistic missiles) and the creation of significantly expanded conventional war capabilities (the doctrine of "flexible response"); (6) former dissenters on military policy within the Eisenhower administration (specifically, Maxwell Taylor) come into the foreground to influence the re-orientation of defense doctrines.

## IV

Narrowing our perspective to the first phase of this evolution of defense policy, the problem immediately presents itself regarding the factors operative within the military itself which would account for the activities of the innovators; or, put differently, are there some general theoretical guidelines which can account for the Taylors and the Gavins? Before beginning such a tentative investigation, though, let us briefly restate certain premises concerning the ultimate nature of the strategic planning process and civil-military relations in the United States which are indispensable for an understanding of the soldier's role in the political system. Firstly, as Huntington correctly pointed out some years ago,[41] given the fact that the American Constitution was written in an era just prior to the evolution of a professional military arm of foreign policy, the founders of the United States system of government were concerned not with the building of fences around the influence of the professional soldier, but with the creation of a system of checks to prevent civilian control over the military by one governmental institution. This, of course, was consonant with the Madisonian theme of equilibrated power which pervaded the document. Yet by equating civilian control over the military with the dispersion of authority over military affairs between the executive and legislative branches (as well as between the national and state levels of government), a government of splintered functions allowing for myriad points of access to the decision process was created.

Furthermore, the military chiefs, being sharply divided over military strategy and priorities of national security to be ordered out of a limited budget, have proven to be fertile ground for exploitation by outside civilian interests. As Janowitz has noted, the Joint Chiefs "have not emerged as a leadership group with a unified theory of war and a consistent set of tactics for influencing executive and legislative conditions."[42] Thus, the military, by the nature of the system in which it must operate and due to its own failure (again, largely systemic in nature) to consistently display a unified façade to outside political forces, has been politicized. As Harry Truman so aptly commented on the ideal of political neutrality for the professional military: "The average career officer learns of his dependence upon 'politics' from the moment he solicits his first application blank for a service academy."[43] The environment in which the military man is compelled to exist is, therefore, inherently politicizing. Just to highlight for the moment the interdependence of "military" and "political" institutions, a brief account offered by one reliable Pentagon reporter concerning the period under investigation should suffice:

> One day during the 'missile gap' hearings I observed to a renowned officer that his latest statement had probably helped the Democrats more than several speeches by their candidates for the [Presidential] nomination. He grinned and said, 'You get the idea, don't you?'[44]

Yet the overall politicizing effects of the system of which the military establishment is an integral part cannot by itself solve the present dilemma; after all, why do some elite members dissent so vigorously from administration policy, seek innovations so tenaciously, and find themselves so favorably disposed toward political action while others of their profession do not? For the answer to this query, we are compelled to look within the military itself for the identification of the factors which would account for the dissension within its ranks and the decisively political orientations of certain of its primary actors.

In attempting to explain the dissension factor, we should perhaps look first to the education variable; that is, can differences in educational experiences among the members of the military elite nucleus account for differing orientations toward political involvement? The first thing to be borne in mind when considering military education is its continuous nature.[45] The importance of formal educational preparation (not to mention the informal socialization process of the profession of arms itself) for high level responsibilities in both military and non-military capacities and entrance into the elite nucleus of the military establishment must not be overlooked. The typical high-ranking career officer has passed through a service academy (the higher up in the military hierarchy one goes, the more likely one is to find service academy education among its members[46]), the Armed Forces Staff College, the Army, Naval or Air War Colleges, the National War College and the Industrial Colleges of the Armed Forces.[47] Field grade officers in the Army, for example, have either some college training (96 per cent), a bachelor's degree (54 per cent), or have done some kind of graduate work beyond the bachelor's (31 per cent); comparable figures for the Air Force are 87 to 95 per cent, 34 to 68 per cent, 20 to 33 per cent, respectively (the higher percentages pertaining to higher rank).[48] The American military has thus evolved from a profession where authority was a result of custom, tradition, law, and heroic achievement to one where academic attainment and military competence have become the chief determinants of promotion and responsibility. This has largely resulted from the gradual transformation of the coercive arm of the state from a rather aristocratic army based upon a simple skill structure and relatively static organization to a massive military establishment, thrust into the decision-making arena and forced to cope with the constantly changing technology of warfare and the governance of a vast bureaucratic infra-structure.[49]

The educational process of the officer corps has undergone a significant change since the Second World War, mirroring the simultaneous drastic modifications which have occurred in the size and complexity of the military establishment as whole. Prior to Pearl Harbor, for example, the service academies (with their emphasis upon discipline, athletics, and engineering) reflected the needs of a small, isolated and tradition-bound military organization which dealt with a less complex and relatively static system of weaponry. The coming of World War II (which brought about a thirty-six-fold increase in the size of the armed forces[50]) and the Soviet-American rivalry of the postwar years (with the concomitant revolution in military technology and strategy) fundamentally altered the nature of service academy training. Reflecting the exigencies of the modern mass army, the academies

experienced a decrease in rigid discipline and isolation, a liberalization of the curricula (with the influx of the humanities), and
a greater emphasis upon organizational management. The necessity of broadening the sphere of military competence in traditionally non-military areas has been fostered by the conversion of
the military chieftains (by civilian authorities) from parochial specialists to what Huntington refers to as "generalists."[51] As has
been noted:

> Anyone who has read testimony of ranking military officers
> before Congressional committees must be impressed by the va-
> riety of matters on which their opinions are sought. They are
> assumed to understand an astonishing array of political, mili-
> tary, economic, scientific, administrative, and even moral issues.
> Further, they are assumed to understand the relation of each
> issue to the others.[52]

The result has been a gradual but inescapable blurring of the
traditional distinction between the "military mind" and the diplomatic or legal mind, especially at the highest levels of power and
responsibility.[53]

The man who most epitomizes the new academic trend which
has pervaded the military academies is Colonel George A. Lincoln. A very atypical career officer, Lincoln (an Oxford educated
Rhodes scholar who was chief of the Strategy and Policy Group
at General George C. Marshall's Operations Division during the
Second World War) relinquished a brigadier commission to assume in 1947 the position as Professor and Deputy head of the
Department of Social Sciences at the United States Military Academy. By 1954, he had become head of the department and a member of West Point's Academic Board, a policy formulating panel.
Colonel "Abe" Lincoln was instrumental in broadening the pro-
spective Army officer's educational horizons by adding new sub-
jects to the standard cadet curriculum (courses in American diplomacy, area studies, comparative government, political philosophy,
comparative economic systems, and cost effectiveness analysis),
inviting eminent civilian academicians as guest speakers at the

Academy, and by instituting programs which were designed to facilitate the interchange of cadets with students at civilian institutions of higher learning. Yet his influence on military education extended far beyond the banks of the Hudson River in New York. His protégé Colonel Robert F. McDermott left Lincoln's department at West Point to become Dean of the Faculty at the newly created Air Force Academy. Lincoln himself has authored several textbooks on international relations and defense policy which have emphasized: (1) the revolution in world politics initiated by the radical implications of military technology and the emergence of the developing nations as a power consideration in the foreign policies of the superpowers; (2) the rise of the military as the principle manager of ever-changing weapons technology and its evolving role in the deterrence of wars; (3) the interrelationship of military policy and domestic politics and economics. Thus, one of his major preoccupations has been with the postwar technological revolution and its implications for the military profession. As the co-author of a well-known text in the field of international politics, he emphasized that, "Since 1900 the pace of history has so quickened that analyses of the supposed present risk being, instead, appraisals of the recent past."[54]

Lincoln was also a direct participant in the strategic debate of the late fifties which we are presently considering, being a panel member for the Rockefeller Brothers Fund report (beginning in 1957), joining in the deliberations of the Gaither Committee (1957-1958) and the deliberations of the Draper Committee (1956).[55] Aiding in the preparation of these reports, Lincoln could have been expected to be a strong influence for increased defense spending, especially in regard to the revolutionary field of missile technology. Several years before he had expressed the conviction that as much as fifty percent of the Gross National Product could be diverted to the defense effort without destabilizing the economy so long as the American people and its political leadership were willing to accept wage, price, and consumption controls; moreover, he viewed "the economic waste of security programs as being 'superficial.' In reality, they are the foundation of social gains."[56]

Perhaps Colonel Lincoln's total impact in the defense realm can be best summed up by two former associates. In regard to the mark left upon military education by Lincoln's academic policies, General Maxwell Taylor (the Superintendant of West Point when Lincoln first joined the faculty) commented in 1966:

> In his Department, Lincoln taught them [i.e., the young instructors at the Academy] the necessity of blending together military and non-military components to form a national strategy of maximum effectiveness. They had acquired from him an understanding of the many facets of national power and the need for flexibility in its application. Such men have become a national asset in preparing the Armed Forces to meet the challenges of evolving world relationships as typified by the complex situation in Vietnam.[57]

At the same time, Secretary of State Dean Rusk, looking back upon the Colonel's long career in military academia, noted: "There is a very long list of men who have looked to 'Abe' Lincoln as their teacher, and I am honored to be counted among them."[58]

# V

However, we are confronted with a perplexing dilemma in attempting to gauge the influence, via the military education process, of the Lincolnian assault upon the tradition-bound service academies. Though it goes without saying that the educational experiences of young officers would obviously differ markedly from those of their seniors, given the fact that it takes on the average some twenty-four years of prior service before an officer can hope to reach the higher echelons of military leadership,[59] Lincoln's former students (and those of his protégés) could not be expected to join the elite nucleus until at least the 1970's or 1980's. Because the effects of the instructional innovations are at best long-run, they would appear to have little direct relevance to the present case study; for example, Maxwell Taylor (a primary actor in the drama) was, as noted above in passing, Superintendent at West

Point when Lincoln began his tenure on the faculty. Yet this is not to dismiss altogether the educational experience variable; Major General John B. Medaris (chief of the Redstone Arsenal at the time of Sputnik) had a very deviant education for a military man, failing to have attended a service academy or its equivalent and being confined in his military training to the field of ordnance.

Perhaps the notions of professionalism and careerism can help us account for the dissension factor; or, put differently, can strategic dissension and political involvement be viewed as a function of differences in the degree of professionalism or varying career orientations within the military? As has been pointed out by both Huntington and Janowitz,[60] the art of the specialist in the application of violence is to be considered a profession in much the same way as those of the lawyer or the physician; in all three cases, the essential characteristics of professionalism are present—namely, expertise, the sense of social responsibility, and corporateness.[61] For the military officer, two elements of professionalism are especially important and can best be illustrated by two brief quotations. As one observer notes:

> Professionals *profess*. They profess to know better than others the nature of certain matters, and to know better than their clients what ails them or their affairs. This is the essence of the professional idea and the professional claim. . . .
> Since the professional does profess, he asks that he be trusted. . . .[62]

But as Huntington adds, the professional soldier "is concerned with only one segment of the activities of his client. Consequently, he cannot impose decisions upon his client which have implications beyond his field of special competence."[63] Thus the true military professional gives advice to his Commander in Chief on purely military matters; his civilian superior, responsible for activity in many overlapping spheres, places this advice in the broad context of the multifaceted nature of the national interest and makes what he feels are appropriate decisions given all the interests and priorities which do not concern the military man in his parochial deliberations. For a member of the military elite to appeal the civilian Commander in Chief's decision to other groups (the press, the Congress, opposition party leaders, the public-at-large) would seem, then, to indicate a lack of professionalism, for he is intruding into areas in which he is not particularly competent—and if he is competent in these areas, he is not, by definition, a strict professional in the military domain.

However, to merely state that a dissenter from strategic policy within the military establishment is being unprofessional is unfortunately no more than a tautological observation and answers, it is to be feared, fewer questions than it poses. The Huntingtonian ideal of a politically sterile military profession is unattainable and, if it were ever approached in the American system, has been a casualty of factors both external and endogenous to the military establishment. The internal elements of non-professionalism (in the specific sense of the proclivity for active dissension) during the later 1950's were primarily: (1) the tendency of officers of unconventional backgrounds to rise to the top of the military hierarchy; (2) the dramatic changes in the nature of the military establishment which had occurred since Pearl Harbor. Those external to the profession itself included: (1) the Constitution and statutes of the United States which have fostered split loyalties among the soldiery; (2) the policies of the Eisenhower administration which, in effect, prodded unprofessional behavior on the part of certain segments of the armed services. Thus, the Gavins and the Taylors are not professional military men who grab for power at the expense of the civilian elements of the government. Rather, they are bureaucrats and technocrats who have served parochial military interests by employing means widely accepted within the framework of the system in which they are compelled to operate by their civilian counterparts.

## VI

As Janowitz has suggested,[64] the members of the military profession who attain nuclear elite status must have innovating perspectives and skills. Thus, the upper echelons of the military estab-

lishment are open to people of "unconventional" career patterns
—that is, those who tend to be less hampered by the traditional-
ism of the profession of arms and, therefore, less professional in
outlook. Presenting brief biographical sketches of General Matthew B. Ridgway and Admiral Hyman Rickover, two well known
dissenters, Janowitz claims that they are highly representative of
the innovating officer in their career patterns. (He also holds that
the key officers in the three services' missile programs—Bernard
Schriever of the Air Force, William F. Raborn of the Navy, and
John B. Medaris of the Army—all conform to this pattern of the
managerial, as opposed to the traditional professional, type.) A
careful examination of the career patterns and backgrounds of our
two prime actors, Maxwell ("flexible response") Taylor and James
("missile lag") Gavin, lend credence to this explanation and, on
the whole, seem to fit Janowitz' model. Gavin's urban Irish background, his early publication (1947) on airborne warfare, his managerial tenure as the Army's chief of research and development,
his dramatic retirement after Sputnik and subsequent populariza-
tion of the missile gap thesis, his diplomatic mission during the
Kennedy administration, his proposal (from retirement) for an
"enclave" strategy in Vietnam, his *volte face* in the late sixties from
a defense advocate to a domestic priorities advocate, his informal role as defense advisor to Senator George S. McGovern in
1972 and the Democratic candidate's serious consideration of him
for the post of Defense Secretary in a new administration—all seem
to indicate a quite deviant professional career and the lack of a
strict professionalism. And Taylor, as well, fits into this scheme,
perhaps even to a more pronounced degree. His reputation as an
intellectual (he is fluent in several languages and holds a host of
honorary degrees from assorted universities dating back to 1946),
his tenure on the faculty of West Point as a language instructor
(1927-1932), his role in diplomatic missions to Peking and Latin
America just before the war, his publication of a manual on Japanese Army tactics, his resignation as Army Chief of Staff and subsequent attacks upon the Eisenhower administration, and his reappearance during the subsequent Democratic administrations in
the high counsels of government[65]—all attest to his lack of tradi-

tional professionalism and proclivities toward political involvement.

Secondly, in regard to the elements in the military which help account for the dissension factor, there is the bureaucratic and technological milieu. The corollary of the perspective which views the military as a profession is that which seeks to approach and analyse it as a vast technical bureaucracy. The two concepts are, of course, highly interrelated, for professionalism is the prerequisite for bureaucratization: The American military is a bureaucratic profession.[66] In his study of the social origins of both military and civilian (business as well as government) executives, Lloyd Warner concluded that,

> Broadly speaking, the backgrounds of the military and civilian executives are similar whether we are considering [father's] occupation, region or state of origin. They are also similar in level of education; but military executives have often attended the United States service academies, where, with their specific purposes, higher education differs as a variety. . . .
> American business executives differ in many respects from American federal executives, but in broad outline they are far more alike than different in social and economic characteristics, including family and occupation as well as education attainment.[67]

Thus, the bureaucratic setting of the military establishment would seem highly comparable to that which exists in any large scale agency of officialdom and, presumably, lends itself to analysis by middle-level organizational theory.[68]

This "civilianizing" of the military—which, conversely, means the "de-professionalizing" of the military bureaucrat—is a rather recent phenomenon resulting from its changing postwar role. As Janowitz observes,

> for some time it [the military establishment] has tended to display more and more of the characteristics typical of any large-scale nonmilitary bureaucracy. The decreasing difference is the result of continuous technological change which vastly ex-

panded the size of the military establishment, increases its interdependence with civilian society, and alters its internal social structure.[69]

The creation of a permanent and vast military establishment, with a mission which has gradually shifted from the implementation of violence to its deterrence through the utilization of complex machinery and advanced technology, has brought about a more rational and managerial and less authoritarian approach among the upper officer corps to the problem of coordinating men and machinery for the modern military role.[70] In the bureaucratic process of legislating defense policy, therefore, strategy emerges less as the rational product of an ideal hierarchy of expertise and competence than as the result of conflict, bargaining, and compromise. And because there are those within the military who seek to protect the interests of their particular service as well as those within each service with a primary loyalty to their technological specialty, we find a clash among technocrats as well as among bureaucrats. Though this may not be a completely novel development—after all, within the Army, for instance, there existed a long rivalry between the cavalry, the infantry and the artillery—it has been accentuated by the ever-changing nature of weapons technology and the life-or-death search of each service arm for a secure role in the nuclear and missile age.

## VII

By no means, of course, have the stimuli for dissension been totally internally generated. Indeed, the exogenous factors have often been paramount. As we have seen, the American system of government not only permits access by the innovators to diverse centers of decision-making power, but actually draws them into the political arena. Given the Constitutional separation of powers and the strange dilemma of the 1950's, where for the first time in over a century a President (and a popular one at that) was faced with opposition party control of both houses of the Congress, it is cause for little wonder that the magnetic nature of the political process vis-a-vis the military elite was intensified. And because the administration was confident of its military expertise (in the person of the Commander in Chief) and due to the tenacious acceptance by the President of a military strategy which could but adversely affect the interests of the Army in particular, it would largely deny the services of their legitimate professional function as the purveyors of advice and wisdom on military matters. Perhaps adding insult to injury, not only would the Eisenhower administration not seek out the advice of those whose job it was to advise, but it would also demand the loyal and ardent support of its programs before the Congress by military men who had had little to do in the developing of programs which were considered by some of dubious merit. In short, then, the Eisenhower administration was demanding that its military chiefs act professionally (that is, loyally) while not treating them as professionals (that is, allowing them to profess). And, finally, it further undermined the professionalism of the military establishment—a professionalism which it needed in a two-party government—by consistently demanding that the military abandon its parochialism and see the whole picture of national security as seen from the White House.

1. This section represents a modified version of a brief article by the author entitled "The American Military: A Reappraisal" which appeared in *Military Review*, Vol. LII (January, 1972), pp. 51-57.

2. From his address as reproduced in the *New York Times*, 2 April 1971, p. 39.

3. For the paranoid "they" syndrome, see David Reisman, et al., *The Lonely Crowd: A Study of the Changing American Character* (New Haven: Yale University Press, 1950), pp. 250-255. A brief, but incisive, consideration of the role of cabalist thinking in American society is presented by Robert E. Lane, *Political Ideology: Why the American Common Man Believes What He Does* (New York: The Free Press, 1967), chapter 7.

4. Representative of this school of historiography are: D. F. Fleming, *The Cold War and its Origins, 1917-1960*, 2 vols. (Garden City: Doubleday & Company, 1961); David Horowitz, *The Free World Colossus* (New York: Hill and Wang, 1965); Gar Alperovitz, *Atomic Diplomacy: Hiroshima and Potsdam* (New York: Vintage Books, 1965); William Appleman Williams, *The Tragedy of American Diplomacy* (New York: Dell Publishing Company, 1962); Frederick L. Schuman, *Cold War: Retrospect and Prospect* (Baton Rouge: Louisiana State University Press, 1962); David Horowitz,

ed., *Containment and Revolution* (Boston: Beacon Press, 1967); John M. Swomley, *American Empire: The Political Ethics of Twentieth Century Conquest* (New York: The Macmillan Company, 1970); Joyce and Gabriel Kolko, *The Limits of Power: The World and United States Foreign Policy, 1945-1954* (New York: Harper & Row, Publishers, 1972).

5.   Samuel P. Huntington, *The Soldier and the State: The Theory and Politics of Civil-Military Relations* (New York: Vintage Books, 1957), chapter 9.

6.   Alexis de Tocqueville, *Democracy in America*, Henry Reeve text as revised by F. Bowen (New York: Vintage Books, 1945), vol. 2, Book 3, Chapter XXII, p. 282.

7.   Wilson C. McWilliams, ed., *Garrisons and Governments: Politics and the Military in New States* (San Francisco: Chandler Publishing Company, 1967), p. vii.

8.   For a survey of the long list of antecedents to the military-industrial complex premise, see Robert H. Ferrell, "The Merchants of Death, Then and Now," *Journal of International Affairs*, vol. 26, no. 1 (1970), pp. 29-39. The present critics, of course, owe a great deal to Harold Lasswell's "garrison state" hypothesis first suggested in the 1930's. For a relevant discussion and critique of Lasswell, see Huntington, *op. cit.*, pp. 346-350. For a recent restatement of the thesis by Lasswell himself, see his "The Garrison State Hypothesis Today," in Samuel P. Huntington, ed., *Changing Patterns of Military Politics* (Glencoe, The Free Press, 1962), pp. 51-70.

9.   Fred J. Cook, *The Warfare State* (New York: The Macmillan Company, 1962); John M. Swomley, Jr., *The Military Establishment* (Boston: Beacon Press, 1964); Richard J. Barnet, *The Economy of Death* (New York: Atheneum, 1970); Sidney Lens, *The Military Industrial Complex* (Philadelphia: Pilgrim Press & The National Catholic Reporter, 1970); C. Merton Tyrrell, *Pentagon Partners: The New Nobility* (New York: Grossman Publishers, 1970).

10.   David M. Shoup, "The New American Militarism," originally published in *The Atlantic Monthly* in 1969 and subsequently reprinted in J. H. Skolnick and E. Currie, eds., *Crisis in American Institutions* (Boston: Little Brown & Company, 1970), pp. 168-177; James A. Donovan, *Militarism, U. S. A.* (New York: Charles Scribner's Sons, 1970).

11.   G. William Domhoff, *Who Rules America?* (Englewood Cliffs: Prentice-Hall, Inc., 1967); Gabriel Kolko, *The Roots of American Foreign Policy: An Analysis of Power and Purpose* (Boston: Beacon Press, 1969).

12.   The estimate of the number of works published on the subject is taken from James L. Clayton, ed., *The Economic Impact of the Cold War* (New York: Harcourt, Brace & World, Inc., 1970), footnote p. 3. Significant critiques which do not fit into our framework include: Seymour Melman's *Pentagon Capitalism: The Political Economy of War* (New York: McGraw-Hill Book Company, 1970); and H. L. Nieburg's *In the Name of Science*, rev. ed. (Chicago: Quadrangle Books, 1966). Both analyses would fit into a mirror image category of our third classification; that is, rather than seeing the military as wards of the corporate rich, they present a picture wherein American industry is a dependent of the Department of Defense by means of the network of defense contracts and subcontracts.

13. See Vernon V. Aspaturian, "The Soviet Military-Industrial Complex —Does it Exist?," *Journal of International Affairs*, vol. 26, no. 1 (1972), pp. 1-28. Indeed, Aspaturian answers the question he poses in the affirmative and apparently sees the Soviet complex as being more powerful in its environment than the American complex in this country.

14. Jack Raymond, "The Growing Threats of Our Military Industrial Complex," *Harvard Business Review*, vol. XLXI (May-June, 1968), p. 56. See also the definition by Julius Duscha, *Arms, Money and Politics* (New York: Ives Washburn, Inc., 1964), p. ix.

15. Domhoff borrowed the term from R. Digby Baltzell, *The Philadelphia Gentlemen* (Glencoe: The Free Press, 1958).

16. C. Wright Mills, *The Power Elite* (New York: Oxford University Press, 1959); also, *Power, Politics and People* edited by I. L. Horowitz (New York: Ballantine Books, 1962), chapter 1. For a collection of critical reviews of Mills' thesis, see G. William Domhoff and Hoyt B. Ballard, eds., *C. Wright Mills and the Power Elite* (Boston: Beacon Press, 1969), especially the critique by Robert A. Dahl.

17. The influence of Bruce Catton's *The Warlords of Washington* (New York: Harcourt, Brace & World, 1948) and Donald M. Nelson's *Arsenal of Democracy* (New York: Harcourt, Brace and Company, 1946) is quite evident. Mills even employs Catton's designation "warlords" in the title of his principle chapter on the military (*The Power Elite*, chapter 8). See also Domhoff, *op. cit.*, chapter 5.

18. Morris Janowitz, *The Professional Soldier: A Social and Political Portrait* (New York: The Free Press, 1960), pp. 378, 347.

19. See also, Tristam Coffin, *The Armed Society* (New York: Penguin Books, 1964), p. 169.

20. Much of the present critique of Domhoff has been suggested by Robert Heilbroner's discussion in his *Between Capitalism and Socialism: Essays in Political Economics* (New York: Vintage Books, 1970), chapter 14.

21. Swomley, *op. cit.*, p. 1 (emphasis added). One would think that Swomley would have been on safer ground if he had suggested merely that the power of the military elite had flowed from circumstances largely beyond its control. But he refuses to take this plausible route and consistently maintains that there is evidently a "power drive" within the military and that its mounting influence has been "a result of a conscious planning for power" (p. 6).

22. Janowitz, *op. cit.*, p. viii.

23. Barnet, *op. cit.*, pp. 167-175.

24. Samuel P. Huntington, *The Common Defense: Strategic Programs in National Politics* (New York: Columbia University Press, 1961), p. 217.

25. Shoup, *op. cit.*, p. 172.

26. For example, see the discussion of Eisenhower's shake-up of the JCS in 1953 in Huntington, *The Common Defense*, chapter 2. See also: Jack Raymond, *Power at the Pentagon* (New York: Harper & Row, 1964), pp. 9-10; Glenn H. Snyder, "The 'New Look' of 1953," in Warner R. Schilling, et al., *Strategy, Politics, and Defense Budgets* (New York: Columbia University Press, 1962), pp. 379-524.

27. Donovan, *op. cit.*, preface.

# The Innovators I

28. *Ibid.*, chapter 6.
29. Alfred Vagts, *A History of Militarism: Civilian and Military*, rev. ed. (New York: The Free Press, 1959), p. 13.
30. See Paul Y. Hammond, "NSC 68: Prologue to Rearmament." in Schilling, *op. cit.*, pp. 267-378; for the traditional hostility of American liberalism to the military, see Huntington, *The Soldier and the State*, chapter 9-11.
31. Raymond, *Power at the Pentagon*, p. 332.
32. Raymond, "The Growing Threat of Our Military-Industrial Complex," *op. cit.*, p. 63.
33. See, for example, Cook, *op. cit.*, chapter 1; Raymond, *Power at the Pentagon*, pp. 137, 160-162, 191-192, 332; Swomley, *op. cit.*, p. 112; Duscha, *op. cit.*, pp. 12-13; Ralph Lapp, *The Weapons Culture* (Baltimore: Penguin Books, 1969), chapter 1.
34. A vociferous critic of the Eisenhower policy of the "long pull" in the late fifties, Fulbright later became disillusioned with the implications of its rejection. In 1974, reflecting on the changing nature of national security since he had taken over as Chairman of the Senate Foreign Relations Committee fifteen years before, he remarked that: "we are in great disarray, our economy is in dreadful condition, in my opinion primarily because of our over-extension, our foreign commitments, and especially the Vietnam war, so that as opposed to 15 years ago in many respects we are in much worse condition." "Interview with Senator J. W. Fulbright," *Meet the Press*, July 7, 1974 (Washington, D.C.: Merkle Press, 1974), p. 7. See also his remarks at the November 1969 Congressional Conference on the Military Budget and National Priorities, reproduced in Erwin Knoll and J. N. Fadden, eds., *American Militarism, 1970* (New York: The Viking Press, 1969), pp. 132-139.
35. For example, see Cook, *op. cit.*, chapter 1.
36. Dwight D. Eisenhower, *Peace with Justice: Selected Addresses*, edited by Grayson Kirk (New York: Columbia University Press, 1961), pp. 37-38.
37. *Ibid.*, p. 36 (emphasis added).
38. Dwight D. Eisenhower, "Farewell Radio and Television Address to the American People, 17 January 1961," *Public Papers of the Presidents: Dwight D. Eisenhower, 1960-1961*, vol. 8. (Washington D.C.: Government Printing Office, 1961), pp. 1035-1039.
39. McWilliams, *op. cit.*, p. 36.
40. Cook, *op. cit.*, chapter 1.
41. Huntington, *The Soldier and the State*, chapter 6.
42. Janowitz, *op. cit.*, p. 16.
43. Quoted in Raymond, *Power at the Pentagon*, pp. 174-175.
44. *Ibid.*, pp. 186-187.
45. John W. Masland and Laurence I. Radway, *Soldiers and Scholars: Military Education and National Policy* (Princeton: Princeton University Press, 1957), especially chapter 3.
46. Janowitz, *op. cit.*, chart p. 59. Academy training appears to be more important in the Navy and least decisive in the Air Force, given the recent origins of its academy at Colorado Springs.
47. See Masland and Radway, *op. cit.*, chapter 8.
48. Kurt Lang, "Technology and Career Management in the Military

Establishment," in Morris Janowitz, ed., *The New Military: Changing Patterns of Organization* (New York: W. W. Norton & Company, 1966), chart p. 56.

49. Morris Janowitz and Roger Little, *Sociology and the Military Establishment*, rev. ed. (New York: The Russell Sage Foundation, 1965), pp. 27-28.

50. Lang, *op. cit.*, chart p. 42. The size of the armed forces increased from 334,473 in June of 1939 to 12,124,418 in May of 1945. During the postwar years, it never dipped below 1.4 million (1948) and reached a peak of nearly 3.7 million during the Korean War. During the Eisenhower years, it steadily decreased to less than 2.5 million by June of 1960; thus the ratio of change between 1939 and 1960 was still nearly 7.5.

51. Huntington, *The Common Defense*, p. 219.

52. Masland and Radway, *op. cit.*, p. 32.

53. See Walter Millis, *Arms and the State: Civil-Military Elements in National Policy* (New York: The Twentieth Century Fund, 1958), pp. 14-141.

54. George A. Lincoln and Norman J. Padelford, *The Dynamics of International Politics* (New York: The Macmillan Company, 1962), p. 561.

55. For a brief biographical sketch of "Abe" Lincoln, see Lt. Colonel Roger H. Nye, "George A. Lincoln: Architect of National Security," in Amos A. Jordan, Jr., ed., *Issues of National Security in the 1970's: Essays Presented to Colonel George A. Lincoln on His Sixtieth Birthday* (New York: Frederick A. Praeger, 1967), chapter 1.

56. George A. Lincoln, *Economics of National Security: Managing America's Resources for Defense*, rev. ed. (New York: Prentice-Hall, 1954), chapters 15 and 16. The quotation is from page 42.

57. Nye, *op. cit.*, p. 15.

58. *Ibid.*, p. 20.

59. Lang, *op. cit.*, p. 51.

60. See the introductory chapters of both Huntington's *The Soldier and the State* and Janowitz' *The Professional Soldier*.

61. Huntington, *The Soldier and the State*, chapter 1.

62. Everett C. Hughes, "Professions," in Kenneth S. Lynn, ed., *The Professions in America* (Boston: Houghton-Mifflin Company, 1962), p. 2 (emphasis in the original).

63. Huntington, *The Soldier and the State*, p. 16.

64. Janowitz, *The Professional Soldier*, chapter 8.

65. Taylor was called upon by President Kennedy to lead an investigation of the Bay of Pigs fiasco and remained in his service first as military advisor to the Chief Executive (1961-1962) and then as Chairman of the Joint Chiefs of Staff (1962-1964). Under Lyndon Johnson, he served as a special counsel (1965-1969); in 1969 he became chairman and president of the Foreign Intelligence Advisory Board. He has authored three major works since his retirement as Eisenhower's Army Chief of Staff.

66. Bernard Barber, "Some Problems in the Sociology of the Profession," in Lynn, *op. cit.*, pp. 15-34; Samuel Huntington, "Power, Expertise, and the Military Profession," *ibid.*, pp. 131-153.

67. W. Lloyd Warner, et al., *The American Federal Executive: A Study of the Social and Personal Characteristics of the Civilian and Military Leaders*

*of the United States Government* (New Haven: Yale University Press, 1963), p. 18.

68. For example, Amitai Etzioni, *A Comparative Analysis of Complex Organizations: On Power, Involvement, and Their Correlates* (New York: The Free Press, 1961).

69. Janowitz and Little, *op. cit.*, p. 17.

70. *Ibid.*, chapter 1; Janowitz, *The Professional Soldier,* chapter 3.

# 4

## THE INNOVATORS II: MILITARY POLITICS

### I

FROM WHAT HAS BEEN STATED THUS FAR, IT IS APparent that the appearance of the strategic dissenters (or innovators) in the late fifties was hardly a surprising aberration. Rather it represented the logical culmination of forces at work both within the military establishment and the political system of which it is a part. The rise of the innovators was the result of: (1) the natural rise to the top of the military hierarchy of men of innovating perspectives; (2) the postwar transformation of the military from a small cloister-like profession to a vast technocratic bureaucracy dominated by those skilled in the management of men and machines; (3) the nature of the decentralized American system which not only permits but actually sanctions and even encourages the involvement of its soldiery in the policy process; (4) the policies of the Eisenhower administration which, ironically, while seeking to restrain the ability of the military to upset its delicate balance of priorities, eventually wound up by politicizing it. In this chapter we will be primarily concerned with the process whereby the innovators were drawn (even if quite willingly) into the debate of the late fifties by both the executive and legislative branches, and with the instruments at the dissenters' disposal to actively influence the course of that debate.

To best understand the overall political context of defense spending in the post-Sputnik years as opposed to that of the years just preceding the "great awakening" of 1957, we should contrast what I choose to term the "lean year syndrome" with the "Pearl Harbor syndrome" and its concomitant "Madariaga effect." Prior to the fall of 1957, the Congress demonstrated a rather parsimonious attitude toward the administration's military budget requests and the President, true to his grand equation of national defense, found himself ardently defending against Congressional criticism programs which he considered both minimal and essential. In such a situation, where the executive served as a bastion against budgetary cuts by the Congress, the military—including dissident Army elements which believed that their service's allocation was already dangerously inadequate—found themselves in a position where their only ally was the extremely miserly Eisenhower administration. Given the realities of the mid-fifties, the service chiefs were compelled in their own interests to embrace the "lesser of the evils" and vigorously supported the administration's budget before the relevant legislative committees. At times, they even seemed to be quite enthusiastic about the merits of the policy of the long haul. While, to be sure, even during the "lean years" the several services maintained commitments to their particular doctrines and peculiar needs, the paramount preoccupation of each appears to have been the protection of what they already had been allotted by the White House, and their contending claims for new roles, functions and funds were distinctly muted. The service strategies during the period of budgetary retrenchment were, of necessity, those of buying time and minimizing losses.

However, in the post-Sputnik period, when the legislative pendulum swings from a niggardly approach to defense spending to a period of prodigal indulgence, we naturally find the military—or, at any rate, significant factions within it—switching allies and devising new strategies of its own to maximize its gains from any potential windfall. While the administration, again out of its sense of balance, sought to prevent additions to (rather than cuts from) its budget by the Congress, the armed services sought to make the most out of legislative generosity and, recognizing that the spending lid was now removed, maneuvered against both the executive and one another to expand their roles and missions rather than merely to conserve them. The "Pearl Harbor syndrome," then, is characterized by the various military branches advancing vociferous claims as to the superiority of their particular doctrines and thus the merit of their arguments in support of greater expenditures at the expense of the competing services' claims and civilian demands in general. Each claiming before Congressional committees to be in sole possession of the ultimate weapon, the service chiefs appear in a situation analogous to Salvador de Madariaga's animals in his famed fable about nature's disarmament conference.[1] A detached observer at the hearings of the Senate and House defense appropriations subcommittees during the period under consideration in this study, might conceivably have devised a Madariaga-like fable of his own:

> When the animals had gathered, the lion looked at the eagle and said gravely, 'the destructiveness of talons has inevitably led to their abolition; thus, we must emphasize claws and jaws in combat.' The eagle looked back at the lion and said, 'Nonsense—the very destructiveness of talons ensures their utility; it is claws and jaws which are now useless.'
>
> Thus each animal in turn proposed the uselessness of the weapons he did not have, until at last the shark rose up and said in tones of sweet reasonableness:
>
> 'Comrades-in-arms, you are all mistaken. All weapons are useful—and in the seas we have them all.'

## II

The contrast between the "lean year syndrome" and the "Pearl Harbor syndrome" is best illustrated by comparing the behavior of the relevant groups during the Congressional budgetary hearings for fiscal year 1958 with that during the first post-Sputnik investigations beginning in November of 1957. Anticipating a critical scrutiny of its defense spending requests by the traditionally cautious House Appropriations Committee, the administration was careful at the beginning of 1957 to frame its budgetary needs in terms of the exigencies of the policy of the long pull. Discussing past treatment of defense matters (that is, by the Truman administration), Defense Secretary Charles E. Wilson pointed to the fallacy of planning for a date of maximum danger. Refusing to define the Soviet threat as a long-term given as was the policy of the Eisenhower administration, short-term planning for successive critical periods of peril had

> forced an artificial peaking of the military effort which, had it been carried to its logical conclusion, would inevitably have resulted in drastic cutbacks once the peaks had been reached. This would have been a reversion to the old pattern of our military history—a succession of peaks and valleys in our national defense effort.[2]

Based upon the premise that though the "threat is still of a high order," the "rise of militant communism has probably reached its peak," the administration had decided as early as March of 1956 that, despite the expected rising costs of defense programs in 1958-1960, the military budget could be kept at the 38-40 billion dollar level. A significant rise in the budget, in addition to meaning a significant rise in taxes and/or inflation as well as extended government controls over a mobilized economy, "would be unreasonable and misunderstood all over the world."[3] Moreover, it was the firm belief of the administration that in the long run the demands of the Russian people would reassert themselves, that the rise of a scientific and industrial intelligentsia within the Soviet Union would bring about such social unrest that the Soviet regime would mellow, become less totalitarian, and redirect its energies into domestic channels. The concomitant of the embourgoisement of Soviet society, declared Wilson, would be the possibility of a working reconciliation between the two superpowers.[4] Until that day, however, "[o]ur basic policy is strength for the long pull until situations have definitely improved or disarmament agreements have been reached under safe inspection."[5] The interim strategy for the military containment of Communist expansion would rest on a foundation of endurable strain upon the American economy and polity—that is, the New Look: "the use of atomic weapons in a major war and . . . the use of such atomic weapons as would be militarily feasible and usable [i.e., tactical nuclear weapons] in a smaller war, if such a war is forced upon us."[6]

On the other hand, while emphasizing the budgetary demands of the long pull, Wilson was quick to voice the opposite concern of the Eisenhower years—the fear of a garrison state. Both he and Admiral Arthur W. Radford (Chairman of the Joint Chiefs of Staff) acknowledged the duty of the service chiefs to press for more and more funds and weapons, but ultimately it was up to the civilian element of the government—both executive and legislative—to place the military demands in the larger context of the general welfare. Wilson, especially cognizant of the extreme criticism he had received from elements within the press and the Congress for his economizing in the Defense Department, was disturbed by the apparent institutionalization of military interests by civilian society: "one of the serious things about this defense business is that so many Americans are getting a vested interest in it; properties, business, jobs, employment, votes, opportunities for promotion and advancement, bigger salaries for scientists, and all that. It is a troublesome business."[7] Thus, while the administration stressed one side of the scales (that is, support for a budget which it claimed was minimal), the nature of its underlying philosophy was such that it could not pass up an opportunity to warn of a possible overemphasis on defense.

Despite Secretary Wilson's attempt to prevent the lower chamber from cutting the defense budget, the House version of the bill reported to the floor by the Appropriations Committee was nearly 2.6 billion dollars less than the administration estimates originally considered,[8] and the administration was forced to appeal to the Senate for restoration. Calling the administration budget "both austere and carefully balanced," Wilson warned that the direct effect of reductions would be felt principally "in the field of aircraft, ships, and missile procurement." As he had before the House, the Secretary outlined the rationale for the strategy for the long pull and emphasized that the Eisenhower program was as austere as it could possibly be without adversely affecting the nation's security interests. As an example of the administration's policy of defense economy, he pointed to the 755,000 man cut in military personnel which had been brought about since 1953, only 400,000 of which was attributable to the end of the Korean war; the balance had been achieved by the New Look's emphasis on the new military technology of nuclear weaponry.[9] In his prepared statement, Admiral Radford also called for a restoration of the cuts which, in his words, would "risk the security of the nation and the free world."[10] The President himself, the committee was informed, had stated the day before that the cuts would adversely affect the country's missile programs. The culprit in rising defense expenditures, Wilson advised, was not new administration programs but simply inflation. In response to queries about trimming the fat from the department's budget, he retorted that the cuts simply could not be absorbed and pleaded with the committee not to "take away the cards and chips from the people who have to try to work something out with the Russians."[11] And, finally, constantly referring to the policy of the long pull and the steady balance which it implied, he alluded to and inverted the phrase about Soviet capabilities which he had employed the previous year in response to the ephemeral "bomber gap" controversy—a phrase to which he would return during the aftermath of the Soviet satellite launching:

> I did not think the Russians were 10 feet tall last year, [but] I don't think they are only 5 feet tall now. I think an orderly sensible approach to the thing has to be done in our country. We cannot have those emotional swings back and forth and do a sensible job.[12]

While the Eisenhower administration was busy asserting what it believed to be the barest essential needs of security before a defense-economy-minded Congress, the military establishment correspondingly adopted a stance designed to buttress the arguments of the executive branch. More fearful of Congressional cuts of their respective budgets than concerned with the opportunities for aggrandizement of their various programs, the civilian and military service chiefs demonstrated a firm commitment to the

105

substance and underlying premises of the President's budgetary requests. In their testimony before the House, neither Army Secretary Wilber M. Bruckner nor Chief of Staff Maxwell Taylor voiced anything like the stinging indictments of White House policy which would characterize their appearances before the committee in later years; indeed, careful examination of their opening statements indicates a preoccupation with the justification of past and present expenditures and the explanation of steps which had been taken to more efficiently spend funds currently appropriated.[13] (The only significant exception to this pattern was General Gavin who sought to emphasize the evolving and expanding role of ground forces in the missile age. Pointing to the traditional role of mobility in the history of warfare as holding out the promise for innovation, he then proceeded to show that, in the era of land-based missiles, control over terrain meant control over the space above it: "The control of land areas will be decisive."[14]) Several months later, before the House unit's counterpart in the Senate, the service's principal spokesmen again reiterated a strong endorsement of the Eisenhower budget—which had now been substantially reduced by the House—as essential to the security of the United States.[15] When queried as to the state of the long-range modernization program of Army equipment, Taylor did matter-of-factly admit that he had originally pressed for greater funding and had been turned down, but without complaining or pressing the point he simply accepted the fact that: "I sit with the other Chiefs . . . on budget matters and I know it is not just a simple matter of the Army saying, 'We need to have some more aircraft.' Because of the question of living within a budget ceiling someone has to decide where the money comes from." As opposed to later years when such an exchange might have served as the departure point for the enumeration of the budgetary starvation of the service, Taylor went no further—nor was he encouraged to do so by his questioner, defense-advocate Stuart Symington.[16] Nevertheless, the Chief of Staff did not forgo entirely a plea for the unique role of his service, stating that the growing reluctance of the Soviet Union to engage in general nuclear war would, in all likelihood, signal a shift in Communist tactics toward subversion and local aggression—"the most likely and most immediate threats to world peace" which, if not arrested "must lead to the erosion of the free world and our piecemeal loss of that which we are pledged to defend." Foreseeing the plethora of limited wars "anywhere on the periphery of the free world," he counselled for American preparedness to "intervene quickly with substantial forces." But once again, his rather perfunctory statement was not elaborated upon nor did it elicit any apparent interest from his listeners. Moreover, it was carefully followed by unqualified support for the President's funding requests and was apparently designed to serve as a leverage for the restoration of House cuts rather than as a means to go beyond previously made executive limitations.[17]

The Congressional testimony of the leaders of the other two services during the budgetary battle of the first half of 1957 also conformed to the ideal of military behavior which the "lean year syndrome" model suggests—namely, enthusiastic support of administration policy and muted (though merely temporarily dormant) inter-service doctrinal controversy. In February, before the House Appropriations Subcommittee, Secretary of the Air Force Donald Quarles unequivocally supported the administration budget and maintained that United States retaliatory capability was more secure than at any time in the past. While both Quarles and Chief of Staff Nathan F. Twining were compelled by the committee to justify their expenditure of funds and attest to the prudent and efficient uses to which their share of the tax dollar had been put, they were doubly on the defensive due to the extra nearly one billion dollars which had been tacked onto administration requests for the Air Force by the Congress for FY1957 in response to the illusive "bomber gap" controversy of the year before. Hard put to explain such a misallocation of resources, Twining explained that new intelligence now indicated a slower rate of Soviet bomber production than previously prophesied, but was quick to add that the Kremlin was still catching up quantitatively. As for the nation's long-range missile program, the General simply assured his audience that, "I know of nothing that could be done to give us operationally effective ballistic missile appreciably sooner."[18] Similarly, three months later before the Senate, the Air Force again defended administration policy, but, at the same time, aware of the less conservative nature of the Senate Appropriations Committee and in the wake of General Taylor's statement on the primacy of limited conventional war forces, the eagle retorted to the lion:

> It is sometimes said that total war waged with modern weapons of mass destruction would be mutual suicide, and that therefore this kind of war has abolished itself. I think this is a dangerous fallacy. We must recognize the fact that total war is no less a potential threat today when both sides possess atomic weapons than it was several years ago when we alone had them.
>
> . . . [O]ur readiness for it must be maintained at the highest peak the resources available will allow.

Moreover, it was suggested that the Air Force had a great (if not paramount) role in possible limited wars as well and, therefore, the greatest investment possible in airpower could deal with both threats: "The most dangerous threat is total war. We must prepare against that above all else and within these preparations we will certainly be able to handle lesser dangers."[19]

And, finally, the Navy as well was quick to demonstrate its loyalty to the threatened administration program and its unique utility in the missile age. A parroting of the Eisenhower policy of the long pull as stated by Secretary Wilson before the House a few days before was presented by Navy Secretary Charles S. Thomas who reminded the committee that the United States simply could not survive as a viable system if either its military armor were allowed to rust or if, in response to some transient danger, it embarked on a policy of prolonged and full mobilization during peacetime. Terming the program before the Congress "a minimum budget" containing only the most essential items, Admiral Arleigh Burke (Chief of Naval Operations) vigorously endorsed the budget which he believed "will give us the maximum in naval power for every dollar requested."[20] Such would have to be the nature of the Navy's strategy in a year when the administration, while not cutting naval expenditures from the previous budget, had refused to increase them and when the military as a whole was generally placed on the defensive even before the usually less fiscally conservative Senate where men like the conservative Allen J. Ellender of Louisiana would demand of the Marine Corps justification as to whether "the world situation warrants the amount [*sic*] of men you presently have."[21] To be sure, however, the Navy would enter the debate between the Army and the Air Force over the paramountcy of either general or limited war forces. In a tone of sweet reasonableness, the shark would rise up before both committees and claim that preparedness for both types of possible scenarios was in order—and that, naturally, the aircraft carrier was just the versatile weapons system needed to wage either type of war.[22]

## III

With the launching of the Soviet Sputniks in the fall of the same year, however, the necessity of military acquiescence to administration policy (and the concomitant need to conserve rather than seek to expand individual service missions) became dysfunctional. In an environment characterized by intense Congressional concern over the state of American defenses, the armed services were moved to disavow the executive branch's attempt to hold the lid down on military spending and openly to press for the expansion of their respective roles and budgets. Indeed, the term "Pearl Harbor syndrome" has been suggested by the analogy consistently drawn by Senate Majority Leader Lyndon Johnson during the post-Sputnik Congressional hearings between the Russian scientific breakthrough and the crushing surprise blow delivered upon American military power a decade and a half before.[23] Reacting to the sense of crisis and imminent peril which gripped the nation's opinion leaders in the wake of the unexpected Communist success of the previous month, Johnson decided immediately after a Pentagon briefing on the military consequences of the satellite to begin an exhaustive investigation into the shortcomings of the administration's military programs—a series of hearings which would run from November of 1957 to July of the following year. And it was apparent after the first half-dozen or so witnesses that the verbal palliatives of President Eisenhower would not suffice to quell the widespread apprehension over the future security position of the country. On the first day of the hearings, Dr. Edward Teller (often referred to as "the father of the hydrogen bomb") warned that the satellite had, despite Eisenhower's frequent assurances, "great military significance"; that the Soviets had demonstrated that they had developed large boosters and a good guidance system which were "quite close to the requirements for intercontinental ballistic missiles." The implication was clear, Teller suggested: the United States was behind in the ICBM race because its programs had received insufficient funding. Similarly, Dr. Vannevar Bush (who had been science advisor to Presidents Roosevelt and Truman) advised that we must "divest ourselves of our smugness and complacency" and "wake up to the fact that we are in a tough competitive race" with the Russians for military superiority and therefore immediately insulate SAC from a surprise missile attack and accelerate missile development. Former General James H. Doolittle called for an urgent build-up of the military establishment and the creation of an aggressive research and development program. And so it went—a parade of scientists, industrialists, educators, and military specialists all reinforcing the crisis-like atmosphere which had abruptly seized the nation.[24]

Confronted with such alarming pronouncements, the administration consistently counselled the Congress against a crash program of military build-up and urged restraint in the authorization of funds for new and ongoing programs. Before the House Defense Appropriations Subcommittee, which with its brief two-day investigation was the first unit of either house to take up the issue, Defense Secretary Neil H. McElroy assured Congressional leaders that the progress of strategic missile development was based upon technical and not budgetary factors. Arguing against "a rather frantic 'crash' program of somewhat dubious effectiveness," he stated forthrightly that there was "little we can do to make a significant change in the date by which we can achieve the first operational ICBM." Deputy Defense Secretary Donald

Quarles similarly refused to sanction a crash program and newly appointed missile director William Holaday reassured the committee that everything feasible was being done in the development of the ICBM and thus the program could not be accelerated. Above all, McElroy claimed that the United States had "ample deterrent" power which was not in any way affected by the Soviet satellites and that steps were being taken to remove the bottlenecks in the missile program.[25] A week later, before the Johnson Subcommittee, the same spokesman returned to the Hill to reiterate and expand upon the cautious wait-and-see policy of the President in regard to new military spending. While elucidating upon the steps taken or planned to remove the non-monetary bottlenecks in the various programs, McElroy steadfastly refused to grant that the Soviets had an edge in either overall military power or even in the field of missiles. Despite attempts by Senator Symington, for example, to show that the Soviet Union had surpassed the United States in "total military strength"—according to the former Air Force Secretary it had ten times as many divisions in the field, five times as many submarines and "thousands more" jet aircraft—McElroy dismissed the claims and refused to admit the need for any major revamping of the country's defense plans, including the acceleration of bomber procurement urged by the Senator. Nor did Quarles admit to a Soviet lead in rocketry; he stood by a recent statement that there was no cause for alarm because of the satellite launchings and that "it is imperative that we not be sidetracked from our prime security objectives by extraneous or irrelevant issues." Holaday as well paraphrased remarks he had recently made before the American Rocket Society: "we are not as far behind as some of our journalistic friends and commentators think we are," he declared. "To listen to some of those so-called experts who are backed by half-information, all seems lost, we have sunk to a position of second-rate power in the world. Such is not the case."[26]

Thus, the administration (with its primary interest in a minimal defense program) and the military chiefs (with their primordial emphasis on maximum preparedness) were bound to part company as the political context which had originally made for strange bedfellows dramatically changed. It was obviously no longer expedient for the military to tie their fortunes to the Eisenhower policy of the long pull when greener pastures beckoned at the other end of Pennsylvania Avenue. The lean years were now over, and as it was no longer a question of conserving but rather one of expanding the military role, the services were more apt to see greater congruence between their respective versions of the national interest and that of a less parsimonious Congress. And while previously a reasonably united front among the services was necessary in confronting a less sympathetic body of lawmakers, it was apparent that temporarily muted rivalries would now be accentuated: to impress upon Congressional leaders the uniquely appropriate function of one's service (or technological interest within a service) in the post-Sputnik era would be of cardinal importance.

Having only a few months before attested to the adequacy of the Eisenhower budget for FY1958 before the appropriate legislative agencies, the three services' civilian and military heads now re-evaluated their stands and found numerous causes for second thoughts. While Army Secretary Bruckner vigorously pushed the Nike-Zeus active missile defense system (a program which the administration had soft-pedaled) and argued that his service should be given primary responsibility for the development of strategic rockets (after all, were not ballistic missiles merely an extension of field artillery?), Chief of Staff Taylor stated in no uncertain terms that he was "not satisfied" with the present state and planned modernization of conventional war forces[27]—despite administration claims to the contrary.[28] General Gavin was even more outspoken in his criticism of his executive superiors (a course of action which would contribute to his controversial retirement a few weeks later), claiming that insufficient funding for the Army as a whole had forced the service to sacrifice the long-overdue modernization of its equipment to the furtherance of its missile program; furthermore, he charged (again in direct contradiction of administration spokesmen) that the lack of money for research and development had been so severe that the balance of military power was finally shifting against the United States. And despite the oft-stated policy of President Eisenhower that the country was concerned with space merely for scientific purposes and was not engaged in a race with the Soviets, Redstone Arsenal chief Medaris and his leading civilian scientist Wernher Von Braun declared unequivocally that the control of space was crucial to the security of the nation and that this security had been sacrificed due to the limitation placed on Army funds by the administration.[29]

In much the same manner, the Air Force performed a virtual *volte face*, and, in marked contrast to their appearances before the Congress but a few months before in defense of the executive budget, service Secretary James A. Douglas and General White called for immediate steps to ensure "a combat ready Air Force with the weapons of today." For immediate consideration (in view of the perceived Soviet edge in rocketry), the airpower spokesmen called for the acceleration of the SAC alert and dispersion programs; for strength in the immediate future, they urged new appropriations to speed up the operational capabilities for both long- and intermediate-range missiles; and, "for the day after tomorrow," the entire space program (which naturally was seen as part of the domain of the Air Force) was to be pushed forward with a new sense of urgency. In response to a question concerning his commitment to current administration policies, Douglas stated flatly that he was "not satisfied with the situation as it exists today," and called for "immediate steps" for the strengthening of SAC and for a missile program which would yield "substantial" ICBM and IRBM capabilities at an earlier date than the administration had previously planned. Contradicting the testimony of the Defense Secretary as well as the assurances of the President, White claimed that the United States was indeed behind in the missile race, but could catch up by greater investment in the Air Force's Titan—an investment which, the General noted, he had advised and the administration rejected. Furthermore, he noted that the President's lack of sympathy for the modernization of the nation's bomber force "gives me cause for a good deal of concern." Finally, calling for "an assured superiority" in strategic nuclear weaponry, White presented a program of increased expenditures which would give the United States more missiles at an earlier date, a vigorous space program and an active missile defense system both under Air Force as opposed to Army direction. In short, both Douglas and White (as well as missile chief Schriever) displayed an unmistakable dissatisfaction with the Air Force budget and endorsed various additional programs the sum total of which would have meant an increase in the administration's requests by some 2.3 billion dollars for FY1959.[30]

Even more critical in his discussion of present policy was Vice Chief of Staff Curtis LeMay whose preoccupation was with the rapid expansion of the manned bomber fleet. A former head of SAC, LeMay noted that his previous pleas for a larger and more rapid procurement of the B-52 stratofortress and demands for at least a minimal dispersion program had fallen upon deaf ears in the executive branch—and even when the Congress had appropriated such funds, the White House merely impounded them despite legislative intent. If the Congress did not provide the added number of planes and bases which were "absolutely necessary" to the security of the country, he warned that the United States would fall behind the Soviet Union in striking power by mid-1959 and would invite a cataclysmic pre-emptive strike by the superior Communist ICBM force at some future date. Terming the Air Force budget "insufficient," he added a word of caution about diverting attention from the strategic situation to the Army's conventional war cause and, restating the classical case for airpower across the wide spectrum of military capabilities, declared: "I do not understand why a force that will deter a big war will not deter a small war too, if we want it to and say it will."[31]

The Navy, for its part, appeared to be the least dissatisfied—or, at any rate, the least outspoken—concerning the Eisenhower budget. Yet at the same time we can discern a progressive hardening of its service line as the hearings before the Johnson committee moved forward. For example, in his initial testimony (following on the heels of Secretary McElroy), Admiral Burke seemed content to merely restate traditional naval doctrine as to the necessity of the United States' controlling the vital sea lanes of the world and the versatile role of seapower in both limited and general conflict. However, returning in late January after the rival air chieftains had presented their case for long-range bombers and land-based ballistic missiles and had deprecated the value of limited war forces, Burke became more forceful in his defense of his service's twin roles. Firstly, he indicated that as far as he was concerned "we are doing just about as well as the Russians are with [land-based intercontinental ballistic] missiles," and that the submarine-launched intermediate-range missile (Polaris) system was the best strategic weapons system available to the United States. Secondly, he emphasized the greater likelihood of limited as opposed to general wars and the necessity of "major increases" in DOD expenditures to prepare adequately for that contingency. Finally, he alleged that administration harassment ("continuous review and review and review") had forced the Navy to submit smaller budget requests (in the order of three to four billion dollars) than it believed necessary. All in all, the executive branch's refusal to raise the total Defense Department budget more than one or two billion dollars from the previous year had brought about severe cutbacks in vital programs—such as the 50 per cent cut in the Navy's anti-submarine warfare (ASW) division. Thus in one stroke Burke sought to counter the Air Force's claim to primacy as well as to prove that, despite the vital and versatile nature of its missions, the Navy had not fared well before the Budget Bureau.[32]

## IV

The Soviet Sputnik thus thrust the American defense policy-making process into a period of disequilibrium with the legislative and executive branches aligned against one another over the question of the adequacy of United States military posture and the three services regrouping for an internecine struggle over future security doctrine and, therefore, the future reallocation of the defense dollar. Not only was there not a single coherent military stance—that is, a set of policies upon which all services could agree—but neither was there a solid alliance between any one service and either the Congress or the White House. To be sure, there was a Henry M. Jackson in the Senate to look after the interests of the Strategic Air Command (the prime production facilities for Boeing's B-52 were located in Jackson's Washington State),[33] and a Daniel Flood in the House to press for limited war forces, and even a Senator Stuart Symington to actively lobby for the defense establishment as a whole. But there was little in the way of a consistently firm commitment by the relevant committees of either chamber to support the interests and doctrines of any particular branch of the armed services. Indeed, beyond what was at times a vague anxiety over administration defense economy, the Congress could not articulate an alternative set of defense doctrines, and its add-on appropriations ran the full gamut from mandatory floors to the manpower levels of the Army and the Marines to increased authorizations for land-based strategic missiles, long-range manned aircraft and the fleet ballistic missile system. If a pattern is to be found here—beyond the obvious predisposition to higher defense spending as a whole—it is not apparent.

Moreover, the administration itself refused to back any particular service doctrine, but instead endeavored to restrain military expenditures as a whole while adhering to the policy of the long pull. To the dismay of the Air Force partisans, Secretary McElroy refused to embrace a strategy of nuclear superiority which would have meant a significant increase in the procurement of missiles and bombers. But at same time, to the chagrin of the Army and Navy, he also rejected a massive expansion of conventional war forces. Before the House Armed Services Committee, McElroy implicitly endorsed a policy of strategic parity; that is, by defining the main objective of defense in terms of the deterrence of a direct assault upon the American homeland, he suggested that the level of deliverable nuclear warheads needed for such a task was in fact absolute and not relative to any increased Soviet capabilities. The primary goal of American strategic power was "to make it obvious to any potential enemy that we have available and are prepared to use weapons of retaliation so devastating that the cost to an aggressor of an attack on us would be unbearable." And inasmuch as the United States, by means of its SAC bombers and carrier based aircraft, had such a capability at the time and would (with the influx of a modest number of land- and sea-based missiles into its arsenal) maintain such a capability for the foreseeable future, it had in effect reached a point of saturation, and thus to build more weapons than planned would be superfluous.[34] JCS Chairman Twining generally concurred and, before the House Appropriations Subcommittee, noted that despite the importance often attached to the relative strength of the two superpowers, "the most important factor is, of course, that you have the proper size force to penetrate the Soviet defenses and destroy the essential targets. . . . This I am confident we can do today."[35] However, while rejecting a policy of assured superiority in the nuclear field as had the Army and Navy, the administration did not see as its corollary the adoption of a policy of limited engagements along the periphery of the non-Communist world. Responding to the charge by Senator Symington that the United States was ill-prepared, given the perennial Soviet threat and America's numerous commitments, to wage conventional warfare, McElroy further developed the premises set forth by the President. Firstly, the Defense Secretary reminded the legislators that the administration did not see a major limited war in the NATO area (that is, Europe and the Middle East) as a realistic expectation given its vital nature to both adversaries: "We just do not see how it can turn out to be a practical possibility." As for the "underdeveloped countries" in less vital regions, in addition to American-trained and equipped indigenous forces "we have a very effective force for limited war with a combination of the paratroop divisions of the Army and the divisions of the Marines." Thus, McElroy noted that the underlying assumption of such limited war advocates as Symington (who urged a 100 per cent increase in Army divisions and a vast expansion of its airlift capacities) was that "there was going to be a quite big engagement of a so-called limited nature, or [the U. S. would have to] be involved in several parts of the world simultaneously." But inasmuch as the President rejected these premises and thereby assumed that major Soviet aggression in Europe and the Middle East and/or myriad aggressions along the periphery of Eurasia would signify an all-out assault upon the free world (and thus

World War III), any increase in conventional capabilities was simply unnecessary.[36]

Meanwhile, the uniformed services had split into two antagonistic doctrinal camps—the finite deterrence/limited war group and the assured superiority/airpower faction. The Army (which along with the Navy comprised the first camp) refused to accept the ICBM as the ultimate weapon in warfare which would make all the other services' roles superfluous. Quite the contrary, Secretary Bruckner maintained that the development of strategic missiles would merely reinforce the nuclear stalemate which had developed between the two super-powers and therefore encourage Soviet aggression at lower levels of intensity. Therefore, the task would pass to the Army to

> see to it that with a standoff of the two giant forces, such as the Soviets and the United States, both having a nuclear power that could destroy the other fellow, . . . that it is suicidal for Russia to undertake it on the basis, that what they are going to do is keep nibbling away, as they are in the Mideast, foment trouble in Indonesia and Syria and those other places around the world, and one by one drag them under the iron curtain, by hook or by crook, that unless we have a ready force to drop in or get in there and do something about it, that is the best way to start one of these global things, and that the limited war . . . that Russia is playing for keeps . . . is the one thing we have to be ready for [*sic*].[37]

Thus the Army Secretary proposed an expanded role for his service which would "permit the precise application of the minimum force to control a specific situation," and by implication appeared to reject administration policy as set forth by the Secretary of Defense.[38] Despite this threat, however, not only had the administration failed to expand its ground forces, General Taylor complained, but it had severely cut back its capabilities by progressively lowering its manpower level and by delaying the already overdue modernization of its equipment. For example, in the budget for FY1959 the Army requested a strength of 925,000 men as the "bare minimum" necessary for American security, but had been authorized only 870,000 by the President; furthermore, after an exhaustive three-year service study which pointed to a requirement of three to four billion dollars a year in additional funds for modernization, the administration refused to concede the money. From the Army's vantage point, then, in an era which would witness the proliferation of conventional war conflicts, the United States had allowed its armies to deteriorate both quantitatively and qualitatively despite the fact that the massive Soviet Army had been re-equipped with a completely new postwar arsenal of weapons and had been trained to fight "either a nuclear or non-nuclear war, large or small, in any kind of terrain."[39]

The Navy for the most part concurred with its sister service's analysis of the international environment. As set forth by Admiral Burke, the Soviet Union had in no way abandoned its ultimate goal of "eventually engulf[ing] the whole world" and, because it had been thwarted in this direction by the American deterrent to global war, it had now adopted the "piecemeal approach to world domination." The "most imminent danger" to the future security of the United States was that "in emphasizing the nuclear general war, this Nation will lose sight of the necessity to maintain adequate strength to combat limited wars in areas remote of this country—limited wars requiring the United States control of the seas. This is the most likely form of future warfare."[40] Thus while a certain portion of the defense budget had to be allocated toward its retaliatory system, inasmuch as "there is a reasonable and finite limit to the amount of deterrent capability required," over-investment was not only superfluous but dysfunctional as it drained funds from the more pressing threat of limited war.[41] With nuclear stalemate a reality, an increase in general war capabilities would in no way serve as an adequate deterrent to conventional conflict which would have to be met on its own terms.[42]

In opposition to the finite deterrence/limited war camp within the military establishment (and, in effect, the finite deterrence/ no limited war group within the Eisenhower administration), one finds the Air Force with a defense doctrine devoid of any connotations whatsoever of the diminishing (let alone negative) utility of investing in greater and greater strategic airpower. Ever since the end of the Second World War, and the concomitant appreciation by both superpowers of the centrality of nuclear weaponry in military strategy, the Air Force—the former bastard son of the Army—had dominated the defense budget, receiving nearly half of military appropriations by the late fifties. The service had definitely come into its own, and its predominance was dependent upon the United States' acceptance of the decisive nature of general war. Thus, the Air Force (quite correctly in terms of its own frame of reference) saw its mission as by far the most vital of the armed services, and as Chief of Staff White would state openly before the Congress,

> . . . the missions now assigned to the Air Force are the most important military missions. I think, quite frankly, that the survival of this Nation does depend on having an Air Force second to none.
>
> The other services have a great part and do *supplement* and *compliment* and in some respects will be paramount, but our survival depends on the retaliatory forces and the air forces of this country today.[43]

In addition to promulgating a doctrine where the critical role of strategic nuclear weapons would have had the effect of reducing the other two services to the roles of mere adjuncts to airpower, the Air Force refused to believe that there could possibly be reached a strategic plateau and standoff between the two rival world powers. The notions of "sufficiency" or "parity" were apparently alien to its philosophy of combat. During the Congressional budgetary hearings of 1959, for example, White categorically dissented from the Army-Navy case for a minimum strategic striking force as set forth by Taylor and Burke, and indicated that an "effective deterrent posture" meant, as far as he was concerned, a significant increase in the number of delivery vehicles for nuclear warheads—in fact, for the 1960 budget nearly twice as many Atlas squadrons as planned by the administration were urged.[44] The Air Force case for the maintenance of massive nuclear superiority revolved about four propositions: (1) that it would take the threat of far greater destruction to deter the Soviet Union than it would to deter the United States inasmuch as the former placed less of a value on human life;[45] (2) that inasmuch as the initiative for surprise attack lay with the Communists, this country would have the capability to absorb a massive Soviet first-strike and still deliver a crushing blow in retaliation if deterrence were to be effective;[46] (3) that an imbalance of nuclear striking power in favor of the United States would allow it to credibly deter non-nuclear aggression as well;[47] (4) that, in the event deterrence should fail, victory in a third world war would go to the stronger of the two gladiators.[48] It is not surprising, then, that the doctrine of finite deterrence and its correlative of limited war were anathema to the roles and missions of the Air Force.

## V

The normal divisions over strategy which pervade the military establishment leave one with a markedly different picture from that painted by certain recent critics. Rather than a monolithic power group in the American political system, the military is in fact a congeries of factions divided over the fundamental issue of what defense policies best serve the security of the nation. The doctrinal schisms are indeed real and there is no reason to doubt that the contending parties sincerely believe that the stands they take are best in terms of the national interest of the United States. That the positions taken also tend to coincide with the institutional interests of the various services or service subdivisions which advance them is less an indication of hypocrisy than it is simply the product of parochialism. And it is even not so much the rationalization of self-interest but this parochialism (a prerequisite of professionalism) which inevitably leads to the politicization of the several factions by the executive branch during the post-lean-year period. Charged with the broadest responsibility—that is, the welfare of the entire polity—President Eisenhower of necessity was forced to weigh military concerns against civilian priorities and at the same time to balance the contending claims within the military. Performing this generalist function, the administration was inevitably compelled to sacrifice certain claims for the realization of the good of the whole as it defined it. Naturally, those charged with the responsibility of executing more specific functions—and generally having been immersed in a particular field for most of their adult lives and having developed the necessarily narrow expertise—tend to see the whole largely in terms of the one part with which they are concerned. Because, as Don K. Price would say, "where you stand depends on where you sit," the generalist and the parochial see things quite differently and are bound to conflict over policy matters.

Yet it is not simply a divergence of views between the generalist Chief Executive and the parochial services. Rather one finds a generalist-parochial continuum with the President at one extreme and the service technocrat (e.g., Army missile-man Medaris or SAC chief Power) at the other. As one moves progressively away from the parochial end of the spectrum, one encounters men who must perform roles which require the consideration of a larger and larger portion of the whole picture: the military chief of staff who while seeking to protect the interests of the service as a whole must also deal with the other service heads, the Department of Defense bureaucracy, and the White House; the civilian service secretary who at the same time serves at the Commander in Chief's discretion but must also keep out a watchful eye for the interests of his agency if he is to effectively oversee it; the Chairman of the Joint Chiefs who must wear two hats—that of the prime military coordinator of the defense establishment as a whole and that of the President's top advisor on military affairs—a function which might cause him to become the President's "party whip" at meetings of the JCS[49]; the Secretary of Defense who, ideally, serves as a loyal member of the administration team, and seeks the implementation of its defense goals.

The extreme parochial vantage point is well illustrated by the testimony of SAC Commander in Chief Thomas S. Power during the Johnson Subcommittee investigations of early 1960. Called upon to reconcile administration reassurances and his own controversial claims that the Soviet Union (with 150 ICBMs and 150 IRBMs) "could virtually wipe out our entire nuclear strike capability within a span of 30 minutes,"[50] he stated: *"as a field commander,* I think we should try to take care of the worst situation,

122

and the worst situation is not one where they [the Soviets] desire peace. The worst situation is one where they are planning to strike us." Moreover, he readily admitted the parochialism of his vantage point noting that his statements "were my own opinions *as viewed from my position* as commander in chief of the Strategic Air Command, and with due consideration for the *responsibilities of that task*," and added that, "I recognize that there are *echelons of responsibility above me which must take other things into consideration than* [*sic*] I do."[51] Similarly, in the same hearings, General White was moved (in his defense of the B-70 bomber which had just been cut back by the President) to declare: "From the *relatively narrow responsibilities* that I have as the Chief of Staff of the Air Force, I felt, and still feel, that it would be highly desirable to go on with this weapons system as rapidly as feasible."[52] And Admiral Burke admitted before the House that though as Chief of Naval Operations he had asked for 60 per cent more in funds than the White House would allow, he could still accept the budget because the President was a generalist and therefore "is responsible for the whole picture."[53]

But it should not be assumed that parochial behavior is indicative of only the military. Quite the contrary, Secretary Bruckner (who was such an ardent advocate of the Army cause that General Taylor later suggested that he was "more loyalist than the King"[54]), considered himself more of a spokesman for his service in the councils of the administration than an agent of the President to carry out the policy of the long pull. Indeed, at one point in an exchange with the chairman of the Senate Appropriations Subcommittee, Bruckner, in his frustration with the administration's defense policies, declared: "I am trying to be a good soldier."[55] Thus, the condition of varied degrees of parochialism exists all down the line of the defense hierarchy. As quite nicely put by General White:

. . . My job is not an easy one as I said before.
General Power, for example, as the Commander in Chief of SAC, would like more money for SAC.

General Partridge of the North American Air Defense Command would like more for his command.

General Weyland of the Tactical Air Command would like more for his command, and so on down the line.

Why is it that each of these people have [sic] a desire to have more? It is because they are charged with a specific responsibility and they are exceedingly dedicated. . . .

He [Gen. Power] sees his problem in black and white.

When it comes to me, and to the [Air Force] Secretary, we must consider other elements of the Air Force. There is not an unlimited amount of funds . . . [and] so let us say instead of seeing it in black and white, we see it in kind of dark gray and muddy white, and we come up with a certain distribution.

This is only one-half my job as Chief of Staff of the Air Force. When I get through with that I have to go down to the Joint Chiefs of Staff. . . . So here, insofar as Air Force requirements are concerned, I am in the relative position of General Power. I see things in black and white from the Air Force point of view.[56]

That the degree of parochialism adheres to the role men are forced to fill rather than being the result of conscious individual decisions is aptly shown by viewing the transformation of behavior as one moves up the hierarchy of command in the defense establishment. That this is equally true of civilians and military men alike will be illustrated by tracing the changing patterns of behavior for both Thomas E. Gates (who rose from Navy Secretary to Defense Secretary) and Nathan F. Twining (who moved from Air Force Chief of Staff to JCS Chairman). In the early post-Sputnik period, for example, while Defense Secretary McElroy was attempting to hold down anticipated increases in defense spending, Gates was concerned for the most part with the expansion of the Navy's role, pressing before the Congress for a "super-acceleration" (that is, one billion dollars) of the Polaris program and urging a threefold increase in the number of missile-launching submarines planned.[57] Just prior to his elevation to Defense Secretary, he continued to be an advocate of greater naval power both for general and limited war and even went so far as to identify the role of his service with the security and well-being of the nation as a whole.[58] As soon as he shifted to the role of Secretary of Defense, however, he proceeded to perform the same function as had his predecessor—namely, a stalwart defender of the administration policy of nuclear sufficiency and the adequacy of its limited war programs.[59] General Twining underwent much the same process. As Air Force chief he was a major figure in the "bomber gap" controversy in 1956 and succeeded in getting near-ly a billion dollars added on to the administration's request for his service for FY1957.[60] Taking over Admiral Radford's post as head of the JCS, Twining found himself taking issue with his for-mer service and defending administration policy on the cutbacks in B-52 production and the development of the B-70 bomber as well as the restraints placed upon the procurement of strategic missiles.[61] Though Twining had originally supported White's (his successor as Air Force chief) position on the B-70, he was com-pelled by his new role as Chairman of the Joint Chiefs of Staff—and thus representative of the President and the Defense Secre-tary—to defend the Eisenhower decision. An interesting exchange between Twining and Symington in 1960 illustrates how the Gen-eral perceived his new role:

General TWINING. I do want you to understand that all these points [in defense of the B-70] were presented strongly by the Air Force, and they had a good hearing. The people who made the decisions had a lot of problems besides purely de-fense, and felt that perhaps we should go a little slower with the Air Force program. . . .

Senator SYMINGTON. Was that the reason you opposed General White's decision?

General TWINING. On the B-70?

Senator SYMINGTON. Yes, sir.

General TWINING. I never opposed his position on the B-70. Well, it depends at what stage of the proceedings you are talk-ing about here now. Initially, of course, I would be for it 100 percent, but when all things come out—

Senator SYMINGTON. Were you for it for military reasons?

General TWINING. Yes.

Senator SYMINGTON. Then you supported it? It is not going ahead. There couldn't have been any other reason for cancelling it but budgetary reasons, could there?

General TWINING. It is a very expensive weapons system.
. . .

Senator SYMINGTON. Can we say that you did feel, because of the cost, after it was turned down [by the President], that you had to differ with General White, and, therefore, oppose it as Chairman of the Joint Chiefs? Isn't that a fair statement?

General TWINING. I think it is a fair statement.[62]

## VI

The division between the generalist and the parochial had the effect, as could be expected, of politicizing the military. Faced with opposition to its programs by the service chiefs and the military technocrats, the Eisenhower administration sought to insulate its policies from the effects of the dissension by: (1) attacking the positions of the dissenters as parochial and, therefore, of dubious validity; and, (2) obtaining from the Chiefs of Staff and Chief of Naval Operations airtight written statements of support for the budget as a whole.

Eisenhower's defense against what he termed the "parochial generals" went back at least as far as 1956, when the Air Force began expressing its fears over the prospect of the United States falling behind the Soviet Union in long-range bombers and the Army charged the administration with sacrificing national security to the fallacious concept of a balanced budget. Responding to a press conference query about the criticisms recently advanced by Army Chief of Staff Matthew Ridgway (who had just retired), the President countered with what was to become a standard reply:

> . . . as all of you know, since back in 1940, I have been receiving advice from every kind of military assistant. Their advice is often expressing their own deeply felt, but let us say narrow fears.
>
> If I had listened to all the advice I got during those years, there never would have been a plan for crossing the Channel. Indeed, I think we wouldn't have crossed the Atlantic. We cer-

tainly would never have invaded Africa and the Mediterranean, and I know we would never have crossed the Channel until yet [*sic*].

So finally there comes places where people in authority must make decisions based upon the best advice they get [*sic*].[63]

Thus, falling back upon his reputation as the nation's foremost military strategist, Eisenhower repeatedly sought to discredit the dissenting voices within the military establishment. Not only was his personal expertise beyond questioning, the President asserted, but his constitutional powers placed him at the apex of the defense hierarchy and if a subordinate commander could not express to him his personal convictions and then loyally carry out the job designated by the Commander in Chief, "then I would say [such] a man isn't capable of carrying out the job he has."[64] Repeatedly in his meetings with the press, the President dismissed the views of his critics—whether they be journalists like Drew Pearson and Jack Anderson, senators like Symington, or military men like Gavin, Power, Taylor, and Medaris[65]—for their inability to advance beyond their distorted preoccupations with minor facets of the whole and refusal to appreciate the entire broad field of the national welfare. As the years—and the charges and counter-charges—progressed, Eisenhower became notably irritated and impatient with the military dissenters, until by the last year of his office he would declare in response to a reporter's request that he comment on General Power's claims on the dangerous vulnerability of the American deterrent:

No; too many of these generals have all sorts of ideas. . . . I have been long enough in the military service that I assure you I cannot be particularly disturbed because everybody with a parochial viewpoint all over the place comes along and says that the bosses know nothing about it.[66]

In order to prevent the military parochials from upsetting the Eisenhower apple-cart, the administration sought from the service chiefs written statement of their support for the defense budget to be signed, sealed, and delivered by the Defense Secretary to the Congressional appropriations committees. Noting that it was certainly "beyond our resources" to "do everything that every individual would like to see done," McElroy would nonetheless assure the Congress that he had in writing the statements of the Joint Chiefs of Staff "that they consider that the fiscal year 1960 proposed expenditure figure is adequate to provide for the essential programs necessary for the defense of the Nation for the period under consideration."[67] Yet the presentation of what was in reality a "treaty" negotiated among quasi-sovereign entities within the executive branch—a course of action, it should be emphasized in passing, made imperative by the division of powers between the White House and the Capitol—had the unexpected consequence of merely further politicizing the military chieftains and encouraging the Congress to exacerbate the divisions within the Pentagon. For, as is the case with many international agreements-in-principle, attempts at clarification merely served to point to the real schisms which had developed between the services and the administration.

Along with the signed approval were deposited the individual reservations of the Joint Chiefs, indicating that their adherence to the decisions of their superiors was highly qualified and depended in large part on varying definitions of "essential programs" and acceptance of the time factor involved—that is, "for the period under consideration." Thus, it would be little comfort to the administration to hear Admiral Burke testify that though he would grant that the present budget would not immediately "jeopardize the security of this country," his fears were directed toward the years ahead—and, given the long lead-time factor in the development of advanced weapons systems, steps not taken now would determine inadequacies in the not-too-distant future. Nor did General White's reservations lend much credence to the administration's claims, for while acquiescing to the Eisenhower budget he noted that the two billion dollars requested by but not granted to the Air Force would mean that the vast majority of SAC's aircraft (the B-47) were rapidly approaching obsolescence and the urgently needed B-58 replacements would not be procured in time—this at a time when the President had depreciated the value of a Soviet missile lead because of the striking power of the Strategic Air Command. And, finally, though Maxwell Taylor would nominally announce halfhearted support of the defense budget as a whole, he would at the same time attach so many reservations that he would eventually be forced to admit that the Army's budget was plainly "inadequate" for the tasks assigned it.[68]

Aware of this obvious incongruence, legislators in both houses (already at odds with the administration over its attempts to keep military spending down) were granted the opportunity of exploiting the divergence between the "treaty" and the numerous reservations attached. By pursuing the stated reservations of the service heads in order to prove that the executive-military agreement was in reality an empty and meaningless shell—a pseudo-agreement—the Congress inexorably further politicized the dissenters. The process which the administration had begun by seeking a façade of support despite the obvious lack of broad-based agreement on fundamentals, the Congress thus completed. And the military, caught between executive and legislative cross-pressures —aware both of the demands of the President for their loyalty and the opportunities which the Congress presented—were inevitably drawn into the political process. Seeking to breech the illusory wall of unity created by the Eisenhower regime, legislators employed two fundamental strategies in their interrogation of military representatives: (1) constant reminders to the military elite that, inasmuch as the Congress served an appellate function in the budgetary process, they were openly invited to submit for legislative review their proposals for additional funds which the Budget Bureau had vetoed; and, (2) incessant attempts to pursue the line of questioning in such a manner so as to compel their sometimes reluctant witnesses to brand the defense budget as obviously inadequate.

Openly attacking the civilian overseers of the defense establishment as "glorified bookkeepers" and instant strategic "geniuses,"[69] ardent limited war advocate Daniel Flood would constantly remind service witnesses that the Constitution had made the House the pivot of the whole appropriations process. Attempting, but failing to get the Air Force chiefs to admit the alleged inadequacy of the Eisenhower budget, he would demand: "I don't want a philosophical statement about your mission. What can you sell me? How many months can you save me and what will it cost?" Unable to entice General White with this inviting hint of a *carte blanche*, Flood persisted in his questioning, as the following exchange will illustrate, until the former was compelled to indicate all the items which he had originally requested of the executive branch but had been denied:

Mr. FLOOD. On January 9 you said, 'I would like to have 1, 2, 3, 4, 5, 6 things.'

General WHITE. And that I had been turned down by the various agencies to whom—

Mr. FLOOD. So you did not get them.

General WHITE. I did not get them.

Mr. FLOOD. You want them this morning?

General WHITE. I do.

Mr. FLOOD. But you have not got them.

General WHITE. I have not got them.

. . .

Mr. FLOOD. . . . Do you want to ask now for what you asked for on January 9 [from the executive branch]?

General WHITE. I think we have stated that we have—

Mr. FLOOD. Do you want it now?

General WHITE. I do.

Mr. FLOOD. Then when you ask this committee for it . . . put in the testimony at this time what you would like to have that you have not gotten in the [President's] budget.

General WHITE. I think I said yesterday—

Mr. FLOOD. Will you do that?

General WHITE. Certainly.

Mr. BOYLE. Let him answer.

Mr. FLOOD. Put it in the record. Put in the record what you want as of 11 o'clock this morning.

(A classified statement was furnished for the use of the committee.)[70]

Similarly seeking to convince the military of the role of the Congress as the court of last resort, Senator Symington would study the individual reservations of the Joint Chiefs, compare them with the administration assertion of adequacy, and reassure them that there was no economic reason at all (contrary to the preachings of the President) why all their requests could not be granted by the legislative branch.[71]

In addition to asserting the appellate function of the Congress, legislators also sought in their investigations to bypass the written testament of the JCS as to the adequacy of the budget by various maneuvers. During the Johnson Subcommittee hearings of 1957, for example, Symington (who had sources of contact within the Air Force) could circumvent the service's civilian and military heads' agreement with administration policy by forcing them to admit that important elements within their commands—such as missile-man Schriever and bomber-man LeMay—did not at all concur with the wisdom of the budget.[72] At the same time, astute special committee counsel Edwin L. Weisl would employ a different technique; finding himself incapable of eliciting a favorable response as to the blatant inadequacy of the budget from Secretary Douglas, he succeeded in getting the same result by couching his inquiry in terms of "satisfaction" with rather than the "adequacy" of the budget.[73] Several months later, before his Senate Appropriations Subcommittee, Senator Chavez directed both the Chairman of the JCS and the Secretary of the Army to give their answers "based solely on military assumptions"—that is, notwithstanding the generalist premises of their superiors.[74] And in much the same manner, Senator Robertson of Virginia tried to get around the standard and cautious military replies on the adequacy of defense expenditures by asking General White for his "personal opinion"—one which, hopefully, would transcend his professional responsibilities to the President as a member of the JCS.[75] And, finally, how could anyone answer in the negative a question—a purposefully suggestive question—like that asked by Symington of Taylor in 1959:

> If we have the right as a government to draft these boys off the farms and out of the cities to come into the Army and be in

uniform when they do not want to leave their homes and jobs, don't you think we have the duty to give them the best possible equipment so that they have the best chance to come back home?[76]

It is apparent then that given the agreements already worked out in the executive budgetary process between the armed services and the administration, the mere involvement of the Congress in scrutinizing the defense budget serves to stimulate military activity in the political process. In fact, even the act by a professional soldier of loyally expressing acceptance of the decisions of his civilian superiors may unintentionally imply a certain degree of dissatisfaction with those decisions. For example, certain listeners drew those very conclusions upon hearing General Lemnitzer agree that,

> when a decision is made, the decision phase ends, as it has to, indeed, in every military organization.
> And when that decision is made, we are good soldiers and we carry out the decision. It is no different with a division in the field against the enemy. Where you are given a mission, you ask for certain things to assist you in carrying out that mission, but just because you don't get everything you ask for you don't leave the field. You do the best you can with what you have.[77]

And if a military man sincerely believes that he simply can no longer attest—in any form whatsoever—to the adequacy of a budget which he deems dangerously inadequate, he should then naturally resign. But it is the nature of the American budgetary process to pose a military parochial with an insuperable dilemma. For, as General Gavin put it when he announced his retirement in early 1958, constitutionally the soldier must acknowledge two superiors—that is, while he owes the executive the loyalty of carrying out its directives, he must also honestly inform the Congress of his views. The two may conflict irreconcilably and leave him no choice other than perjury or insubordination—or, as Gavin saw it, "if neither of these are acceptable to you turn in your suit."[78] And, to be sure, such an action itself may be an extreme form of political behavior.

## VII

The instrumentalities at the disposal of the politicized innovators to influence the course of the strategic controversy of the late fifties were varied and numerous, but we will briefly examine the most important: (1) Congressional testimony; (2) the information "leak"; (3) addresses and interviews; (4) publications; (5) retirement.

Though we have dealt at length with the testimony of the period's military spokesmen before the several legislative committees concerned with defense policy, we heretofore approached the matter from a different angle—namely, the politicizing effects of the budgetary process. However, at this point we are concerned less with the way in which the political process tends by its very nature to draw often reluctant members of the military elite into the debate than with the role of the Congressional hearing as a forum for those who (for whatever reasons) have become active participants in controversy. The two who probably most effectively employed the committee investigation (in conjunction with the other means of influence—particularly resignation) were Gavin and Taylor. Leaving his post as the Army's chief of research and development due to frustration with the policies of the Eisenhower administration and with the firm belief that he could be a more effective advocate of the Army's cause from outside the military establishment than from within, Gavin announced his retirement in early January, 1958, a time which coincided with the extensive investigations being conducted by the Armed Services Committees of both houses. Outraged by the news, Lyndon Johnson ordered an immediate inquiry into the General's decision vowing: "This committee and its chairman are not going to tolerate any Administration rubber-hose tactics or any effort to put committee witnesses in a strait-jacket."[79] Having announced his decision at a rather propitious moment, Gavin proceeded to attack the state of America's defenses from two sides. Firstly, he charged the President with having allowed the armed services (and especially the conventional forces) to deteriorate, arguing that the Army would have to be virtually doubled in size and provided with a much greater mobile capacity. Secondly, he warned that the Soviet Union was on the threshold of a significant ICBM capacity and had outpaced the United States in the control of space meaning that this country was "entering an extremely critical period" in its history. Having placed all its eggs in one basket (and not even enough there), the administration had permitted the Soviets to acquire missile superiority and, while they might not launch a surprise attack with nuclear weapons, the Communists could be expected by means of limited war, subversion, and the blackmail of "sputnik diplomacy" to threaten the peripheries of the free world. All in all, Gavin presented a frightening prophecy of the state of things to come: "it seems clear starting a year or two from now that we are going to live and conduct our international negotiations under a canopy of fear."[80]

Similarly having resigned his post during the immediate post-Sputnik period, Taylor would return, unencumbered by allegiance to the Commander in Chief, "to express my personal views as a civilian on our military posture." Echoing the charges of his colleague, the former Army Chief of Staff levelled a vehement attack against the entire policy of the New Look which he alleged was dominated by budgetary considerations and not by security factors at all and which had forced the Joint Chiefs to "abdicate their authority" and thus left "someone less qualified perhaps to make the decision." The major reliance placed upon weapons of mass destruction, he warned, "has lost all justification in view of Soviet progress in atomic weapons and long-range missiles," the limited size of the American missile force, and the dwindling asset of our manned bomber. In addition to the marked decline in U. S. capability to deter deliberate general nuclear war, moreover, this decline had been accompanied by "a continued neglect of the requirements of limited or non-atomic war despite the increasing probability of this form of challenge with the growth of Communist strength and self-confidence." Rather than matching our military capabilities to our worldwide commitments, Taylor suggested, "we tailor our forces to the means, largely the budgetary means available." Calling for a policy of "flexible response" to replace the Dulles doctrine of "massive retaliation," he reminded the committee that it would cost an additional appropriation of three billion dollars a year for the next five years just for the Army alone to be modernized and expanded to wage limited war; add to this the expenditures necessary to build "a small, mobile and secure missile force," and the total defense budget would have to be raised to perhaps 55 billion dollars annually for the next half decade.[81]

Another widely used but less direct means of influencing the policy-making process—and one which lends itself to manipulation by the dissenter who remains within the administration—is the "leak." A weapon employed throughout officialdom in interagency or interpersonal power struggles, the leak provides a source of intelligence to the Congress—information on policy differences among executive agencies that are often blurred over or ignored in formal testimony or submissions from the White House.[82] Particularly plagued by leaks from within the Defense Department, President Eisenhower had at times become so irritated that he had taken his Defense Secretaries severely to task.[83] But to stop a leak at its source—which, of course, are those interests adversely affected by the decision—was found to be difficult if not impossible. And understandably so, for those who are committed to a course of action which they believe to be vital to the well-being of the country (and what parochial official honestly believes that his agency's programs are *not* in the national interest?) will employ all legitimate avenues in search of allies. Thus, when General Ridgway decided to retire as Army Chief of Staff in 1955 after having submitted as an unclassified document his final report to Secretary Wilson—a paper highly critical of the doctrine of massive retaliation—and when the latter requested that it be classified in order to suppress its contents, the report not very surprisingly came into the possession of the *New York Times*.[84] And when his successor's appeal for three billion dollars to deploy the Nike-Zeus anti-ballistic missile system was turned down by the President in 1957, Taylor subsequently divulged the top secret proposal to strategic members of the press corps, thereby hoping to expand the arena of decision-making and compel the administration to reconsider.[85] Nor was the Army the only service to indulge in such machinations; indeed, during the controversy over the alleged missile gap during the late fifties, the military services consistently informed friendly newspapermen and Congressmen of their particular intelligence estimates as to the nature of the Soviet threat. And as one would expect the Air Force consistently found "evidence" of Soviet missiles which the Army and Navy had missed. (In 1961, for example, Air Force intelligence leaked its estimates to the press which claimed the existence of three hundred deployed missiles in Soviet Russia, while Naval intelligence could confirm but ten.) Moreover, much of the debate led in the Senate by Stuart Symington was based upon the inflated Air Force figures, while the administration based its case on the much lower estimates of the Central Intelligence Agency.[86]

A third means of publicizing one's dissenting view is the use of speaking engagements which, while superficially directed toward a limited audience, are utilized as forums for the broadest dissemination possible. Of all the numerous addresses by the military (many of which have been cited previously) the one which stands out for its decisive importance is General Power's speech of 19 January 1960. On that occasion he announced that America's retaliatory force could be dealt a crippling blow by a surprise Soviet missile attack. Such an alarming and forthright assessment by the commander of SAC was bound to have momentous repercussions, especially in an election year when the Democrats (who, of course, also controlled the national legislature) had made defense a dominant campaign issue. Indeed, coming at the beginning of the new session of the Congress, Power's charges set the tone for the important Johnson Subcommittee hearings of February and March and forced virtually all the administration's witnesses to deal with the problem as he had defined it.[87] Of similar intent was the interview which Gavin had granted to the *New York Times'* Hanson Baldwin two years before.[88] Coming as it did on the heels of the General's announced retirement and testimony before the Senate, it served as an added reminder to the Congressional investigators of the Army's frustrations.

The publication by retired dissenters of books critical of the Eisenhower administration also flourished during the period under consideration, especially those by the partisans of the Army.[89] Moreover, the works were often timed for release so as to have the greatest impact possible on the political arena; Taylor's book, for example, was at his request to be published in time for the reconvening of the Congress at the beginning of the Presidential election year.[90] The arguments presented should be familiar to the reader by now, but perhaps a brief summary of the two most important works would be helpful given the role of the doctrines in the 1960 election campaign rhetoric. For the most part, Gavin reiterated and refined the many points he had made before the Johnson Subcommittee earlier that year. Most importantly, Gavin emphasized "that the broad spectrum of their [the Soviets'] capabilities, as well as their specific strength in many areas, puts them in a position of clear advantage. As a consequence, they now have the initiative and they continue to outmaneuver us, diplomatically and strategically." Specifically, he identified what he referred to as the "missile lag"; that is, "a period, and one we are now entering, in which our own offensive and defensive missile capabilities will so lag behind those of the Soviets as to place us in a position of great peril." The critical period of the lag would coincide with the administration of the next President, years which would require a new leadership capable of guiding the United States through dark days when it would be at a significant disadvantage in both general and limited war capabilities. Ridiculing the "sugar-coated reassurances" of the Eisenhower people, he maintained that during the years of the lag the Russians would so increase their ICBM striking ability that American retaliation in kind would become "rather meaningless." Furthermore, Gavin urged that the closing of the strategic gap was a prerequisite to the development of the conventional capabilities necessary to prevent the erosion of the non-Communist world:

A much discussed topic today is limited war. Much of it, I fear, is wishful thinking. For a limited war concept is only valid within an impressive overall capability to wage general war. No opponent will ever accommodate us to the extent of allowing us to fight a limited war merely because that is what we want to fight. . . . Actually, a nation dare not risk a limited undertaking without possessing the obvious capability of fighting a general war. And to the extent that we have the latter capability we may indulge ourselves in the former.

All factors of national power considered, Gavin concluded with the ominous warning that "we are in second place militarily and in second place in the exploration of space. . . . If the present patterns continue the only peace that we will find will be that peace of Carthage."[91]

The following year, Taylor published his biting attack upon the doctrine of massive retaliation—a policy which, in his view, "could offer our leaders only two choices, the initiation of general war or compromise and defeat." Adapting Gavin's argument, he asserted that the United States was "probably inferior to the USSR in numbers of ballistic missiles," and thus, if the threat of massive retaliation had ever been credible as a response to conventional aggression, it was obviously no longer so. Attacking the administration for its progressive diminution of the Army's share of the defense budget, he called for the recognition of "the need for the capability to react across the entire spectrum of possible challenge, for coping with anything from general atomic war to infiltration, aggression such as threatened Laos and Berlin in 1959." A new strategy of "flexible response," Taylor assured, would deal with our "piecemeal attrition" under the long haul policy. Thus, though the link between the missile gap and inability to wage limited wars is to be found in Gavin as well, the former is added by Taylor almost as an afterthought to justify the need for a conventional build-up. Moreover, he fuses the two concepts—inadequate preparation for both general and limited warfare—into a sort of missile-manpower gap. Referring to Gavin's missile lag, he notes:

the United States faces a period of several years in which we will be inferior to the USSR in general war and in conventional, counterattrition forces. It will be a period in which our leaders will be hard put to maintain our world position in face of the probably increased Soviet pressures. These adverse conditions will tend to loosen the bonds of our alliances and to increase the trend toward neutralism and compromise among the weak.[92]

The primary problem, then, as singled out by both Gavin and Taylor was twofold: the Soviets could be expected to gain strategic superiority (by means of their alleged ICBM advantage) and retain and exploit a tactical (i.e., conventional) superiority. Thus, the dwindling credibility of the American deterrent to both general and limited wars might conceivably invite a Soviet first-strike against the United States or, more likely, present this country with the prospect of *faits accomplis* along the peripheries of the free world by limited proxy or insurgency conflicts. It was here, along the rimland of Soviet-dominated Eurasia, that the United States must be prepared to employ conventional forces so as to deter or wage limited wars. What this would necessitate, naturally, was the adoption of a new defense doctrine more attuned to the changing circumstances of the 1960's—one which would reject the priorities of the Eisenhower years and substitute for its alleged complacency a new sense of urgency. Out of the apparently perennial internecine struggle within the military establishment, then, emerged a set of security policies which vigorously dissented from the orthodoxy of the administration and suggested an alternative course of action. The shock of the Soviet satellite launching of late 1957 had abruptly thrust the political system into a period of disorientation in regard to defense policy. And it was this disequilibrating stimulus which served as a catalyst for the convergence of the several deprofessionalizing influences (both internal and external to the military establishment) which had until then remained latent. Compelled to search for new secure functions in the missile age, the several services propagated defense doctrines which had the effect of rationalizing their respective parochial institutional interests. What was now missing was the broader debate among the nation's communication and political elite necessary to transform the dissenting opinions of the innovators into a viable and legitimate policy alternative. Conception was now a reality, and the gestation period was not long in following.

1. It will be recalled that at the World Disarmament Conference in 1932, Madariaga of Spain replied to the Soviet proposal for complete and total disarmament with a fable:

When the animals had gathered, the lion looked at the eagle and said gravely, 'we must abolish talons.' The tiger looked at the elephant and said, 'we must abolish tusks.' The elephant looked back at the tiger and said, 'we must abolish claws and jaws.'

Thus each animal in turn proposed the abolition of the weapons it did not have, until at last the bear rose up and said in tones of sweet reasonableness:

'Comrades, let us abolish everything—everything but the great universal embrace.'

2. U. S. House of Representatives, Committee on Appropriations, Subcommittee on Department of Defense Appropriations, *Department of Defense Appropriations for 1958*, part 1, 85th Congress, 1st Session (Washington, D.C.: Government Printing Office, 1957), pp. 3-4. (Hereafter cited as *House: DOD FY1958*.)

3. *Ibid.*, pp. 4-5.
4. *Ibid.*, p. 19.
5. U. S. Senate, Subcommittee of the Committee on Appropriations, *Department of Defense Appropriations for 1958*, 85th Congress, 1st Session (Washington, D. C.: Government Printing Office, 1957), p. 24. (Hereafter cited as *Senate: DOD FY1958*.)
6. *House: DOD FY1959*, p. 36.
7. *Ibid.*, pp. 47, 50, 52-53, 74.
8. *Senate: DOD FY1958*, introductory statement by committee chairman Dennis Chavez of New Mexico, p. 2.
9. *Ibid.*, pp. 3-9.
10. *Ibid.*, p. 9.
11. *Ibid.*, pp. 34-35, 43.
12. *Ibid.*, p. 25.
13. *House: DOD FY1958*, pp. 399 ff.
14. *Ibid.*, pp. 501 ff.
15. *Senate: DOD FY1958*, pp. 147-148.
16. *Ibid.*, p. 136.
17. *Ibid.*, pp. 141-144.
18. *House: DOD FY1958*, pp. 902 ff.
19. *Senate: DOD FY1958*, testimony of General Twining, pp. 328-329.
20. *House: DOD FY1958*, pp. 589 ff.
21. *Senate: DOD FY1958*, p. 262.
22. *Ibid.*, testimony of Admiral Burke, p. 237; *House: DOD FY1958*, testimony of Secretary Thomas, pp. 589-594.

23. Some one-half-dozen times, at critical junctures during his Preparedness Investigating Subcommittee hearings, Senator Johnson unmistakably
compared the Soviet Sputniks (and the resulting plight for America's defense) with the devastating attack upon Pearl Harbor by the Japanese Navy
in 1941. U. S. Senate, Preparedness Investigating Subcommittee of the Committee on Armed Services, *Inquiry into Satellite and Missile Programs*, 85th
Congress, 1st-2nd Sessions (Washington, D. C.: Government Printing Office, 1958), part 1 (pp. 2, 342, 1004), part 2 (pp. 1311 and 1975), part 3
(p. 2474). (Hereafter cited as *Senate: Inquiry*).
24. *Ibid.*, part 1, testimony of Dr. Edward Teller, pp. 4-20; testimony
of Dr. Vannevar Bush, pp. 57-68; testimony of James H. Doolittle, pp. 111 ff.
25. U. S. House of Representatives, Committee on Appropriations, Subcommittee on Department of Defense Appropriations, *The Ballistic Missile
Program*, 85th Congress, 1st Session (Washington, D. C.: Government Printing Office, 1958), pp. 5 ff.
26. *Senate: Inquiry*, part 1, testimony of Neil McElroy, pp. 194 ff.; testimony of Donald Quarles, pp. 261 ff.; testimony of William Holaday, pp. 345
ff.
27. *Ibid.*, testimony of Wilber Bruckner and Maxwell Taylor, pp. 462 ff.
28. U. S. House of Representatives, Committee on Armed Services, *Investigation of National Defense Missiles*, 85th Congress, 2nd Session (Washington, D. C.: Government Printing Office, 1958), testimony of Secretary
McElroy, p. 3976. (Hereafter cited as *House Armed Services: Missiles*.)
29. *Senate: Inquiry*, part 1, testimony of James Gavin, pp. 485 ff.; testimony of John B. Medaris, pp. 539 ff.; testimony of Wernher von Braun, pp.
479 ff.
30. *Ibid.*, testimony of James Douglas and Thomas White, pp. 837 ff.;
testimony of Bernard Schriever, pp. 1607 ff.
31. *Ibid.*, testimony of Curtis LeMay, pp. 900 ff. An even more extreme
version of the airpower doctrine was presented to the committee at a later
date (20 January 1958) by aeronautical consultant and author Major Alexander P. De Seversky who levelled an unqualified attack against the limited
war advocates. Calling for a quadrupling of the Strategic Air Command and
sole Air Force jurisdiction in space, Seversky maintained that the victor in
the next major war would be the nation which controlled air and space. To
fight in any conventional contest would play into the hands of the Soviets,
he warned: "Thus, in a limited warfare, they want us to fight an air war
without air superiority; a surface war with inferior manpower without a
chance of scoring a decision; to lose our supporting Navy without even attempting to neutralize the source of attack. The whole thing is preposterous."
(Pp. 1297 ff.)
32. Compare Admiral Burke's testimony of 14 December 1957 (*ibid.*,
pp. 644 ff.) with that of 20 January 1958 (pp. 1925 ff.). Also, for the different
emphases of those within the Navy concerned with different aspects of the
service's overall role, see: testimony of Rear Admiral Charles E. Weakley
(Director, Undersea Warfare Division), pp. 711 ff.; testimony of Rear Admiral Hyman G. Rickover (Assistant Chief of the Bureau for Nuclear Pro-
pulsion), p. 1382 ff. Placing these two presentations in juxaposition, one
gets an excellent indication of the parochial interests of the military technocrat

—Weakley defending the ASW program and Rickover the nuclear-powered Polaris submarine.

33. Senator Jackson, who was not a member of the Johnson Armed Services subcommittee, was notably inconspicuous during the post-Sputnik hearings. His only participation in the hearings occurred during the testimony of William M. Allen, President of the Boeing Airplane Company, where Jackson favorably interrogated the industrial executive so as to demonstrate that the corporation's Seattle plant could produce three times as many B-52 bombers a month as it currently was producing. *(Ibid.,* pp. 1256-1268.)

34. *House Armed Services: Missiles,* testimony of Secretary McElroy, pp. 3975-3890.

35. U. S. House of Representatives, Committee on Appropriations, Subcommittee on Department of Defense Appropriations, *Department of Defense Appropriations for 1959,* 85th Congress, 2nd Session (Washington, D. C.: Government Printing Office, 1958) testimony of Nathan F. Twining, pp. 31-32. (Hereafter cited as *House: DOD FY1959.*)

36. U. S. Senate, Subcommittee of the Committee of Appropriations, *Department of Defense Appropriations for 1959,* 85th Congress, 2nd Session (Washington, D. C.: Government Printing Office, 1958), testimony of Secretary McElroy, pp. 31-34. (Hereafter cited as *Senate: DOD FY1959.*)

37. *House Armed Services: Missiles,* testimony of William Bruckner, p. 4233.

38. *Senate: DOD FY1959,* testimony of William Bruckner, p. 46.

39. *Ibid.,* testimony of Maxwell Taylor, pp. 77-84, 106-108; also, *House: DOD FY1959,* pp. 254-257.

40. *House: DOD FY1959,* testimony of Arleigh Burke, pp. 442-444.

41. *Senate: DOD FY1959,* testimony of Arleigh Burke, p. 143.

42. *House: DOD FY1959,* testimony of Arleigh Burke, p. 444.

43. *Ibid.,* p. 129. (Emphasis added.)

44. U. S. Senate, Subcommittee of the Committee on Appropriations, *Department of Defense Appropriations for 1960,* 86th Congress, 1st Session (Washington, D. C.: Government Printing Office, 1959), testimony of Thomas White, pp. 253 ff. (Hereafter cited as *Senate: DOD FY1959.*) While the Eisenhower administration planned no more than 9 Atlas ICBM squadrons for FY1960, the Air Force sought 16 or 17 squadrons.

45. *Ibid.*

46. See, for example, Nathan F. Twining, *Neither Liberty Nor Safety: A Hard Look at U. S. Military Policy and Strategy* (New York: Holt, Rinehart and Winston, 1966), pp. 110-111.

47. See, for example: U. S. House of Representatives, Subcommittee on Department of Defense Appropriations of the Committee on Appropriations, *Department of Defense Appropriations for 1960,* 86th Congress, 1st Session, part 2 (Washington, D. C.: Government Printing Office, 1959), testimony of Thomas Power, pp. 380 ff. (Hereafter cited as *House: DOD FY1960.*)

48. In a book first written in 1959 but subsequently banned by the Defense Department, SAC commander Power forcefully attacked the "fallacy" of finite deterrence and urged that the United States "maintain a credible capability to achieve a military victory under any set of conditions and circumstances." Power then went on to define the winner in a nuclear war as

the side which "manages to retain sufficient strength after the nuclear exchange to terminate hostilities on its terms and force the surrender of the other side." (The General did not consider whether such a traditional military evaluation of victory was any longer meaningful in the age of nuclear weapons.) See his *Design for Survival* (New York: Coward-McCann, 1965), chapter 7.

49.   The apt phrase "party whip" was employed by retired Army Chief of Staff Maxwell Taylor in his attack upon the Eisenhower defense program; however, when he became John Kennedy's Chairman he performed the same function—only on behalf of his doctrine of "flexible response" rather than the Dulles policy of "massive retaliation" and the long pull. See Maxwell Taylor, *The Uncertain Trumpet* (New York: Harper & Brothers, 1959), pp. 37-38.

50.   Power's speech in New York on 19 January (followed within a week by a similar one in Washington) was reported in the press alongside Defense Secretary Gates' declaration that, "There is no deterrent gap." See the *New York Times*, 20 January 1960, p. 1.

51.   U. S. Senate, Preparedness Investigating Subcommittee of the Committee on Armed Services, in conjunction with the Committee on Aeronautical and Space Sciences, *Missiles, Space and Other Major Defense Matters*, 86th Congress, 2nd Session (Washington, D.C.: Government Printing Office, 1960), testimony of Thomas Power, pp. 18-19 (emphasis added). (Hereafter cited as *Senate: Joint Hearings 1960*.)

52.   *Ibid.*, testimony of Thomas White, pp. 125-126 (emphasis added).

53.   U. S. House of Representatives, Subcommittee on Department of Defense Appropriations of the Committee on Appropriations, *Department of Defense Appropriations for 1961*, part 2, 86th Congress, 2nd Session (Washington, D. C.: Government Printing Office, 1960), testimony of Arleigh Burke, p. 103. (Hereafter cited as *House: DOD FY1961*.)

54.   Maxwell Taylor, *Swords and Ploughshares* (New York: W. W. Norton & Company, 1972), p. 167.

55.   *Senate: DOD FY1960*, testimony of Wilber Bruckner, p. 100.

56.   *House: DOD FY1960*, part 1, testimony of Thomas White, pp. 825-826.

57.   *House Armed Services: Missiles*, testimony of Thomas Gates, pp. 4490 ff.

58.   *Senate: DOD FY1959*, testimony of Thomas Gates, pp. 113 ff.; also *Senate: DOD FY1960*, pp. 153 ff.

59.   See, for example, his first appearance as Secretary of Defense before the Congress, *House: DOD FY1961*, pp. 2 ff. also *Senate: Joint Hearings 1960*, pp. 437 ff.

60.   For Twining's explanation of his role in the "bomber gap" controversy, see his testimony, *House: DOD FY1958*, part 1, pp. 911-913.

61.   *Senate: Inquiry*, part 3, testimony of Nathan Twining, pp. 1824 ff.

62.   *Senate: Joint Hearings 1960*, p. 278.

63.   "News Conference, 19 January 1956," *Public Papers: DDE*, vol. IV, pp. 168-169.

64.   "News Conference, 23 May 1956," *ibid.*, p. 514.

65.   For the President's rejoinder to Gavin's "missile gap" charges, see

"News Conference, 20 August 1958," *ibid.*, vol. VI, p. 649; for Eisenhower's response to the Pearson-Anderson allegation that he had slowed down ICBM development thus setting the U. S. back ten years, see "News Conference, 22 July 1959," *ibid.*, vol. VII, p. 542; and, finally, for defense against Medaris' indictment of the Eisenhower space program, see "News Conference, 22 October 1959," *ibid.*, pp. 733-734.

66. "News Conference, 3 February 1960," *ibid.*, vol. VIII p. 145.

67. U. S. Senate, Preparedness Investigating Subcommittee of the Committee on Armed Services and the Committee on Aeronautical and Space Sciences, *Missile and Space Activities*, 86th Congress, 1st Session (Washington, D. C.: Government Printing Office, 1959), testimony of Neil McElroy, p. 5. (Hereafter cited as *Senate: Joint Hearings 1959.*) Also, *Senate: DOD FY1960*, pp. 4-16.

68. *Senate: Joint Hearings 1959*, testimony of Arleigh Burke, pp. 57 ff.; testimony of Thomas White, pp. 68 ff.; testimony of Maxwell Taylor, pp. 97 ff.

69. *House: DOD FY1959*, p. 266; *House: DOD FY1960*, p. 578.

70. *House: DOD FY1959*, pp. 181-184.

71. See: U. S. Senate, Committee on Appropriations, *Supplemental Defense Appropriations Bill, 1958*, 85th Congress, 2nd Session (Washington, D. C.: Government Printing Office, 1958), pp. 26-36, 103; *Senate: Inquiry*, part 2, pp. 2015 ff.

72. *Senate: Inquiry*, part 1, pp. 71-73.

73. *Ibid.*, p. 844.

74. *Senate: DOD FY1959*, pp. 40, 52-53. Interestingly, while Chavez failed to get an attack on administration policy from General Twining, Secretary Bruckner was very accomodating, declaring:

we have seen nothing in the intervening time [since the Army's original requests of DOD] . . . to change the logic or the basis of our decision.

On the contrary, we see many things that support the decision we made at the time, and while I am not here in any sense, as you appreciate, to carry a flag or to solicit or start a crusade against what the Secretary of Defense has decided, in answering your question I can say that the recommendation that we made at that time is correct. I have seen many, many things that corroborate our judgment that the recommendation was correct—and based upon a solid premise from a military standpoint.

75. *Ibid.*, p. 402. It should be noted in passing that the Air Force Chief of Staff indicated that there was no divergence whatsoever between his "personal" and "professional" judgments—and that, therefore, the President's budget was adequate.

76. *Senate: Joint Hearings 1959*, p. 104.

77. *House Armed Services: Missiles*, p. 4252.

78. *Ibid.*, pp. 4350-4355.

79. *The New York Times*, 6 January 1958, p. 1.

80. *Senate: Inquiry*, part 2, testimony of James Gavin, pp. 1445 ff.; *House Armed Services: Missiles*, pp. 4333 ff.

81. *Senate: Joint Hearings 1960*, testimony of Maxwell Taylor, pp. 186 ff.

82. Charles R. Dechert, "Availability of Information for Congressional Operations," in Alfred de Grazia, ed., *Congress, the First Branch of Government: Twelve Studies in the Organization of Congress* (Garden City: Doubleday & Company, 1967), p. 170; also, Douglas Cater, *The Fourth Branch of Government* (New York: Random House, 1965), pp. 128-141; U. S. House of Representatives, Committee on Government Operations, *Government News from Anonymous Sources*, 88th Congress, 2nd Session, (Washington, D. C.: Government Printing Office, 1964), pp. 17-171.

83. Robert J. Donovan, *Eisenhower: The Inside Story* (New York: Harper Brothers, 1956), pp. 10-11.

84. Matthew B. Ridgway, *Soldier: The Memoirs of Matthew B. Ridgway* (New York: Harper & Row, 1956), chapter 38.

85. Jack Raymond, "The Growing Threats of Our Military-Industrial Complex," *Harvard Business Review*, vol. XLXI (May-June, 1968), p. 61. Though he does not state so, Raymond (*New York Times* Pentagon correspondent) may quite conceivably have been the journalist informed of Taylor's proposal.

86. Roger Hilsman, *To Move a Nation: The Politics of Foreign Policy in the Administration of John F. Kennedy* (Garden City: Doubleday & Company, 1967), pp. 162-163; Stewart Alsop, *The Center: People and Power in Political Washington* (New York: Harper & Row, 1968), pp. 219-220; Stuart Symington, "Where the Missile Gap Went," *The Reporter*, 15 February 1962, p. 26; Edgar M. Bottome, *The Balance of Terror: A Guide to the Arms Race* (Boston: Beacon Press, 1971), chapter 3.

87. The joint hearings of the Johnson Preparedness Investigating Subcommittee and his Aeronautical and Space Sciences Committee began with Power's speech being placed in evidence and the General himself called to testify. Subsequently, Defense Secretary Gates, JCS Chairman Twining, and all the service chiefs found themselves obliged to comment on Power's calculations. See *Senate: Joint Hearings 1960*, especially Power's testimony, pp. 3-54, 81-113.

88. *The New York Times*, 12 January 1958, pp. 1, 14. Less than a week later, Gavin delivered a follow-up address wherein he continued to press his case before the public (16 January 1958, p. 13).

89. The principal works by the leading Army spokesmen, all of whom retired from office during the Eisenhower administration, were: Ridgway, *op. cit.*; James M. Gavin, *War and Peace in the Space Age* (New York: Harper & Brothers, 1958); Taylor, *The Uncertain Trumpet*; John B. Medaris, *Countdown for Decision* (New York: G. P. Putnam's Sons, 1960).

90. *The New York Times*, 7 November 1959, pp. 1, 10.

91. Gavin, *op. cit.*, pp. 3-4, 6-7, 12, 288.

92. Taylor, *The Uncertain Trumpet*, pp. 5-7, 78, 139.

# 5

## THE POPULARIZERS I: THE PRESS

### I

THE PRESS DURING THIS PERIOD EXERTED SIGNIFI-
cant influence over the course of events. As Bernard C. Cohen
has noted in regard to the media's influence: "the press is significantly more than a purveyor of information and opinion. It may
not be successful much of the time in telling people what to think,
but it is stunningly successful in telling people what to think
*about.*"[1] By defining what is "news"—that is, what the important
issues of the day are—the fourth estate is often decisive in re-
shaping the priorities of government itself. In the nation's capital
one finds "a separate and quasi-official branch of government"[2]
—the Washington press corps, a group comparable in size to the
national legislature—which successfully monopolizes the coverage and reporting of events in political Washington. (Behind,
or under, this small elite stand approximately sixty thousand people across the country who write and edit the observations and
interpretations of this prestigious group for dissemination to the
general public through the press, radio, and television.[3])

Moreover, there is the tendency among the Washington press
to, in the words of columnist Steward Alsop, "travel in a pack";
that is, "when one political journalist writes something which is
—or which seems to be—new or important, the rest of the press

corps immediately begins to follow the same story." This "herd instinct" is partially explained (or, in any case, reinforced) by the peculiar professional society in which the press corps functions (rather incestuously), the outward manifestations of which are such venerable institutions as the National Press Club, the Grid-iron Club, and the various luncheon clubs. In constant intellectual and social contact, the country's leading journalists are provided with the means for exchanging information and discerning the latest news "fashions" in the profession.[4] In addition to the closed nature of Washington press circles, the standardization of news in the United States—a country without a national newspaper—is also brought about by the influence of certain papers normally designated the "elitest" or "prestige" press. The *New York Times*, for example, as (in Joseph Kraft's words) "a basic source of news to editors, writers, politicians, statesmen and professional men all over the country," does much to account for this phenomenon.[5] Newspaper editors and reporters throughout the country are heavily reliant upon the prestige press for the definition of "news" and the interpretation of contemporary problems. Also, the specialization which has occurred in the journalistic profession in recent years has brought individual expertise to the foreground of influence. Correspondents anywhere contemplating a story in a particular field are apt to look for insights to the reports and analyses of the given area's respected dean—for example, Bernard Nossiter of the Washington *Post* in economics, James Reston of the *New York Times* in foreign affairs, John Finney (also of the *Times*) in science. In fact, as one observer notes, "all *Times*men are influential" inasmuch as all correspondents are highly dependent upon a handful of papers, of which the *Times* is by far the most important.[6] In short, then, those national issues deemed significant or newsworthy by the communications elite are those which will probably be debated by the influential in and out of government and, by framing the alternatives available to decision-makers, the press in effect is able to set the parameters governing legitimate outcomes of the policy process.[7]

Yet the power which the press wields in American society is still of a special and limited nature, for the gentlemen of the press operate on the periphery of power. They have influence, but as Alexander Hamilton pointed out, 'Influence is not power.' Real power means the power to make the great decisions, and although Washington's press corps may praise or criticize or explain or even sometimes obliquely affect those decisions, the press does not make them.[8]

Aside from the press' rather dubious influence on the masses (the average adult reads but one-half column daily on foreign affairs[9]), its sway with America's foreign and defense establishment elite (those whom Gabriel Almond referred to as the official policy leadership, policy and opinion elites, and the attentive public[10]) is much more relevant for our purposes. In addition to the underlings in the media themselves, government officials and the intellectual community are influenced by the prestige press and its leading commentators. The *Times*, for example, is "read by virtually everyone in the government who has an interest or responsibility in foreign affairs." The Congress, especially, is highly dependent upon the press for information and interpretation, for while the State Department and other executive agencies may turn to the press for basic factual data about international politics (the news tickers often beat official cables with pertinent information by several hours, or even a day), Senators and Representatives are even more dependent on the media, lacking alternative sources or expertise of their own. Given the fact that even highly placed Congressmen in specialized committees find access to sensitive information from the executive branch like a "trickle—intermittent, specialized, partial," the press has come to perform a critical role for the legislature, serving as the hub of the Congressional intelligence system and the chief provider of information. It is the major columnists who provide the ideas, insights, and policy analyses for the bulk of the members of the legislative branch and their staff assistants. (And as is to be expected, many a Congressman's speech has had its origins in a nationally syndicated column.) Furthermore, members of both Houses tend to look to the editorials of the *Times* and *Post* as indices of elite public opinion, having little notion of the true feelings of their constituents on complex policy alternatives.[11] Therefore, as James Reston has noted,

> What influence the press has on the conduct of foreign policy usually comes indirectly, not through the mass of the people but mainly through the Congress of the United States. The relationship between well informed reporters in Washington and influential Congressmen are quite different from the relations between reporters and officials of the executive branch of government.[12]

The direct influence of the mass media on the Chief Executive is negligible when compared with its role vis-a-vis the Congress. Indeed, the press' influence on mass public opinion is probably even less than that of the President. Whenever the people in this country are confronted with a controversy and the "torrents of confusing and often contradictory information" which it normally entails, the "tendency is to assume the government is right."[13] As was the case when the prestigious and popular Dwight Eisenhower held the reins of government, the "public listens to the Administration, not the critics, and the reassurances of the Administration induce mass acquiescence in its policies."[14] In such confrontations with a critical press and Congress as occurred over defense policies in the wake of the Sputnik launching, the President retains the upper hand with the public-at-large, for the issues tend to be so removed and so complex and the facts so obscure that the people are quite willing to delegate to the President more discretion than, perhaps, is normally the case with purely domestic programs.[15] Yet one must be careful not to gainsay entirely the significance of the relationship between the press and the executive branch, for in a presidential system of government, where the questioning of officials by the legislative branch is not institutionalized, the Presidential news conference largely (if inadequately) serves the same function as the "question period" in a parliamentary system. It was during the weekly or bi-weekly

149

encounters between President Eisenhower and his critics in the press corps that the latter could compel the embattled Commander in Chief to respond publicly to the charges of his critics in the Congress, the military, or the media themselves and deal with the very issues which Eisenhower would have preferred to ignore rather than to dramatize.

## II

If it is indeed true that there is a discernible and meaningful pattern of standardization of news reporting and analysis in the United States, and that this definition of relevant issues has an impact on the Congress (as well as other significant publics) and is generated largely by the prestige press, then it would follow that we should carefully examine the coverage and editorial themes (as well as the outstanding columns) of the nation's pace-setting paper—the *New York Times*. To be sure, a truly exhaustive study of news coverage would require a careful examination of other lesser elite papers as well (such as the Washington *Post* and *Star*); moreover, an ideal study would reflect a thorough content analysis of all elite papers for the entire span of some five years which constitutes the time frame of the present case study. But inasmuch as we are concerned with the influence of the media as but one aspect of our multifaceted approach, we shall content ourselves with a selective examination of the coverage allotted the defense controversy during the four or five months following the Sputnik launching of 4 October 1957 in the *Times*; the relevant editorial positions of the paper will be more extensively considered and will take us up to the endorsement of the candidacy of John F. Kennedy in late October, 1960; finally, we will trace the arguments of leading commentators as well.

As was suggested previously (chapter two), the immediate aftermath of the Soviet satellite launching might generally serve as an adequate microcosm of the debate which would culminate in the Presidential election campaign three years later. Yet because this brief period affords the observer such an excellent microcosmic view of the contending forces and arguments of the years to follow, one cannot simply project the extensive news coverage of defense issues during this period to the years 1957 to 1961 as a whole. It is quite probable that no news story from the end of the Korean war to the intensification of the Southeast Asian conflict so preoccupied the nation's political and communications elite for so long a stretch of time (Presidential election campaigns notwithstanding). Indeed, even a superficial scanning of the *Times'* headlines from October, 1957, to February of the following year would leave one with the impression that the United States for a brief time in its 171-year history lived in a world which consisted only of rockets and satellites. So while a word of caution is in order in regard to the typicalness of news coverage during the post-Sputnik period, the intensity of the initial preoccupation should serve nonetheless as an indication of the magnitude of the shock and help us understand the unique durability of the issues involved.

From the initial banner headline reporting of the event on 5 October and its displacement of the racial tensions in Little Rock, Arkansas, as the major news story, Sputnik and related issues (e.g., space, defense missiles, Khrushchev's rocket-rattling in the Middle East) thoroughly dominated the *New York Times* until, by late February of 1958, the nation's deepening recession took precedence. Indeed, not until 15 October was defense not carried as the main feature (this was to be a temporary aberration) and not until the thirtieth did it actually fall from page one (also a brief interlude). Though a subsidence of the initial shock is evident by the closing days of October, November was to begin with another banner headline announcing the launching of Sputnik II —a much heavier vehicle carrying a canine cosmonaut—and the month was to continue at a furious pace as momentous events followed quickly on the heels of one another: the Soviet leader's ominous fulminations, Eisenhower's reassurance addresses, the disturbing revelation of the secret Gaither Committee report, the beginning of Congressional investigations, and finally, the President's stroke. Nor was December to be anticlimactic what with the hearings of the Johnson Preparedness Subcommittee intensifying, the ignominious and spectacular failure of America's hastily-as-

151

sembled Vanguard launching (which was to have placed in earth orbit a poor orange-sized counterpart to the massive Sputniks), and the picture of an aging President, still recovering from his stroke, scurrying off to Paris to reassure America's NATO allies. (Things seemed to be going from bad to worse and even the long-apathetic American people were beginning to express anxious concern about the future.[16]) There was, in effect, but one issue presented by the prestige press in late 1957-early 1958: the waning defense posture of the United States. Not only was it the top priority—it was the only priority.[17]

The *New York Times'* editorial policy during this period was entirely consistent with the extensive news coverage allotted the defense issue. Before examining the themes presented in its editorials, however, we should perhaps first add a further word on the influence that the *Times* could be expected to have had on an emerging actor in the debate who would eventually fulfill the crucial role of midwife to the newly articulated alternative defense doctrines. For if most Congressmen and bureaucrats closely followed the events of the day as reported and interpreted by the *Times*, Eisenhower's future successor, John Kennedy of Massachusetts, normally paid very careful attention to both its news reports and editorial views. As former special counsel to the late President, Theodore C. Sorensen informs us about Kennedy:

He thought the *Times* one of the most influential newspapers in the nation, less guilty of bias and sensationalism in its news stories than any other publication. He had read it regularly since his days in Choate, which may be one reason why he would be worried more over its editorials than those of a dozen more widely distributed newspapers combined.[18]

The first thing one should bear in mind when reconsidering the editorial stance of the *Times* during the post-Sputnik period is that the paper which is now normally associated with a vigorous and consistent endorsement of an American foreign policy geared to detente and restraint—a paper which has become a forum for criticism of the burgeoning military establishment and its expanded role in the 1960's—was in the 1950's an accurate reflection of the cold war psychology which gripped the nation as a whole and a leader in the liberal community's battle with the Eisenhower administration for higher defense expenditures. Indeed, the *New York Times* was a proud and enthusiastic "cold warrior" only a few years before it became unfashionable to be one. During the fall and winter of 1957-1958, the *Times* constantly warned of the dangers facing the United States in a world witnessing the sudden and ominous growth of Soviet military power and technology; it was taken as axiomatic that the Soviet Union was a ruthless and demonic power not at all interested in arms limitation or accommodation with the West, but rather bent on dividing the forces of freedom in the world in order to attain universal dominion. America was confronted with the specter of "barbarism armed with Sputniks," intent on fomenting instability in the international system and, through the instigation of crises and the rattling of its rockets, seeking to divide the guardians of the free world so as to "take over all of it." Thus, the *Times* would sanction all necessary and expedient means to protect the threatened security of the United States, including the maintenance of firm links with such distasteful allies as Franco's Spain.[19]

Espousing such a widely accepted world view, the *Times'* editorial policy in the wake of the Russian propaganda coup is, therefore, easily comprehended. Four interrelated themes dominated its editorials, all of which lent aid and comfort to the growing ranks of those opposed to the Eisenhower policy of the long pull and afforded a rallying point for a new orientation in military doctrines around which defense critics of every hue could coalesce: (1) the indisputable evidence of Soviet missile power, coupled with the greatly enhanced stature of Communism brought about by the scientific breakthrough, signalled a new era of aggressiveness on the part of the Kremlin which now could be expected by means of Sputnik diplomacy to seek the intimidation of both America's allies and neutrals and thus expand its influence at the expense of the United States; (2) the administration of Dwight Eisenhower was dangerously complacent and was needlessly sacrificing the security of the country to outmoded notions of economy in government, and what was now in order were massive new expenditures for arms and weapons technology; (3) the President's critics—especially those in the Democratic party —were advancing sound alternatives which were more in harmony with the security interests of the West than the myopic policies currently pursued; (4) it was time that the United States rejected any notion of mere parity with the Soviets and adopted a plan to attain (and maintain) clear-cut American superiority all across the board in military power, the contest for scientific and technological supremacy, and the race for the conquest of space.

The *Times* immediately assessed the significance of Sputnik as predominantly political rather than scientific and was quick to point out that "[t]he rocket motors which sent it into the upper atmosphere . . . can be incorporated into intercontinental ballistic missiles delivering hydrogen bombs upon defenseless millions." The intent of the Soviet leader in launching the satellite was made unmistakably clear by the simultaneous interviews that Khrushchev had granted to both James Reston of the *Times* and a group of British M. P.'s in which he declared that bombers were now obsolete ("You might as well throw them in the fire.") and that the Soviet Union—armed with its arsenal of rockets—was now in a position of strength to deal with the United States. Furthermore, the *Times* pointed to the Russian premier's thinly veiled threats of missile attack on Turkey during the current Middle Eastern crisis as proof that the Soviets had now taken the offensive and would not rest until they had completely isolated the United States from its major allies.[20]

The *Times* immediately took President Eisenhower severely to task for allegedly "putting domestic budgetary and political considerations ahead of security," and called for a "maximum effort" in the field of space and military rocketry which would utilize "all the rich resources of our science, technology, and industry." The Soviet Sputnik, its editorials warned, "raises questions of the gravest character regarding the correctness of our present and past national policies," and, indeed, presages a "radical change in the military balance of power." The administration, while creating the illusion of movement, simply refused to make the necessary reassessment of past policy and, in failing to do so, subjected

154

the country to grave peril: "Survival in a rapidly changing world requires that nations, as well as individuals, adapt quickly to changes. Those who cannot, or will not, adapt in good times are destroyed or defeated." A "feeling of emergency grips the people of the free world," suggested the *Times*, and "our people will not hesitate to make whatever sacrifices are needed." What was urgently needed now was leadership from the White House—leadership which would bravely acknowledge that the United States was indeed in a "race for survival," not an outer space basketball game (as administration spokesmen had cavalierly suggested), and which would realize that what was needed was a new Manhattan project. The American people were ready for the challenge, but unfortunately their President was not. With the shock caused by the second Sputnik launching in a month, the paper's editorial writers charged Eisenhower with being "seriously remiss" in not educating the public as to the need of spending more money on defense, "even if it's 'only' a billion or two more" a year. In successive reviews, it was charged that the country was two or three years behind the Soviet Union in the missile race, that time was quickly running out to rectify the situation, and that the United States must be willing to make "whatever financial sacrifices necessary." By the time of Eisenhower's stroke a few weeks later, Democratic newspapers across the land (but not the *Times*) called upon him to resign and turn the country over to a new and younger leadership.[21]

Given the *Times'* obvious dissatisfaction with the Eisenhower defense program, its concomitant support for the administration's Democratic critics was, of course, natural—and was directed toward both the Presidential and Congressional wings of the party.[22] In regard to the critics in the Presidential party, the *Times* favorably received a stinging indictment by the Democratic Advisory Council, terming the statement "several thousand well-chosen words." (In its statement issued two weeks after the first Sputnik launching, the DAC charged the administration with having embarked on a course of "unilateral disarmament" for reasons of domestic economy. Noting that the American economy "permits sizable additional defense expenditures," the defense critics called for a level of spending determined solely by the requirements of security, as they defined them.) A month later, in an editorial entitled "The Loyal Opposition" (a term favorably connoting a degree of party responsibility normally not found in this country), a second DAC indictment (which accused Eisenhower personally of complacency) was termed "not primarily a partisan statement." At the same time, *Times* support was lent to the Congressional Democrats who (under the leadership of Senate Majority Leader Lyndon Johnson) were also hacking away at the administration's program. In an early review of the Johnson Committee investigation (then still in progress), the editorial staff maintained that it had been demonstrated by the hearings that "our country has been allowed to slide into a position of grave though not irretrievable military (as well as political) danger," and that there was an immediate need for "imaginative leadership" (presumably to be supplied by the Senate Democratic majority). At the beginning of the new session of the Congress in early 1958, the *Times* favorably received Senator Johnson's own "state-of-the-union" message as a "valuable send-off for the new session" and a "timely call" for Americans to "wake up." (In an address to Senate Democrats summarizing the findings of his Preparedness Investigating Subcommittee, Johnson criticized current White House policy and called for a program designed to conquer space inasmuch as "control of space means control of the world.") And a few weeks later, when Johnson outlined a seventeen-point defense program which called for significant spending increases on both strategic and conventional military means necessary in the "race for survival,"—the same phrase the *Times* had employed—it was warmly praised while, at the same time, Sherman Adams' criticism of the administration's Democratic rivals was denounced as blatantly "partisan."[23]

The *New York Times*, then, explicitly rejected the basic tenets of the administration's defense policy, not the least of which was the President's long-standing acquiescence to a position of relative American inferiority in strategic missiles (at least for the short run) and overall strategic parity vis-a-vis the Soviet Union (in the long run). Casting aside Eisenhower's counsel for moderation and balance, the *Times* called for an immediate crash program to "assure our superiority in missiles." Warning that a "stand-off . . . is not enough," its editorials endorsed "unchallengeable free world superiority" in the "decisive weapons of the future." Not only in strategic weaponry must the United States stay ahead, but also in science, engineering, and overall technology. And in the race for the domination of space—a race which the President would not even acknowledge—it was "imperative" that this country be the leader for it was simply "unthinkable" for the American nation to be second.[24]

Moreover, the editorial policy of the nation's leading prestige paper demonstrated a remarkable consistency for the remainder of the second Eisenhower administration right up to its endorsement of the candidacy of John Kennedy (who had made defense a major campaign issue) in the 1960 Presidential contest. At several critical junctures during the defense posture debates of 1959, the *Times* questioned whether "we [are] doing all we can do to assure that the 'missile gap' specter never becomes a reality."[25] Later in the same year, following the Soviets' launching of the first unmanned probe designed for lunar circumnavigation, the paper's editorial page was filled with criticism for the Eisenhower space program's failure to close the space gap, charging that its nearsighted policy "would doom this country to permanent inferiority in space research with all the potentially unhappy consequences this would imply."[26] But a few months later, and in the wake of another Russian missile success, it again questioned the veracity of administration assurances that all was well with defense asking:

> would it not be wiser in our interests for our leaders to tell us bluntly whether the Soviet Union is substantially ahead of us in the item of rocket power and, if so, to mobilize our resources to wipe out that gap as soon as possible? The latest Soviet rocket demonstration suggests that the burden of proof now rests with those who would answer this question in the negative.[27]

When the executive branch cited new and improved intelligence estimates (probably based on information yielded by the top-secret U-2 flights) which downgraded Soviet missile capabilities, the *Times* apparently placed little faith in them, suggesting that it would be more prudent to err on the safe side.[28]

Just prior to the quadrennial convention of the Democratic party in 1960, three daily editorials were published sequentially on the defense problem presenting proposals which closely paralleled the future defense planks in the party's platform. Concerning the space program, the basic criticism of the last two and one-half years was reiterated; the budget of the National Aeronautical and Space Administration (NASA) would have to be drastically increased, to the tune of twelve to fifteen billion dollars for the 1960's. Addressing itself to the "missile gap," the *Times* appeared somewhat equivocal, on the one hand chastising some Congressional elements (presumably Stuart Symington) for playing "the numbers racket," but at the same time endorsing the expansion of the deterrent force by means of the Polaris submarine fleet and the B-70 supersonic bomber (which the President had just vetoed); in a matter of "life or death," it declared, "budgetary considerations must not be a limiting factor." But above all, the "greatest weakness" in American strength was insufficient provision for conventional forces to deal with the prospect of limited warfare—"by far the most likely kind of military emergency we face."[29] And in regard to Presidential hopefuls, official and de facto endorsements were consistent with the paper's line on defense policy. Though no official endorsement was given New York Governor Nelson Rockefeller in his sporadic bid for the Republican nomination, the *Times* (which had demonstrated an affinity for the views of its home state's chief executive going at least as far back as the Rockefeller Fund report on national security in January of 1958) gave unequivocal support to his position on the immediate need of increasing the military budget by some three and one-half billion dollars and flatly endorsed his hard-line defense doctrines over the more pro-administration stand of Vice President Nixon.[30] And, of course, the *Times* did firmly endorse Senator Kennedy's bid for chief of state, and, while not citing defense policy as a primary reason, it reprinted its endorsement in the same edition in which there appeared Nixon's rather vague response to the paper's questionnaire on national security.[31]

The Popularizers I

## III

Much of the pre-Sputnik debate over strategic policy planning may be attributed to a handful in the military, political, and communications elite, the foremost of which among the press were not connected with the *New York Times* at all. Though their charges were forthright and incessant, nationally syndicated columnists like the Alsop brothers failed to expand their base until, under the impetus of the Soviet space spectacular, their ranks swelled and their cause became a national issue. As Joseph and Stewart Alsop explain the failure of the press to join them in their crusade: "Barring exceptional circumstances such as the Sputniks created, our press is generally contented to leave defense problems to the Generals, the Administration and the members of the National Security Council. The official administration line is published, and so are the competing service claims; but that is about all."[32]

The first thing which should be noted in discussing the significance of the Alsops is the distinctly political conception they had of the role of columnists in contemporary America, for they viewed themselves as a necessary part of the policy process—as the guardians of the public interest whose primary duty was to serve as "the people's eyes and ears" vis-a-vis government. Indeed, the notion of political sterility or neutral observation was alien to their philosophy of journalism:

> Above all reporting offers the sense of being *engagé* in the political process of one's own time. The reporter who is not consciously *engagé* is in fact likely to be a bad and unsuccessful reporter. . . . [H]e must . . . be *engagé* if only because he himself is a most necessary part of the political process.[33]

Thus, the Alsops (through their nationally syndicated column, "Matter of Fact") battled two administrations over the course of a decade over the question of national defense. From their first column in 1945 to their last in 1957, the two brothers attempted to mobilize informed opinion against what they believed was a dangerously deteriorating posture and, by 1960, the defense situation had for them become so intolerable that the younger partner declared: "the Eisenhower regime has dismally failed to maintain a genuine balance of power with the Communist bloc."[34] The ultimate cause of United States military decline was, from their point of view, the fatal tendency to underrate the Soviets; as early as 1949 they wrote in their column that,

> the intelligence services of the Western powers have now proved to be just as wrong about other Russian technological capabilities as they were about the time schedule of the Russian atomic energy program. This means, very simply, that the other grounds for Western complacency were going the same way as the American atomic monopoly.[35]

As partisans of airpower, their primary concern was with long-range bombardment, either by aircraft or missiles (for which they had the foresight to assess a preponderant role in future warfare as early as 1946), and they vividly predicted the implications of a Soviet lead in this field with their publication of the substance of the 1951-1952 Lincoln Report. In the early months of the first Eisenhower administration, they concluded their summary of the findings of the Lincoln group (the most important of which was that the United States for the first time, in the Alsops' words, "became nakedly vulnerable to Soviet air attack with atomic weapons") by illustrating the country's meager investment in long-range missiles as compared to that of the Soviets and warned that we were "running the risk of falling behind Soviet development of these dreadful weapons, which in themselves may decide the world power struggle."[36] And the following year, they prophetically warned of the Soviet development of an ICBM before 1958 (despite official predictions to the contrary) which would represent for the United States "the final stage of the journey into danger." Two years before the trauma of Sputnik, the Alsop brothers, in discussing the findings of the National Security Council's Killian Committee, framed the "missile gap" argument (though they did not use that exact phrase) in the form it would essentially retain for the next half-decade:

> . . . the Soviet Union is now overtaking the United States in the air-atomic weapons race.

As of now, by this report's estimate, the frequently mentioned 'America lead' may be expected to become a Soviet lead in the period 1960-1965. The basis of this estimate is the expectation that in 1960-1965, the Soviet Union will enjoy a decided superiority in intercontinental missiles.[37]

For the Alsops, the tragedy of America's future lay in the fact that while Soviet advances indicated that the world balance of power was being overturned in Moscow's favor, the Eisenhower administration pursued a "business-as-usual" policy. Ever since 1949, when the Soviet Union broke the American atomic monopoly, Communist power had grown more menacing every year, and now there was every indication that they would surpass the free world in the vital field of missiles. The first concrete evidence of the coming gap was reported by them in January of 1956 when they announced that the Soviets possessed a 1500-mile intermediate range ballistic missile—a weapon which not only signified a giant step in the race for the ICBM, but one which would place four-fifths of the Strategic Air Command's medium-range B-47 bombers (largely dependent on overseas bases) under the threat of instant annihilation.[38]

In addition to the military implications of missile superiority, the first nation into space would gain, as the Alsops foresaw, an immense psychological advantage by demonstrating for all to see its technological edge. Thus, simultaneous with their exhortation for an acceleration of the American ballistics program came admonishments pressing for a more intensive space program—one which would beat the Russians in the race for an earth satellite. Pointing to the invaluable propagandistic value of a man-made moon, the Alsops warned two and a half years before Sputnik would capture the imaginations of the American people that, "the most cogent pro-satellite argument can best be understood in terms of a couple of headlines: SOVIETS CLAIM SUCCESSFUL LAUNCHING OF EARTH SATELLITE, and U. S. RADAR CONFIRMS EXISTENCE OF SOVIET SATELLITE." And when the monumental event of October, 1957 did come to pass, it was for them (in conjunction with the Soviet test of the

161

first ICBM two months before) the "worst single piece of news of the post-war years."[39]

The Alsops' indictment of the Eisenhower administration was largely indictment by historical analogy. The post-World War II era was to the two columnists a repetition of the struggle between "democracy" and "totalitarianism" in the 1930's. In a life and death struggle with an aggressive enemy, to let down one's guard—as Chamberlain had done then and Eisenhower was doing now— was to senselessly invite defeat. And so they drew the parallels: the President's arguments were "so wonderfully reminiscent of the days of Chamberlain and Baldwin"; the administration presented the nation with "the policies of Baldwin and Chamberlain"; the future would hold only "American-made Munichs."[40] The Alsops concluded their collaboration only a few months after Sputnik, but they had ably laid the groundwork for those in the journalistic profession and elsewhere who would now embrace what until then had been their lonely crusade.[41]

Another columnist who was involved in the early stages of the missile gap debate and is worthy of consideration was the inimical Drew Pearson. Author of the highly popular column, "Washington Merry-Go-Round" (published since 1932—since 1948 with the collaboration of Jack Anderson—and syndicated in the Washington *Post* and over six hundred other newspapers), Pearson warned of the imminence of a Soviet satellite and ICBM lead as early as May of 1956 and predicted the actual date of the Sputnik launching with a good deal of accuracy in August of the following year.[42] His post-Sputnik consideration of American defense policy was notable both for the harsh (but typically Pearsonian) nature of the personal attacks directed at the President and the nature of his sources—which were primarily from the Department of Defense bureaucracy (civilians such as former Assistant Defense Secretary Trevor Gardner, military men like retired General Gavin, scientists like Wernher von Braun) and the Congress (Senators Symington and Jackson, among others).[43] Thus, in Pearson we find a clear indication of the triangular nature of the coalition of defense critics in the late 1950's—the press, the Congress, the DOD bureaucracy.

In his book-length indictment of, not just the Eisenhower administration, but Eisenhower himself, published in 1958, Pearson attributed the sorry state of America's security[44] to

> the personality of the Commander in Chief. He . . . wanted to be loved. And during the course of his military career in Europe and his campaigning for the Presidency, he had built up a public love and devotion and prestige that amounted to a father image. Because of that image and because of his long service in the army, the nation trusted him. He could do no wrong. They did not know he was complacent, easygoing, unwilling to spend the long hours of grueling grind which any President must spend if he is to lead the nation. That Dwight D. Eisenhower was not willing to do these things, that he honestly believed he could serve as a part-time President, that he did not have the courage to deal forcefully with his old buddies in the Pentagon or the budget cutters in the Treasury Department, is one of the reasons why the United States today finds itself in the gravest danger in history.[45]

In Pearson's eyes, Eisenhower was guilty not only of dereliction of duty but also of deliberately misleading the American people, and the columnist even went so far as to suggest that the President's three illnesses had impaired his faculties, making him "fuzzy and confused on major issues."[46]

To be sure, the columnists of the *New York Times* were a good deal more reflective than their impetuous colleague and sought to deal with the defense issue in terms of its own inherent logic and merit, but in the end they too were disenchanted with the President's policies. And because of the degree of specialization characteristic of the prestige press, each approached the defense issue from a different angle: science editor J. W. Finney was primarily concerned with the United States' poor showing in the space race and consistently lobbied for increased spending for NASA and a program designed to overtake the Russians[47]; Arthur Krock, whose chief concern was domestic politics, saw the Soviet Sputnik as evidence that this country was losing the psychological war for the loyalties of foreign peoples[48]; Kremlinologist Harry

Schwartz focused on the more aggressive foreign policy being pursued by the Soviets as a result of their reassessment of the balance of power[49]; Washington correspondent James Reston was generally critical of the administration's imprudent economy and lack of movement[50]; and, perhaps most significantly, military editor Hanson W. Baldwin was most apprehensive about the deterioration of conventional forces and the misplaced emphasis on missiles. Of all the *Times* columnists, Baldwin deserves further note, for his approach made him a leading spokesman in journalistic circles for what was to become the doctrine of "flexible response."

In much the same manner that the military establishment was seriously divided over strategic doctrine and budgetary priorities, the press then also failed to present a monolithic front. While columnists like the Alsops and Pearson (not to mention many of the *Times*' columnists as well as its editorial staff) were hammering away at the defense issue as it was reflected in the Sputnik launching—that is, the space and missile lags—Baldwin maintained from the beginning of the controversy an imperturbable skepticism regarding the significance of the Soviet accomplishment and its ramifications for the future of American foreign policy. Within a week after Sputnik, Baldwin began a series of articles on the significance of the satellite by noting that "the extreme reactions in the United States to the Soviet satellite are not justified by a calm appraisal of the technical and military progress in both countries," and concluded with a rather optimistic assessment of the relative state of the American missile program.[51] And while space and missiles dominated the attention of the nation's leaders, he continued to emphasize a countertheme: the waning effectiveness of United States conventional war forces in an era where the greatest risks would come from limited, not general nuclear, war.[52]

In fact, by the end of the year, Baldwin articulated a defense policy consonant with that of the limited war/finite deterrence group within the military, arguing that a nuclear stalemate was developing between the two superpowers and calling for a "flexible strategic concept" capable of "multiple responses to multiple threats."[53] Throughout the new year the *Times*' foremost military

specialist continued expounding upon the same theme, beginning with his extensive (and favorable) interview with General
Gavin and soon followed by another long series of articles in which
he emphasized the "unbalanced" nature of our military strength—
"a tremendous capability for massive retaliation," but too little for
a swift reaction to small-scale conventional aggression.[54] Also in
1958, he had published a book-length comparison of Soviet and
American military power, a sober analysis which rejected the notion of Communist strategic superiority and, in fact, pointed to
an overkill capacity on the part of the United States: "even allowing for misses, aborted missions, and effective enemy defense,
the U. S. has, as far as piloted aircraft and giant nuclear weapons
are concerned, a factor of safety many times larger than many
observers believe is either necessary or desirable"; however, he
maintained that the armed forces' ability to meet limited probes
was diminishing and therefore the problem of defense planning
was "largely a problem of balance."[55] Throughout 1959 and 1960
as well, Baldwin consistently argued against the exaggeration of
Soviet strategic power suggested by the missile gap advocates, instead urging that the primary dilemma was the underemphasis
on conventional war forces.[56]

## IV

Though the views of the fourth estate mirrored in many ways
the divisions within the military establishment over defense policy, it is nonetheless true that the press did manage to focus
attention on the issue of national defense and the need for a re-
orientation of military policy. If there was one common denomina-
tor to be found among the dissidents within the military services,
the communications media, and elements within the Congress,
it was the sheer desire for change.

In addition to popularizing the several service doctrines and
generally framing the contours of the national public debate, the
press had substantial influence on the substance of congressional behavior. Though we will focus on the sway which the media
had over legislative action, it should not be assumed that there
was but a one-way interaction between the two institutions. Quite

the contrary, for often Congressmen obtained official responses to queries posed publicly by correspondents which would otherwise have gone unanswered.[57]

The press' influence on the Congress was three-fold: (1) it provided legislators with general information on the actions and views of those involved in the controversy; (2) it gave Congressional critics of administration policy intelligence on dissension within the executive branch; (3) it supplied "documentation" or "proof" which could be used to buttress the arguments of those opposed to the administration. The general information—or primary sources—which came into the possession of the nation's legislators were for the most part reports on or transcripts of the speeches and interviews of other participants in the debate, especially the innovators. Thus, throughout the Congressional hearings of this period we find the members of investigating committees questioning witnesses from the executive branch on the views set forth by military and civilian bureaucrats—Representative Jamie L. Whitten (Democrat-Mississippi) quoting from a speech by administration stalwart Admiral Radford; the chief counsel of the Johnson Committee citing the television statement of General Ridgway; Senator Symington citing a *Life* magazine article by Trevor Gardner, quoting from a television interview of Admiral Burke, or referring to a telecast involving the Air Force Secretary.[58]

In addition to being purveyors of general information, the media also served another intelligence-gathering function for the Congress—namely, that of discovering and publicizing rifts which arose in the "enemy" camp. In this regard, one finds such incidents as: House Defense Appropriations Subcommittee chairman George H. Mahon quoting from a *New York Times* article by John B. Morris which indicated that Air Force chief White had vigorously protested within the administration against what he considered to be an inadequate budget—a budget he was then defending on the Hill; Senator Saltonstall placing into the Senate Appropriations Subcommittee record a Washington *Post* article indicating that the Air Force had argued for more missiles squadrons than the administration would allow; a Washington *Evening*

*Star* account of the struggle within the early Kennedy administration between the forces favoring finite deterrence and those espousing the counterforce doctrine cited during hearings before the House.[59] And, finally, besides merely gathering intelligence for the legislative branch, the press also served to sift through its content, digest it, and present incisive analyses of its significance. So highly regarded were certain papers and journalists that often a member of either chamber would cite their views as authoritative evidence—equally as, if not more, authoritative than the testimony of administration witnesses. Thus we find limited-war advocate Flood inserting into official committee record material from the *Times* and the *Post* supporting the conventional war strategy; Symington quoting a *Times* article which maintained that the American space program had still not moved off of "dead center" a year after Sputnik; Senator Cannon (Democrat-Nevada) referring to a recent column by Joseph Alsop criticizing the administration's handling of the country's alleged missile inferiority; Senator Chavez, chairman of the Senate's defense appropriation committee, citing the comments of a number of reporters chastising President Eisenhower's preoccupation with balanced budgets rather than balanced security.[60] Naturally, the administration itself was not averse to calling upon the expertise of the profession of journalism (when such expertise could be usefully employed), and one even witnesses such a bizarre occurrence as the Chairman of the Joint Chiefs of Staff pointing to the conclusions of Hanson Baldwin to reinforce his own arguments.[61]

As has been mentioned, the relationship between the media and the Chief Executive differs greatly from that between the press and the Congress. Unlike his foes at the other end of Pennsylvania Avenue, the President is reliant upon the gentlemen of the press for neither information, expertise, nor analysis. Moreover, while the legislators and the correspondents, both seeking to affect the policies of the executive branch and limit its power, are natural allies, the Presidency and the nation's newspapers are normally in an antagonistic state, and for the same reasons. During the Eisenhower years, the chief point of encounter between press and President occurred at the regularly-held news conferences. Ideally, perhaps, a President proficient in the rites of journalism (especially the primordial desire for copy) or one more adept at the give-and-take of the friendly adversary relationship can manipulate the conference so as to communicate his views to the general population and keep his policies constantly in the public eye. Yet, in the final sense, it is the press and not the President who, through the pattern of questioning, sets the theme for the encounter. And when the White House is generally placed on the defensive (as was the case during the late Eisenhower years), the press is likely to bring into the foreground many of the issues which its star witness would rather keep in the background. And whether he chooses to meet such matters head on or circumvent them, he is in effect compelled to deal with them, and his responses (evasive or otherwise) will be treated by the press as newsworthy.

During the first Eisenhower administration, when the country was still experiencing the after-effects of the trauma of Korea, the issue of defense (as raised by the journalists) frequently revolved about the possibility of a Commander in Chief once more committing the nation to war. And time and again, whether the initial impetus for renewed concern might be crises in the Far or Middle East, Eisenhower consistently assured his questioners that, in his philosophy of government, only the Congress could commit the United States to war and that he would not subvert the intent of the Constitution.[62] Moreover, as we have seen,[63] the President usually managed during this early period to lecture the press on the merits of the policy of the long pull—a doctrine framed while the memory of the frustrations of limited war were all too fresh. Beginning in 1955, however, the views of defense critics like Ridgway and Symington began to find their way to the President's ear by means of the conference, and Eisenhower, for the first time, found himself on the defensive on his home territory.[64] The following year, an election year with the Symington Committee investigating the alleged bomber gap, the press continued confronting the Commander in Chief with the charges of his Democratic foes on Capitol Hill and Eisenhower continued to defend the long haul doctrine.[65] From late 1957 to the end of his public service, the President was literally deluged with the charges of his many critics, and scarcely a meeting with the press went by without at least one question being devoted to the defense issue. And as could be expected, his temper grew progressively shorter, for as soon as one charge was dismissed another was raised until he found even his personal motives and integrity under question.[66] Moreover, because so many of the assumptions of his critics had by his last year become so widely accepted, he became irritated when questions were so framed as to box him into a corner in his response, as the following exchange illustrates:

Q. William McGaffin, Chicago Daily News: Mr. President, in view of the international prestige at stake, why are we not moving with a greater sense of urgency to catch up with Russia in the field of space exploration?
THE PRESIDENT. Just start at that again. How did you start it, how did you start that question?
Q. Mr. McGaffin: I said, in view of the international prestige at stake.
THE PRESIDENT. Is it?
Q. Mr. McGaffin: Well, sir, do you not feel that it is?
THE PRESIDENT. Not particularly, no. . . .[67]

Despite Eisenhower's annoyance with the recurring theme, however, he was (to his chagrin) virtually powerless to stem the tide of circumstances. What began with the disgruntled mumblings of the innovators had now, with the stimulus of the Soviet invasion of space, been transformed (with the invaluable assistance of the country's press) into a national issue. With the intervention of academia it would soon become a legitimate policy alternative.

1. Bernard C. Cohen, *The Press and Foreign Policy* (Princeton, N.J.: Princeton University Press, 1963), p. 13. (Emphasis in the original.)
2. Douglass Cater, *Power in Washington* (New York: Vintage Books, 1964), pp. 225-226.
3. James Reston, *The Artillery of the Press: Its Influence in American Foreign Policy* (New York: Harper & Row, Publishers, 1966), p. 13.

4. Stewart Alsop, *The Center: People and Power in Political Washington* (New York: Harper & Row, Publishers, 1968), pp. 172-175.

5. Cohen, *op. cit.*, p. 129.

6. William L. Rivers, The *Opinionmakers* (Boston: Beacon Press, 1965), pp. 52-55. See also Cohen, *op. cit.*, pp. 56-60.

7. Because of its notable influence on the course of national debate, the press has frequently been subjected to severe criticism by those dissatisfied with its frame of reference. And because of its self-perceived role as the "watchdog" of government, the press often finds itself at odds with the powers that be who periodically mount counterattacks against its privileged—but largely undefined—status in the polity. Thus, it should come as little surprise that the verbal attacks upon the press issued in recent years by Vice President Agnew were substantially similar to those levelled by New Dealers in the 1930's except for the fact that it was then seen as a Tory stronghold rather than as a bastion of Eastern liberalism. See Harold L. Ickes, *America's House of Lords: An Inquiry into the Freedom of the Press* (New York: Harcourt, Brace and Company, 1939).

8. Alsop, *op. cit.*, pp. 17-171.

9. Cohen, *op. cit.*, p. 251.

10. Gabriel Almond, *The American People and Foreign Policy* (New York: Harcourt, Brace and World, 1950), pp. 137-143.

11. Cohen, *op. cit.*, pp. 134, 141-161, chapter 7; V. O. Key, Jr., *Public Opinion and American Democracy* (New York: Alfred A. Knopf, 1961), chapter 4; Charles R. Dechert, "Availability of Information for Congressional Operation," in Alfred deGrazia, ed., *Congress, The First Branch of Government: Twelve Studies in the Organization of Congress* (Garden City, N. Y.: Doubleday & Company, 1967), pp. 154-203.

12. Reston, *op. cit.*, p. 71.

13. *Ibid.*, p. 70.

14. Samuel P. Huntington, *The Common Defense: Strategic Programs in National Politics* (New York: Columbia University Press, 1961), p. 238.

15. Theodore C. Sorensen, *Decision-Making in the White House* (New York: Columbia University Press, 1963), p. 48.

16. According to surveys conducted by the American Institute of Public Opinion, only one-quarter of the general population was "satisfied with the present defense policies of the United States" by the end of November, 1957. Also, by January of 1958, a majority of a national sample expressed the belief that the Soviets could decimate most American cities with ICBMs—a capability it would not possess for several years. This marked a dramatic shift in opinion from the year before when less than a fifth of the population believed the Soviet Union further advanced in nuclear weaponry than the United States. These AIPO findings are cited in Paul Y. Hammond, *The Cold War Years: American Foreign Policy Since 1945* (New York: Harcourt, Brace & World, 1969), appendix to chapter 5.

17. This brief survey of the news coverage of the Soviet Sputnik, the American reaction and related defense issues is drawn from a careful examination of the *New York Times*, 1 October 1957 to 16 February 1958, inclusive.

18. Theodore C. Sorensen, *Kennedy* (New York: Harper & Row, Publishers, 1965), p. 318.

19. *The New York Times*, 12 October 1957 (p. 18), 13 October (section 4, p. 10), 4 November (p. 28), 8 November (p. 28), 20 November (p. 34), 21 November (section 4, p. 18).

20. *Ibid.*, 6 October 1957 (p. 10), 9 October (p. 34), 10 October (p. 32), 11 October (p. 26), 12 October (p. 18), 13 October (section 4, p. 10), 18 October (p. 22).

20. *Ibid.*, 7 October 1957 (p. 26), 8 October (p. 34), 10 October (p. 32), 14 October (p. 26), 16 October (p. 34), 17 October (p. 32), 18 October (p. 22), 4 November (p. 28), 5 November (p. 30), 10 November (section 4, p. 10), 19 November (p. 32), 29 November (p. 27), 30 November (p. 8), 7 December (p. 20).

22. The terms "Congressional" and "Presidential" parties are used here in the sense first suggested by James MacGregor Burns in his *The Deadlock of Democracy: Four Party Politics in America* (Englewood Cliffs, N. J.: Prentice-Hall, 1963).

23. For the editorials referred to, see the *New York Times*, 21 October 1957 (p. 24), 18 November (p. 26), 27 November (p. 30), 9 January 1958 (p. 32), 24 January (p. 27). For the texts of the two statements of the Democratic Advisory Council, see 20 October 1957 (p. 3) and 17 November (p. 82); for Senator Johnson's addresses, see 8 January 1958 (p. 10) and 24 January (p. 6).

24. *Ibid.*, 4 October 1957 (p. 26), 18 October (section 4, p. 22), 26 October (p. 20), 29 October (p. 30), 11 November (p. 28), 2 December (p. 26), 5 December (p. 34).

25. *Ibid.*, 16 January 1959, p. 26.

26. *Ibid.*, 6 October 1959, p. 38.

27. *Ibid.*, 22 January 1960, p. 26.

28. *Ibid.*, 27 January 1960, p. 32.

29. *Ibid.*, 3 May 1960 (p. 38), 4 May (p. 44), 5 May (p. 34).

30. *Ibid.*, 9 June 1960 (p. 32) and 11 June (p. 20).

31. *Ibid.*, 30 October, section 4, p. 10. The text of Mr. Nixon's response to the Times questionnaire is on page 56; the news story is on page 1 ff.

32. Joseph and Stewart Alsop, *The Reporter's Trade* (New York: Reynal & Company, 1958), p. 60.

33. *Ibid.*, pp. 10, 42-43.

34. Stewart Alsop, *Nixon and Rockefeller: A Double Portrait* (Garden City: Doubleday & Company, 1960), p. 7.

35. *The Reporter's Trade*, p. 140.

36. *Ibid.*, pp. 59 and 197.

37. *Ibid.*, pp. 238 and 276.

38. *Ibid.*, p. 282.

39. *Ibid.*, pp. 255, 337.

40. *Ibid.*, pp. 61, 83, 106; also pp. 63, 90.

41. In addition to preparing the foundations for the "missile gap" controversy, the Alsops may have had a more direct influence on the course of events. The elder Alsop was a close friend of both John Kennedy and his

security advisor McGeorge Bundy; in fact, Joseph Alsop had urged the choice of Lyndon Johnson as a running mate upon candidate Kennedy. To what extent Kennedy was influenced by the views of the Alsops, both before and after he became President, can only be guessed, and no attempt to do so will be made here. For the relationship of Alsop and Kennedy, see: Arthur M. Schlesinger, Jr., *A Thousand Days: John F. Kennedy in the White House* (Boston: Houghton-Mifflin Company, 1965), p. 42; Bernard L. Collier, "The Joe Alsop Story," *The New York Times Magazine*, 23 May 1971, pp. 23 ff.

42. "Washington Merry-Go-Round," 31 May 1956 and 31 August 1957, as reproduced in Drew Pearson and Jack Anderson, *U. S. A.—Second Class Power?* (New York: Simon and Schuster, 1958), pp. 2-3.

43. *Ibid.*, p. x.

44. Whatever his sources, Pearson propagated wildly exaggerated figures on Soviet missile capability, claiming that they were producing 2000 missiles a month and already had in operation at least 20 missile bases and 400 missiles. Though the author fails to identify these operational missiles as IRBMs (which would have been a bit more reasonable) or ICBMs, the context in which the estimates are given suggests that he did indeed mean intercontinental missiles. *Ibid.*, pp. 15-17.

45. *Ibid.*, pp. 19-20.

46. *Ibid.*, pp. 129.

47. The *New York Times*, 13 October 1957 (section 4, p. 5), 4 October 1959 (p. 1), 11 October 1959 (section 4, p. 6), 15 December 1959 (p. 1), 17 January 1960 (p. 7).

48. See, for example, his "Why We Are Losing the Psychological War," *New York Times Magazine*, 8 December 1957, pp. 12 ff.

49. See Harry Schwartz, *The Red Phoenix: Russia Since World War II* (New York: Frederick A. Praeger, Publishers, 1961), pp. 205 ff. Also, the *New York Times*, 6 October 1957 (p. 43) and 20 October (section 4, p. 4).

50. The *New York Times*, 10 November 1957 (section 4, p. 10), 8 November (p. 12), 17 November (section 4, p. 10), 3 December (p. 23), 1 January 1958 (p. 1), 15 January (p. 18).

51. *Ibid.*, 15 October 1957 (p. 17) and 16 October (p. 17).

52. See, for example, "The U. S. Defense Cuts: A View of How Economy is Slashing Fat, Muscle, and Bone of the Forces in Europe," *ibid.*, 29 October 1957, p. 9.

53. Hanson W. Baldwin, "A Military Policy for the Missile Age," *New York Times Magazine*, 3 November 1957, pp. 13 ff.; *New York Times*, 21 December 1957, p. 2.

54. The *New York Times*, 12 January 1958 (interview with General Gavin, pp. 1 ff.), 2 February (pp. 1 ff.), 3 February (pp. 1 ff.), 4 February (pp. 1 ff.), 5 February (pp. 1 ff.), 6 February (pp. 1 ff.).

55. Hanson W. Baldwin, *The Great Arms Race: A Comparison in U. S. and Soviet Power Today* (New York: Frederick A. Praeger, Publishers, 1958), p. 42-43.

56. See, for example: "Missile 'Gap' Debate Blurs Broader Issues," The *New York Times*, 17 January 1959 (section 4, p. 9); "Big Defense Issue: What Kind of Deterrent?," 1 February 1959 (section 4, p. 3); "U. S. Military Confident of Superiority Now," 5 April 1959 (section 4, p. 3); 5 July

172

1959 (section 4, p. 8); 11 October 1959 (pp. 1 ff.); "The 'Missile Gap'—I," 22 January 1960 (p. 4); "The 'Missile Gap'—II," 23 January 1960 (pp. 1 ff.); 14 February 1960 (section 4, p. 3).

57.   An example of this intermediary function of legislators vis-a-vis the press on the one hand and the executive branch on the other would be the role which Representative Daniel Flood (Democrat-Pennsylvania) played during House appropriations hearings in early 1957. After having placed into the record a copy of Stewart Alsop's column in which the latter suggested that a missile gap would soon develop which would make "sitting ducks" out of SAC's bomber fleet, Flood demanded and received a written reply from the office of the Secretary of Defense answering the journalist's charges. U. S. House of Representatives, Committee on Appropriations, Subcommittee on Department of Defense Appropriations, *Department of Defense Appropriations for 1958*, part I, 85th Congress, 1st Session (Washington, D. C.: Government Printing Office, 1957), pp. 554-556.

58.   See, respectively: U. S. House of Representatives, Committee on Appropriations, Subcommittee on Department of Defense Appropriations, *Department of Defense Appropriations for 1959*, 85th Congress, 2nd Session (Washington, D. C.: Government Printing Office, 1958), pp. 87-88 (hereafter cited as *House: DOD FY1959*); U. S. Senate, Preparedness Investigating Subcommittee of the Committee on Armed Services and the Committee on Aeronautical and Space Sciences, *Joint Hearings: Missile and Space Activities*, 86th Congress, 1st Session (Washington, D. C.: Government Printing Office, 1959, p. 101; U. S. Senate, Subcommittee of the Committee on Appropriations, *Department of Defense Appropriations for 1959*, 85th Congress, 2nd Session (Washington, D. C.: Government Printing Office, 1958), p. 250 (hereafter cited as *Senate: DOD FY1959*); U. S. Senate, Subcommittee of the Committee on Appropriations, *Department of Defense Appropriations for 1960*, 86th Congress, 1st Session (Washington, D. C.: Government Printing Office, 1959), p. 168 (hereafter cited as *Senate: DOD FY1960*); U. S. Senate, Preparedness Investigating Subcommittee of the Committee on Armed Services, in conjunction with the Committee on Aeronautical and Space Sciences, *Missiles, Space and Other Major Defense Matters*, 86th Congress, 2nd Session (Washington, D.C.: Government Printing Office, 1960), p. 475 (hereafter cited as *Senate: Joint Hearings 1960*).

59.   See, respectively: *House: DOD FY1959*, p. 129; *Senate: DOD FY1960*, pp. 24-243; U. S. House of Representatives, Committee on Appropriations, Subcommittee on Department of Defense Appropriations, *Department of Defense Appropriations for 1962*, part 3, 87th Congress, 1st Session (Washington, D. C.: Government Printing Office, 1961), pp. 143-144.

60.   See, respectively: *House: DOD FY1959*, pp. 338-345; *Senate: DOD FY1959*, p. 238; *Senate: Joint Hearings 1960*, pp. 38-39; U. S. Senate, Subcommittee of the Committee on Appropriations, *Department of Defense Appropriations for 1961*, part I, 86th Congress, 2nd Session (Washington, D. C.: Government Printing Office, 1960), p. 1.

61.   U. S. House of Representatives, Committee on Appropriations, Subcommittee on Department of Defense Appropriations, *Department of Defense Appropriations for 1960*, part I, 86th Congress, 1st Session (Washington, D. C.: Government Printing Office, 1959), p. 42.

62. See, for example, U. S. Presidents, *Public Papers of the Presidents of the United States: Dwight D. Eisenhower, 1953-1961*, 8 vols. (Washington, D. C.: Government Printing Office, 1960-61): "News Conference, 17 February 1953," vol. I, pp. 51-52; "News Conference, 29 April 1954," vol. II, p. 427; "News Conference, 19 January 1956," vol. IV, p. 164; "News Conference, 4 April 1956," vol. IV, p. 380.

63. Chapters 2 and 4.

64. "News Conference, 2 February 1955," *ibid.*, vol. III, p. 226; "News Conference, 2 March 1955," p. 303; "News Conference, 18 May 1955," p. 508; "News Conference, 6 June 1955," pp. 78-79.

65. "News Conference, 19 January 1956," *ibid.*, vol. IV, pp. 168-169; "News Conference, 6 February 1956," p. 235; "News Conference, 25 April 1956," p. 433; "News Conference, 4 May 1956," pp. 433 ff.; "News Conference, 9 May 1956," p. 74; "News Conference, 5 September 1956," p. 739.

66. See, for example, the angry exchange between Eisenhower and a reporter, "News Conference, 13 January 1960," *ibid.*, vol. VIII, pp. 25-26.

67. "News Conference, 26 January 1960," *ibid.*, p. 127.

# 6

## THE POPULARIZERS II: ACADEMIA

### I

IN MUCH THE SAME MANNER IN WHICH BOTH THE military establishment and the press were divided over the priorities of a new American defense policy, academicians concerned with security doctrine were also initially at odds with one another over the means which would best serve the foreign policy interests of the United States in the decade of the sixties. Even if the defense intelligentsia had not progressed beyond the anomic dissatisfaction evident in these other circles, it would still have wielded considerable influence over the course of the controversy by simply having capped the innovating perspectives with the legitimacy of wisdom which is the distinguishing characteristic of academia. Given the mounting disenchantment with the Eisenhower policy of the long pull, even an anarchic onslaught on the New Look could have served only to further undermine confidence in the prudence of existing policies. Yet, in time, the civilian strategists were able to significantly transcend the doctrinal schisms which plagued other actors, and the common elements upon which they could eventually agree would serve as the core for a new alternative conventional wisdom. In this chapter, then, we will trace the progressive convergence of views which occurred in the late 1950's between those strategic theorists primarily concerned with general war scenarios and those preoccupied with the needs for limited war.

Gauging the influence of those academicians who lent credence and structure to the innovating arguments is, unfortunately, a more difficult and tentative task than was the case with their fellow popularizers in the journalistic profession. Unlike the succinct and readily available views of their brethren in the prestige press, the theoretical speculations of the defense intellectual elite were probably less apt to be studied by the members of the Congress and their administrative aides. Indeed, aside from relatively rare allusions to and brief quotations from the findings of certain strategic theorists, legislative hearings were devoid of any notable reference to their works,[1] committee members and counsel presumably being more concerned with the revelations of military specialists and Pentagon correspondents than with the complicated deductions of armchair strategists.[2]

Yet, to be sure, there are other (and more direct) avenues of access to the policy-making process. Unlike President Eisenhower, who by nature and temperament distrusted intellectuals (at one time he defined an intellectual as "a man who takes more words than is necessary to say more than he knows"[3]), John Kennedy and his Defense Secretary, Robert McNamara, gathered around them a team of advisors which included a number of university professors profoundly influenced by the theoretical premises outlined by their colleagues during the preceding years.[4] Moreover, virtually all of the civilian thinkers to be considered in this chapter were, at one time or another during the period under investigation, associated with the various research organizations or "think tanks" under contract to the several armed services and the Department of Defense[5]; indeed, several served as consultants to the White House or the Defense Department during the Kennedy-McNamara years.[6] The new Democratic administration had, in fact, so internalized the alternative defense doctrines articulated by the strategic thinkers that its more partisan defenders subsequently made it appear that the various academicians had appropriated the long-held views of John Kennedy rather than vice versa.[7] In any event, we are justified in echoing the observation of one student of defense politics who maintains that the views of such theorists as Henry Kissinger and Herman Kahn provided the new administration with an "intellectual basis for a major shift in United States strategic thinking."[8]

## II

The limited war debate among academicians began as a direct reaction to Secretary of State John Foster Dulles' enunciation of the doctrine of massive retaliation in early 1954 and came prominently into the foreground in 1956 and 1957; however, by 1958 the general anxieties over a Soviet missile lead led to new concerns over American strategic capabilities and, thus, a new emphasis on the prerequisites for successfully deterring (or, in the event that this failed, waging) general nuclear war. By the time the new administration came to power in 1961, academia had available a set of strategic concepts which incorporated both levels of conflict.

Setting the tone for the strategic war debate of the last Eisenhower years was a trenchantly critical article on current policy by Albert Wohlstetter published in *Foreign Affairs* in January of 1959,[9] in which the author sought to dispel "the nearly universal optimism about the stability of deterrence." Maintaining that the shock of the Soviet Sputnik of October 1957 had "almost dissipated," Wohlstetter criticized both administration advocates of nuclear parity as well as limited war theorists (such as Henry Kissinger and James King) for assuming that there was an automaticity of thermonuclear balance between the two superpowers. Quite the contrary, he argued, for the balance of terror "is in fact precarious, and this fact has critical implications for policy. Deterrence in the 1960's is neither assured nor impossible but will be the product of sustained effort and hard choices, responsibly made."[10] The delicate nature of the present nuclear stalemate rested ultimately on the known capacity of United States retaliatory forces to survive a Soviet surprise attack, reach enemy territory, overcome its defenses, and destroy the programmed targets. However, given the growing destructive power of the Kremlin's first-strike capability (with the influx into its strategic arsenal of more and more ICBMs), the "soft" nature of SAC bases (both vulnerable bomber complexes in the continental United States and overseas IRBM squadrons), the radical decrease in warning time brought about by long-range missiles, and the mounting difficulties in overcoming Russian defenses (with increased enemy emphasis on manned interceptors and civil defense programs)—with all these new factors in the strategic balance operative, it would be a "formidable hurdle for the greater part of our deterrence force" to complete its missions over hostile territory at least until the mid-1960's at which time this country would have a sizable fleet of second-generation ICBMs in hardened underground silos. Indeed, given new Soviet active and passive air defenses alone, Wohlstetter suggested that it might take a full sixty half-megaton American delivery vehicles to assure the destruction of at least half the population of a relatively small city of some 900,000. Therefore, the Eisenhower policy of simply seeking to match Soviet capabilities for a first-strike would make deterrence difficult to achieve for the next administration. Thus, warned Wohlstetter,

> we must expect a vast increase in the weight of attack which the Soviets can deliver with little warning, and the growth of a significant Russian capability for an essentially warningless attack. As a result, strategic deterrence, while foreseeable, will be extremely difficult to achieve, and at critical junctures in the 1960's, we may not have the power to deter attack. Whether we have it or not will depend on some difficult strategic choices as to the future composition of the deterrent forces as well as hard choices in its basing, operations and defense.[11]

Moreover, given the values, experience, and goals of Communist leadership, the United States would be tragically mistaken in gearing its survival to the peaceful and reasonable intentions of its adversary:

> Russian casualties in World War II were more than 20,000,000. Yet Russia recovered extremely well from this catastrophe. There are several quite plausible circumstances in the future

when the Russians might be quite confident of being able to limit damage to considerably less than this number—if they make the sensible strategic choices and we do not. On the other hand, the risks of not striking first might at some juncture appear great to the Soviets, involving, for example, disastrous defeat in a peripheral war. . . .[12]

The implications of Wohlstetter's analysis were unmistakable: given the possibility (perhaps the probability) of a Soviet first-strike, the major priorities of United States defense policy would have to be a major expansion of its retaliatory forces coupled with a "more energetic provision for active and passive defenses to limit the dimensions of the catastrophe in case deterrence should fail." Concluding with a grim warning, he noted that if this country failed to provide itself with an adequate deterrent in the early 1960's, "general war is likely."[13]

Another respected figure from the academic world concerned with the deterrent posture of the United States during this period was Bernard Brodie, who had originally established his reputation in military theory as a naval power strategist during the Second World War. As at first a civilian at the Institute for Advanced Study at Princeton University and later as a naval reserve officer, Brodie severely criticized the doctrine of strategic bombing as promulgated by the intellectual heirs of Douhet in this country, and played down the significance of airpower in modern warfare.[14] However, with the quantum jump in destructive power realized by atomic power in 1945, Brodie revised his earlier consideration of airpower and acknowledged that a revolution had indeed taken place in modern warfare. Moreover, he foresaw as early as 1946 that nuclear weaponry had made it "theoretically feasible to produce rockets capable of several thousands of miles of range," and that soon "any world power [would be] able from bases within its own territory to destroy most of the cities of any other power."[15] Yet while granting that "there can no longer be any dispute about the decisiveness of strategic bombing," he believed that the prospect of nuclear plenty and the concomitant unlikelihood of any power developing a perfect air-defense system made superiority in airpower of little significance, for even an inferior air force could wreak havoc on a country possessing a quantitative edge. Therefore, multilateral possession of the bomb would make future general warfare irrational ("no victory . . . would be worth the price"), and the role of the military establishment would be transformed from that of waging and winning war to deterring it:

> Thus, the first and most vital step in any American security program for the age of atomic bombs is to take measures to guarantee to ourselves in case of attack the possibility of retaliation in kind. The writer in making that statement is not for the moment concerned with who will *win* the next war in which atomic bombs are used. Thus far the chief purpose of our military establishment has been to win wars. From now on its chief purpose must be to avert them. It can have almost no other purpose.[16]

While prophetically presenting the case for nuclear parity and stalemate some three years before the Soviet Union even possessed an atomic bomb, however, Brodie acknowledged that in the early stages of the coming missile age, before the point of saturation had been reached which would nullify the significance of a quantitative disparity, there would be a political-psychological advantage to superiority in numbers:

> the development of rockets is not likely to proceed at an equal pace among all the larger powers. One or several of them will far outstrip the others, depending not alone on the degree of science and engineering talent available in each country but also on the effort which the government causes to be channeled into such an enterprise. In any case, the possibilities of an enormous lead on the part of one power in the effective use of the atomic bomb are inseparable from technological developments in vehicles—at least up to a certain common level, beyond which additional developments may matter little.[17]

From the dawn of the atomic age to the beginning of the space age, Brodie continued to discuss the implications of nuclear and thermonuclear weaponry for military policy, and while he remained critical of the claims made for airpower as the ultimate deterrent to all forms of aggression, he nonetheless displayed a consistent primary concern for general warfare.[18] And though he believed that the limitations of airpower necessitated a capability for limited conventional war on the part of the United States, he did not waver from the firm position that "while total war is the one kind of war we cannot afford to fight, it nevertheless must continue to claim, indefinitely, a first-priority call upon our resources." This preoccupation stemmed from his premise that "if the Soviet leaders should ever decide that by a surprise attack they could confidently count on destroying our strategic air force, whose very purpose it is constantly to threaten their existence, it would be their duty as good Bolsheviks to launch that attack."[19] As with Wohlstetter, then, we find a concern with developing the capacities for conventional war subordinated to the vigilance necessary to preserve the dynamic nuclear balance of terror.

In 1959, Brodie (now a senior staff member of the RAND Corporation[20]), had published a major work on the problems of maintaining the free world's deterrent to Communist aggression.[21] Restating and refining many of the points in strategy which he had made during the previous two decades, he accepted the dictum that general war was irrational and amounted to mutual suicide —but only if both sides (especially the party likely to suffer a surprise attack) maintained a defensible retaliatory force. Once general war was successfully held in check by the threat of unacceptable reprisals, conflict would inevitably move to lesser (that is, conventional) levels. And here aggression would have to be deterred by the ability and willingness to intervene locally with limited war units inasmuch as the threat of massive retaliation would no longer appear credible for anything less than an attack on the United States itself. "Where our interests are not vital," reasoned Brodie, "how can a general threat of this kind be believed?"[22] But, to be sure, the build-up in conventional forces was, in view of the Soviet lead in missiles and the resulting disequilibrium of strategic balance, to be ranked behind the necessary measures to ensure the security of America's second-strike capabilities. Given the fact that the United States explicitly rejected the doctrine of preventive war, it committed itself to a pure deterrence (that is, strike-back) strategy which meant a readjustment in policies and willingness to "pay the full price of such a strategy." With growing Soviet strategic power, it was "absolutely essential" that the administration provide massive expenditures for the protection (through dispersal, active defenses, increased warning, and strong underground shelters) for the Strategic Air Command's long-range bombers—the security of which "is taken too much for granted by almost everybody, including our highest national policy-makers."[23] In addition, a vigorous fallout-shelter program was a necessary supplement to these measures in order to reinforce the credibility of America's nuclear deterrent, to keep limited wars from escalating, and to preserve at least half the population in the event deterrence should fail. Moreover, Brodie suggested that the protection and expansion of SAC, a sizeable civil defense effort, and the creation of a capacity for conventional war "would require quite considerable funds beyond those already provided." Attacking the defense budgetary ceilings of the New Look, he argued that the economy could easily withstand an expenditure of 15 per cent of its G. N. P. for security measures without suffering ill-effects; indeed, he suggested that such increases in defense spending (twelve to fifteen billion dollars annually) would serve to stimulate the economy and blamed much of the stagnation of United States economic growth in the 1950's on Eisenhower's niggardly approach to military spending.[24]

By far the most controversial of the works published by the strategic war theorists during this period was Herman Kahn's *On Thermonuclear War*,[25] a collection of a series of lectures delivered at the Center of International Studies at Princeton in 1959, the substance of which grew out of the studies of the RAND Corporation. Extremely critical of both the view that deterrence was a simple consequence of the sheer existence of hydrogen bombs and that general nuclear war must end in mutual suicide, he suggested that the deliberate initiation of a nuclear exchange might be a reasonable course of action on the part of a state prepared for such a contingency. "A thermonuclear war is quite likely to be an *unprecedented catastrophe* for the defender," declared Kahn. "Depending on the military course of events, it may or may not be an unprecedented catastrophe for the attacker. . . ."[26] In support of this view, systems analysis demonstrated that "for at least the next decade or so, any picture of total world annihilation appears to be wrong irrespective of the military course of events. Equally important, the picture of total disaster is likely to be wrong even for the two antagonists."[27] The study of the genetic effects of thermonuclear war and the concomitant radioactivity conclusively proved to Kahn's satisfaction that a good number of Americans would survive and that even the complete decimation of the fifty largest metropolitan areas in the country "does not seem to be a total economic catastrophe. It may simply set the nation's productive capacity back a decade or two plus destroy many 'luxuries.'" Given this fact that the tragedy of the postwar environment "would not preclude normal and happy lives for the majority of survivors and their descendants,"[28] there was thus an important difference between victory and defeat in such a contest:

> Once one accepts the idea that deterrence is not absolutely reliable and that it would be possible to survive a war, then he may be willing to buy insurance—to spend more money in preparations to decrease the number of fatalities and injuries, limit damage, facilitate recuperation, and to get the best military result possible—at least 'to prevail' in some meaningful sense if you cannot win.[29]

Having thus indicated that it was not only possible to wage and survive Armegeddon, but actually to walk away the victor (presumably in the traditional sense of being able to impose one's will on the vanquished), Kahn then set out to examine the parameters of the future international environment and the best possible defense policy for the United States. With the potentially crucial Russian edge in missiles, the Soviets were likely to move toward a first-strike capability—that is, an ability to launch a surprise attack against American strategic forces which would leave the United States disarmed and defenseless before Soviet threats of annihilating the country's population centers. Indeed, he suggested that a mere 125 fairly accurate missiles might be sufficient to contain American retaliation to tolerable levels: "thus he might find it the path of caution to attack while the opportunity to rid himself of his dangerous opponent was still available."[30] In any event, the inadequate measures taken by the Eisenhower administration meant that the survival of the United States might in the immediate future "depend on extreme responsibility and caution on the part of Soviet decision-makers or on Soviet inability or unwillingness to carry through the kind of crash program for ICBMs which they previously carried through for their . . . bomber programs . . . ."[31] Thus, it was the "imprudent" policy of present American leaders to, in effect, leave the decision as to whether there was to be a deterrent gap in the hands of the enemy. Arguing that we could not base our survival on Soviet intentions, Kahn urged that immediate steps be taken to insulate SAC from a first-strike by the Soviet Union.[32] For the coming decade, he proposed that a new policy be adopted which would provide for enough flexibility in posture to change capabilities to a first-strike capacity on short notice if the international situation should deteriorate, and which would leave the United States with enough forces to deter a direct attack, decrease the incidence of extreme provocations by the Soviet Union in Europe, and keep limited wars limited by taking away from the Communists any incentive for escalation. This expansion of strategic power would, he conceded, lead to an increase in the national budget by 10 to 20 per cent and a lower standard of living than would otherwise be the case, but this was the only alternative to taking "desperate gambles" in gauging Soviet intentions.

## III

Before the Soviet Sputnik launching and resulting claims of missile superiority diverted the energies of many academicians to the problems of strategic power, the dissatisfactions of most theorists with the Eisenhower defense program revolved around its very over-emphasis on strategic forces. Indeed, the case for flexible response (or limited war capabilities) was justified by many as the liberal community's alternative to the doctrine of massive retaliation,[33] for it was generally assumed that a military stalemate between the two superpowers all across the continuum of likely military conflict would force the Communists to seek an accommodation with the West. As Oskar Morgenstern nicely put it: "The matching of technical capabilities must be preserved from strategic bombers on downward to specific limited-war capabilities in order to shift the area and domain of conflict primarily to the political, diplomatic, economic and ideological sphere."[34]

One of the early proponents of conventional military capabilities, William W. Kaufmann, aptly summed up the goal of limited war as "obtain[ing] a passage between the Scylla of nuclear holocaust and the Charybdis of interminable retreat."[35] With the loss of American impunity from nuclear retaliation by the early 1950's, the threat of American strategic airpower in response to less than a direct attack on the United States was no longer a tenable policy, and thus "if one side has an advantage in conventional means and all the other factors of traditional military power, it has open to it the possibility of employing that power without undue risk and at a cost that is bearable whatever the outcome of the ensuing conflict."[36] However, if the United States demonstrated "a willingness and ability to intervene with great conventional power in the peripheral areas, after the manner of Korea, we will have a reasonable chance of forestalling enemy military action there."[37]

Much of the reasoning behind the forecast of likely enemy behavior during a period of relative nuclear parity was deduced by students of Soviet military strategy, the foremost of whom was Raymond L. Garthoff. As early as 1953, in a study for the RAND Corporation, he identified Soviet military (and political) doctrine as a derivation of the "fundamental Bolshevik conflict-image of the world." Surveying the writings of prominent Marxist theoreticians as well as Russian military strategists, Garthoff fell back upon the Leninist notion of "the relation of forces" as the central explanation of Soviet long-term global designs:

> The criterion for determining offense or defense as being the strategy for any given situation (and no situation is viewed as

being static) is a calculation of the relation of forces between the opponents. In case of a favorable relation of forces, one in which the Soviets have the capability for effective advance, the offensive is mandatory, with the only reservation that this be viewed strategically.[38]

Thus, he maintained that the Soviets embraced a plan for expansion which recognized the need for tactical flexibility in accordance with the ebb and flow of historical events—that is, a policy of advance when the circumstances were favorable and retreat when superior force dictated the prudence of such action. Several years later, Garthoff suggested that the Kremlin had secured the means to wage both general and limited war and had therefore attained a degree of flexibility for "meeting any war contingency with whatever military forces are most expedient, without having their hands tied by an over-specialized capability which permits only a narrow choice or none at all." Moreover, unlike the United States, the Soviet Union did not see a mutual stalemate between the major powers, but rather believed they had neutralized the West in strategic weaponry and thus could gradually extend their power through a variety of means—military and non-military—short of general war on the Eurasian periphery:

the Soviets favor the use of non-military substitutes such as political and economic pressures, inducements and blandishments, military demonstrations and threats, subversion, colonial rebellion and guerrilla warfare, over direct military means as a strategy to extend Soviet influence and control.[39]

By the late 1950's, then, the Soviet leaders had come to believe that the relation of forces had finally shifted in their favor, for

the *employment* of nuclear and thermonuclear weapons is *necessary* in the United States concept, but *not* in the Soviet one. The Soviets thus retain greater freedom of choice. If a genuine stalemate in intercontinental capabilities is achieved in a prehostilities period, the United States might be endangered by the neutralization of its entire strategy, and hence its ability to act, whereas the Soviet strategy would be served by this development.[40]

Robert Osgood approached the problem of limited war from the vantage point of the "realist" school which sees the use of force in the pursuit of the power and interests of the state as endemic in the quasi-anarchic environment politics.[41] Given the decentralized nature of the system in which sovereign states are compelled to interact, all actors can be expected to protect their interests as subjectively defined through the utilization of all expedient means. But the simple fact was that, by the mid-1950's, general war was no longer an expedient means of foreign policy. "It is safe to assume," wrote Osgood, "that so long as the United States and the Soviet Union maintain their capacity for mutual destruction and neither can be sure of preventing the other from exercising it, then neither government will rationally and deliberately choose to fight a total war, except as an act of desperation." While it was not likely that the Soviets would consciously engage in general war with the United States, neither was it likely that they would renounce their cherished goals of spreading their ideology and influence into vulnerable areas. Quite the contrary, for along "the arc of nations contiguous or nearly contiguous to the Sino-Soviet perimeter from Iran to Korea," we "must assume that they will use limited force as a means of attaining their ambitions."[42] And herein lay the foremost dilemma for American security, for a gradual overturning of the balance of power could be accomplished without the overt challenge of all-out war:

> To the extent that American national strategy is supported by a diversified military capacity, capable of countering Communist aggression under a variety of contingencies, the nation will enhance the flexibility of its diplomacy and promote favorable political positions. To the extent this diversified capacity is lacking, the nation will incur the serious political and psychological disadvantages that rigid diplomacy is bound to impose in competition with a resourceful diplomacy of an unscrupulous power.[43]

187

What was urgently needed, therefore, was a thorough reorientation, not merely of United States military policy, but of the psychology of American leadership which tended to dissociate military power from diplomacy and could not separate the concept of warfare from such outworn notions as total victory and unconditional surrender. If policy makers in Washington failed to embrace in the future the doctrine of limited warfare prevalent in the state system from Westphalia to the French Revolution and from Vienna to Sarajevo (that is, limited war to achieve marginal adjustments in the balance of power), Osgood warned that they would eventually face the same grim consequences that the West had with the coming of the Second World War. Drawing an historical analogy, he declared: "If France and Great Britain had been willing to take the risk of fighting limited wars at an early date—for example, in 1936, when Hitler's troops reoccupied the Rhineland—they might have avoided the terrible choice between acquiescence and total war later."[44]

Similar conclusions (and prescriptions) were reached in what was perhaps the most important treatise on limited war published during the period, Henry A. Kissinger's *Nuclear Weapons and Foreign Policy*.[45] The present Secretary of State arrived at his judgment on the basis of an analysis of the patterns and regularities of state behavior evident from the study of diplomatic history.[46] According to Kissinger, there are two fundamental types of international orders: a legitimate and stable one, and a revolutionary and inherently instable one. While the first international system is characterized by an acceptance of the general structure of power by all the major powers, the second exists when one power (that is, Napoleonic France, Hitler's Germany, Soviet Russia) is so dissatisfied with the existing order that it seeks to completely overturn the given equilibrium. In such a revolutionary system as existed during the post-World War II era, diplomacy and negotiation (which imply compromise, functional appeasement of limited demands, and moderate adjustments in the balance of power), become not merely useless but self-defeating for the dominant status quo power, for the conciliation sought by the revolutionary state is simply a tactical maneuver in which it engages as it jockeys for hegemony. Moreover, status quo powers (because they have much to lose from conflict) tend to be reluctant to accept a revisionist state for what it is and retort with the proper policies of containment. And while in the past certain insular powers (like the United Kingdom) had a margin of safety adequate to allow them to misperceive the machinations of its foes until the eleventh hour, the chief defender of the present international order (the United States) could indulge in no such luxury in the age of bipolarity and nuclear weapons.[47]

For Kissinger the vital national interests of the United States depended on a secure world balance of power which ultimately hinged on "our ability to deny the resources and manpower of Western Europe to an aggressor." The national interest revolved about

> the geopolitical fact that in relation to Eurasia the United States is an island power, inferior at present only in human resources though eventually even in industrial capacity. Thus, we are confronted by the traditional problem of an 'island' power—of Carthage with respect to Rome, of Britain with respect to the Continent—that its survival depends on preventing the opposite land mass from falling under hostile control.
>
> If Eurasia were to be dominated by a hostile power or group of powers, we would confront an overpowering threat. And the key to Eurasia is Western Europe. . . . If the United States were ever confined to 'Fortress America,' . . . we would [at best] be forced into a military effort incompatible with what is now considered the American way of life. At worst we would cease to be masters of our policy.[48]

Thus the interventionist policies of necessity pursued by Continental statesmen like Austria's Metternich in the post-Napoleonic period were more appropriate for the United States than the more restrained approach of England's Castlereagh.

The Soviet Union's quest for absolute security (that is, the defeat of non-Communist states, which are enemies by definition) confronted the West with, in Kissinger's words, "a contest without quarter." While the relation of forces is unfavorable (as was the case with general war in the nuclear age), direct assault would be avoided, but the inherent dynamism of their ideology would force the Soviets to adopt a "strategy of ambiguity"—to tilt the balance of power in their favor by constant, almost imperceptible pressures: subversion, guerrilla warfare, aggression by proxy. The tactics may shift to suit changing circumstances, but permanent and protracted warfare based on a vision of inevitable triumph was seen as the fundamental strategy of the Kremlin:

> Neither an all-out showdown nor a permanent peace are part of the Soviet theory except as the former may be forced upon them by all-out attack. . . . Rather, the Soviet concept is one of seeking to manage the inevitable flow of history, to bring about the attrition of the enemy by gradual increments and not to stake everything on a single throw of the dice.[49]

Only by a vigorous and consistent policy of containment of Soviet power could the United States prevent the piecemeal loss of Eurasia and hope eventually to dissipate the messianic élan of Bolshevism. However, the present doctrines of the Eisenhower administration merely played into the hands of the Soviets by posing incredible threats in response to ambiguous and limited probes. Though Kissinger granted that the United States had a superiority in strategic power, nuclear stalemate was still a reality because America was still vulnerable to even Russia's inferior forces. Thus, the policy of massive retaliation could only "paralyze the will" of the West to resist Soviet encroachments, "actually encourage the Soviet leaders to engage in aggression" and "absorb the peripheral areas of Eurasia by means short of all-out war." What was needed, of course, was a new strategic doctrine (limited war) which would allow us to avoid the choice between Armegeddon and defeat on the installment plan.[50] At this point, Kissinger consistently played down the threat of Soviet strategic power and discounted the significance of a numerical lead in ICBMs, indicating that he believed the nuclear stalemate to be a given for the foreseeable future:

What does 'being ahead' in the nuclear race mean if each side can already destroy the other's national substance? What is the strategic significance of adding to the destructiveness of the nuclear arsenal when the enormity of present weapons systems already tends to paralyze the will?[51]

## IV

Prior to Sputnik (and the related missile gap controversy), then, the limited war partisans had pinned their case for a funneling away of funds from strategic to conventional forces on the premise that nuclear stalemate existed despite the obvious American superiority in striking power. Moreover, this stalemate was assumed to be one of the constants of the future international system. However, with the anxieties over Soviet missile capabilities voiced in the post-1957 period, the limited war strategists reframed their arguments to include the necessity of a new strategic build-up while, at the same time, faithfully adhering to the doctrine of a conventional build-up.

Perhaps the best illustration of the transformation in the limited war theorists is to be found in Henry Kissinger. In January of 1958, the Rockefeller Brothers Fund published its report on the military aspects of national security, prepared under the direction of Kissinger.[52] In many ways, the widely disseminated report was merely an updating of his *Nuclear Weapons and Foreign Policy* published only the previous year, and it allowed Kissinger to revise his previous stand so as to take into account the effects of the Soviet Sputnik. Reversing his stand on the almost automatic self-regulating nature of the strategic balance, he now conceded its precarious nature:

> The growth of nuclear stockpiles on both sides has been aptly described as the 'balance of terror.' It is a condition that some [for example, Kissinger himself in 1957] have incorrectly interpreted as a static, unchanging, nuclear 'stalemate' or 'stand-off.' Nothing could be further from the truth.
> Nuclear deterrence is immensely complicated, since each

new scientific advance, if applied by one side and not the other, is capable of overturning the strategic equation. In a dynamic situation, we must continually strive to improve our technological position lest an accumulation of advantages by an aggressor ultimately confront us with overwhelming strength.[53]

Pointing to the ominous Russian lead in both short- and long-range missiles, the report warned that "all of our air bases, at home and abroad, are vulnerable to surprise attack, particularly as Soviet missiles become operational." Thus, the first priority of defense planning was to create a retaliatory force "so well protected and numerous" that it would be able to survive, "no matter what the scale of the enemy attack," overcome any potential defense, and return a blow "which will inflict an intolerable amount of damage." Therefore, the administration was urged to: "press for the most rapid development and procurement of operational intermediate-range and intercontinental ballistic missiles"; reduce the SAC alert to fifteen minutes; accelerate the early warning and anti-missile defense systems. Inasmuch as deterrence depends on a combination of power and the will to use it, a significant civil defense program was also in order as the second priority of defense: "the ability to afford reasonable protection to our population may enable us to act with firmness and resolution in times of crisis. In the age of the ballistic missile, the known capability of a society to withstand attack will become an increasingly important deterrent."[54]

For the most part, though, Kissinger's re-evaluation of the needs for strategic deterrence was consonant with his long advocacy of limited war, for a Soviet lead in nuclear striking power would, it was urged, serve as "a shield behind which to expand by more limited means." It was still maintained that the most likely threat to the free world would come from a gradual Communist infiltration and domination of the vital peripheral areas "through steps each of which is so small and seemingly so insignificant that it does not seem to justify overt intervention"; therefore, preparedness for all-out war was seen as a prerequisite for allowing the United States to contain limited probes on their own terms, without the fear of escalation by the Soviet Union. Counselling for major increases in the defense budget, the report called for a military establishment adequately prepared to discharge two distinct though related tasks: "one, to discourage an all-out attack through the existence of a powerful, instantly ready retaliatory force, and, two, to react effectively to limited aggression through the ability to make our response fit the challenge."[55]

Two years later, Kissinger published another major work on security strategy[56] focusing on the new era of the 1960's, a period of acute danger which would require a new and vibrant leadership attuned to the fact that

> the United States cannot afford another decline like that which has characterized the past decade and a half. Fifteen years more of a deterioration of our position in the world such as we have experienced since World War II would find us reduced to Fortress America in a world in which we had become largely irrelevant.[57]

After "a decade of almost continuous decline" in American power, the next administration would face the grim problem of a Soviet Union made belligerent by the weakness of the United States. Specifically, during the first half of the coming decade, the new President would be confronted with a missile gap. At worst, the Soviets might be tempted to overwhelm our vulnerable retaliatory force with a massive missile attack; at best, the Communists will be given a free hand to blackmail all contiguous areas. Moreover, the long lead-time involved prevented the United States from closing the gap for several years—that is, a missile gap in the period 1961-1965 was now unavoidable. But the crux of the matter was simply that, even in the best possible world (that is, where the Soviet Union did not attain a first-strike advantage), the United States would not be able to deter limited aggression with the "reckless" threat of all-out war:

> The missile gap will therefore reduce substantially, perhaps completely, the threat of our retaliatory force against any chal-

lenge to our survival, except the most direct. Even if the missile gap is never sufficient to enable the Soviet Union to attack the United States, it should provide increasing opportunities for the kind of blackmail of which the crisis over Berlin is but an augury.[58]

And in the period of stable mutual deterrence which would arise in the late '60's (assuming that it survived the missile gap years), the United States would be no better off than where it had been before Sputnik when Kissinger had first argued for a conventional capability.

Thus, in Kissinger[59] we see the convergence of many of the arguments of both the strategic- and limited-war enthusiasts. Though perhaps not proposing a strategic force as large as that suggested by the damage-limitation (or counter-force) strategists of which Herman Kahn is the best example, he nonetheless embraced a policy geared to both strategic and conventional build-ups. In academia, then, we find the intellectual justification for the fusion of the two concepts which previously, both within the military establishment and the press, had remained largely distinct.

1. See, for example, the respective citations from the works of Henry Kissinger and Oskar Morgenstern during the joint Senate hearings of 1960: U. S. Senate, Preparedness Investigating Subcommittee of the Committee on Armed Services, in conjunction with the Committee on Aeronautical and Space Sciences, *Missiles, Space and Other Major Defense Matters*, 86th Congress, 2nd Session (Washington, D.C.: Government Printing Office, 1960), pp. 225, 464.

2. It is interesting to note, however, that when the views of strategic theorists were channelled through projects which reflected the input of a panel of respected scientists and former military men and were presented by a prestigious political figure, they received a good deal of Congressional attention. See, in this regard, Nelson A. Rockefeller's testimony concerning the findings of his Special Studies Project, prepared under the direction of Henry Kissinger: U. S. Senate, Preparedness Investigating Subcommittee of the Committee on Armed Services, *Inquiry into Satellite and Missile Programs*, 85th Congress, 1st-2nd Sessions (Washington, D. C.: Government Printing Office, 1958), pp. 1005 ff.; U. S. House of Representatives, Committee on Appropriations, Subcommittee on Department of Defense Appropriations, *Department of Defense Appropriations for 1959*, 85th Congress, 2nd Session (Washington, Government Printing Office, 1958), pp. 44 ff.

## The Popularizers II

3. Quoted in Walter LaFeber, *America, Russia, and the Cold War, 1945-1966* (New York: John Wiley and Sons, Inc., 1967), p. 183.

4. See, for example, the discussion by Raymond Aron, *The Great Debate: Theories of Nuclear Deterrence*, translated by Ernst Panel (Garden City: Doubleday & Company, Inc., 1965), chapter 3.

5. The primary research institutions related to defense policy during this period were: the RAND Corporation (the chief client of which was the Air Force); Johns Hopkins University's Operations Research Office (ORO), which served the Army; the Navy's Operations Evaluation Group administered by the Massachusetts Institute of Technology; the Institute for Defense Analysis, which was under contract with the Office of the Secretary of Defense and the Joint Chiefs of Staff. Numerous other private institutions (such as the Council on Foreign Relations and the Center of International Studies at Princeton University) also provided research facilities for the strategic theorists. Of all the above, though, the RAND Corporation was by far the most important and of those academicians treated in this chapter the following were, in one way or another, associated with it: Herman Kahn, Albert Wohlstetter, Henry Kissinger, Bernard Brodie, Thomas Schelling, W. W. Kaufmann, Raymond Garthoff, and Herbert Dinerstein.

6. Henry Kissinger, for example, served as a consultant to the White House and the U. S. Arms Control and Disarmament Agency; W. W. Kaufmann was an advisor to the Defense Department and the Air Force during the same period.

7. In his lucid, if biased, recollection of the "New Frontier," Arthur M. Schlesinger, Jr., relates Kennedy's long-standing advocacy of limited war doctrine in such a manner as to leave the reader with the distinct impression that the intellectual community joined the young Senator's crusade against the Eisenhower doctrine of "massive retaliation." See his *A Thousand Days: John F. Kennedy in the White House* (Boston: Houghton Mifflin Company, 1965), pp. 310-311. Actually, as we shall see in subsequent chapters, Kennedy did not emerge as a major political figure in the doctrinal controversy until just prior to the 1960 Presidential election.

8. Jack Raymond, *Power at the Pentagon* (New York: Harper & Row, Publishers, 1964), pp. 248-249; also, Aron, *op. cit.*, chapters 2 and 3.

9. Albert Wohlstetter, "The Delicate Balance of Terror," *Foreign Affairs*, vol. 37, no. 2 (January, 1959), pp. 209-234.

10. *Ibid.*, p. 209.

11. *Ibid.*, p. 215.

12. *Ibid.*, p. 219.

13. *Ibid.*, pp. 230-231. While his primary concern was with general war capabilities, Wohlstetter did not totally neglect the need for meeting lesser threats: "nothing here should suggest that deterrence is in itself an adequate strategy. The complementary requirements of a sufficient military policy . . . certainly include a more serious development of power to meet limited aggression" (p. 230). However, his paramount concern was obviously with buttressing United States strategic capabilities.

14. Bernard Brodie, *Sea Power in the Machine Age* (Princeton: Princeton University Press, 1941), especially chapters 19, 20; also, *A Layman's Guide to Naval Strategy* (Princeton: Princeton University Press, 1942), espe-

cially chapter 7. (This last work was revised and re-published in 1944 under the title, *A Guide to Naval Strategy*, in which the earlier attacks upon the role of airpower in modern warfare were somewhat muted.)

15. Bernard Brodie, "War in the Atomic Age," in Brodie, ed., *The Absolute Weapon: Atomic Power and World Order* (New York: Harcourt, Brace and Company, 1946), p. 36.

16. Bernard Brodie, "Implications for Military Policy," *ibid.*, pp. 71, 75, 76. (Emphasis in the original.)

17. *Ibid.*, p. 79.

18. See, for example, the following contributions by Brodie: *The Atomic Bomb and American Security*, Memorandum No. 18 (New Haven: Yale Institute of International Studies, 1947); *The Atomic Bomb and the Armed Services*, Public Affairs Bulletin No. 55 (Washington, D.C.: Government Printing Office, 1947); "Navy Department Thinking on the Atomic Bomb," *Bulletin of the Atomic Scientists*, vol. 3 (July, 1947), pp. 177 ff.; "War Department Thinking on the Atomic Bomb," *ibid.*, (June, 1947), pp. 150-155; "Strategic Bombing: What it Can Do," *The Reporter*, vol. 3 (15 August 1950), pp. 23-31; "Some Notes on the Evolution of Air Doctrine," *World Politics*, vol. 7, no. 3 (April, 1955), pp. 349-370.

19. Bernard Brodie, "More About Limited War," *World Politics*, vol. 10, no. 1 (October, 1957), p. 121; also, "Strategy Hits a Dead End," *Harper Magazine* (October, 1955), pp. 32 ff.; "Unlimited Weapons and Limited War," *The Reporter*, vol. 2 (18 November 1954), pp. 16 ff.; "The Anatomy of Deterrence," *World Politics*, vol. 11, no. 2 (January, 1959), pp. 173-191.

20. Before joining the RAND Corporation, Brodie had been: Professor of International Relations at Yale University; a member of the original faculty at the National War College in 1946 and later a member of its advisory board; lecturer and consultant at the Air, Army, and Naval War Colleges.

21. Bernard Brodie, *Strategy in the Missile Age* (Princeton: Princeton University Press, 1959).

22. *Ibid.*, p. 255.

23. *Ibid.*, pp. 205, 255, 282.

24. *Ibid.*, chapter 10. It is interesting to note that prior to the 1960's, most economists agreed with Brodie's assessment and saw high military spending as beneficial to the expansion of the American economy (contrary to Eisenhower's view). Only with the war in Vietnam was this accepted position questioned, as concern with the question of resource allocation (i.e., national priorities) replaced the preoccupation with growth per se. See James L. Clayton, ed., *The Economic Impact of the Cold War* (New York: Harcourt, Brace and World, Inc., 1970), especially the editor's introduction.

25. Herman Kahn, *On Thermonuclear War* (Princeton: Princeton University Press, 1960); also, by the same author, *Thinking About the Unthinkable* (New York: Horizon Books, 1962), and *On Escalation: Metaphors and Scenarios* (New York: Frederick A. Praeger, Publishers, 1965).

26. *On Thermonuclear War*, p. 10 (Emphasis in the original.)

27. *Ibid.*, p. 22. (Kahn placed this entire passage in italics.)

28. *Ibid.*, pp. 77, 81.

29. *Ibid.*, p. 24.

30. *Ibid.*, p. 195. (In the original, the entire passage is italicized.)

## The Popularizers II

31. *Ibid.*, p. 201.

32. His program called for: (1) an increased ground alert for SAC bombers; (2) a "crash hardening program" for planes as well as missiles; (3) an "emergency dispersal program" for bases; (4) a "full airborne alert" for strategic bombers; (5) an increase in the number of first-generation Titan, Atlas, and Polaris missiles to be deployed; (6) the repair of any "holes" in our air defenses; and, (7) "at least moderately effective" civilian defense programs. (*Ibid.*, pp. 204-205.)

33. See, for example; John P. Roche, "Can a Free Society Fight a Limited War?" *The New Leader*, 21 October 1968, pp. 6-11; Arthur M. Schlesinger, Jr., *Kennedy or Nixon: Does It Make Any Difference?* (New York: The Macmillan Company, 1960); Roger Hilsman, *To Move a Nation: The Politics of Foreign Policy in the Administration of John F. Kennedy* (Garden City: Doubleday & Company, 1967), pp. 149-150. As Hilsman put the issue:

> The real issue is whether there is to be an accommodation, however painfully and slowly arrived at, between the Communist and especially the Chinese Communist world or a final showdown in which only one emerges dominant.
>
> A final showdown would present a test of will and require a grim determination in picking the time and the place. An accomodation would take equally steady nerves and require a willingness to make the sacrifices and live with frustrations of a limited use of force and political compromise. But the point is that the Korean War, Dienbienphu, the two Laos crises, and Vietnam are only the opening guns of what might well be a century-long struggle in Asia. . . .

34. Oskar Morgenstern, *The Question of National Defense* (New York: Random House, 1959), pp. 143-144.

35. William W. Kaufmann, "Limited Warfare," in Kaufmann, ed., *Military Policy and National Security* (Princeton: Princeton University Press, 1956), p. 136; also, *The Requirements of Deterrence*, Memorandum No. 7 (Princeton: Center of International Studies, 1954), and "The Crisis in Military Affairs," *World Politics*, vol. 10, no. 4 (July, 1958), pp. 579-603.

36. William W. Kaufmann, "Force and Diplomacy," in Kaufmann, ed., *Military Policy and National Security*, p. 237.

37. William W. Kaufmann, "The Requirements of Deterrence," *ibid.*, p. 29. See also, James E. King, Jr., "Nuclear Plenty and Limited War," *Foreign Affairs*, vol. 35, no. 2 (January, 1957), pp. 238-256.

38. Raymond L. Garthoff, *Soviet Military Doctrine* (Glencoe, Illinois: The Free Press, 1953), pp. 9 and 72. See also, Herbert S. Dinerstein, *War and the Soviet Union: Nuclear Weapons and the Revolution in Soviet Military and Political Thinking* (New York: Frederick A. Praeger, Publishers, 1958), p. 206.

39. Raymond L. Garthoff, *Soviet Strategy in the Nuclear Age* (New York: Frederick A. Praeger, Publishers, 1958), pp. xii, 98, 103.

40. *Ibid.*, p. 187 (emphasis in the original.) Also, see Garthoff's *The Soviet Image of Future War* (Washington, D. C.: Public Affairs Press, 1959). It is interesting to note in passing that the introduction to this volume was by former General James M. Gavin.

197

# American Defense Policy

41. Robert E. Osgood, *Ideals and Self-Interest in America's Foreign Relations: The Great Transformation of the 20th Century* (Chicago: University of Chicago Press, 1953); "The Uses of Power in the Cold War," in Robert A. Goldwin, ed., *America Armed: Essays on United States Military Policy* (Chicago: Rand-McNally & Company, 1963), pp. 1-21; with Robert W. Tucker, *Force, Order and Justice* (Baltimore: The Johns Hopkins Press, 1967), especially chapter 1.

42. Robert E. Osgood, *Limited War: The Challenge to American Security* (Chicago: University of Chicago Press, 1957), p. 26.

43. *Ibid.*, p. 7.

44. *Ibid.*, pp. 98-99.

45. Henry A. Kissinger, *Nuclear Weapons and Foreign Policy* (New York: Harper & Brothers, Publishers, 1957). This volume grew out of the discussions of a group assembled under the auspices of the Council on Foreign Relations; prominent members of the panel included such limited war advocates as Hanson W. Baldwin, James M. Gavin, Paul H. Nitze and two men who would be influential in the high circles of the Kennedy administration—McGeorge Bundy and Roswell L. Gilpatric.

46. Henry A. Kissinger, *A World Restored: Europe After Napoleon* (Boston: Houghton Mifflin Company, 1957).

47. *Ibid.*, especially chapters 1-3; *Nuclear Weapons and Foreign Policy*, chapter 10.

48. *Nuclear Weapons and Foreign Policy*, pp. 269-270.

49. *Ibid.*, pp. 133-134.

50. *Ibid.*, pp. 192-4. See also Henry A. Kissinger, "Military Policy and Defense of the 'Grey Areas,'" *Foreign Affairs*, vol. 33, no. 3 (April, 1955), pp. 416-428; "Force and Diplomacy in the Nuclear Age," *ibid.*, vol. 34, no. 3 (April, 1956), pp. 349-366; "Reflections on American Diplomacy," *ibid.*, vol. 35, no. 1 (October, 1956), pp. 37-56; "Strategy and Organization," *ibid.*, vol. 35, no. 3 (April, 1957), pp. 378-394; "Missiles and the Western Alliance," *ibid.*, vol. 36, no. 3 (April, 1958), pp. 383-400; "Nuclear Testing and the Problem of Peace," *ibid.*, vol. 37, no. 1 (October, 1958), pp. 1-18; "The Search for Stability," *ibid.*, vol. 37, no. 4 (July, 1959), pp. 537-560.

51. *Nuclear Weapons and Foreign Policy*, pp. 60, 92, 95, 123, 132-133.

52. Rockefeller Brothers Fund, *Prospects for America: The Rockefeller Panel Reports*, Report II: "International Security: The Military Aspect" (Garden City: Doubleday & Company, 1961), pp. 93-155.

53. *Ibid.*, p. 146.

54. *Ibid.*, pp. 107, 110, 111, 150, 138-139.

55. *Ibid.*, pp. 128, 113, 101. Highly critical of the Eisenhower budgetary ceilings, the report called for substantially increased defense expenditures; indeed, not including foreign aid and the civil defense program proposed, it was estimated that effective security "will require *successive* additions on the order of $3 billion each year for the next several fiscal years" (p. 152, emphasis added).

56. Henry A. Kissinger, *The Necessity for Choice: Prospects of American Foreign Policy* (New York: Harper & Row, Publishers, 1960). This work grew out of the deliberations of several groups which included both academicians and future members of the Kennedy administration—e.g., Thomas

# The Popularizers II

Schelling, Albert Wohlstetter, Klaus Knorr, Jerome Weisner, Arthur Schlesinger, Jr., Dean Rusk, Townshend Hoopes, William C. Foster, H. Rowan Gaither.

57. *Ibid.*, p. 1.
58. *Ibid.*, pp. 6, 36, 37.
59. Other academicians who synthesized the two views during this period include: Gordon B. Turner and Richard D. Challener, eds., *National Security in the Missile Age: Basic Facts and Theories* (New York: Frederick A. Praeger, Publishers, 1960); and, Glenn H. Snyder, "Balance of Power in the Missile Age," *Journal of International Affairs*, vol. 14, no. 1 (1960), pp. 31-34; also, by Snyder, *Deterrence and Defense: Toward a Theory of National Security* (Princeton: Princeton University Press, 1961). See, also, by Kissinger, "Limited War: Conventional or Nuclear? A Reappraisal," in Donald G. Brennan, ed., *Arms Control, Disarmament and National Security* (New York: George Braziller, 1961), pp. 138-152.

# 7

## THE CAPITALIZERS I: CONGRESSIONAL POLITICS

### I

THUS FAR IN OUR STUDY OF THE DOMESTIC FORCES which precipitated the shift in United States security policy from the Eisenhower-Dulles to the Kennedy-McNamara doctrines, we have focused upon those actors (the innovators) who initiated the strategic controversy and those (the popularizers) who disseminated these dissenting views and afforded them with intellectual justification. To be sure, by the end of the 1950's an alternative set of legitimate defense policies had been vigorously propagated, but this is not to say that future American decision-makers were therefore irrevocably committed to a rejection of the policies of the Republican interregnum. Quite the contrary, for so long as Dwight Eisenhower (or a successor committed to the same strategy) remained at the helm of government, the long pull would remain the official approach of the American polity to national security. When we speak of the capitalizers, then, we are identifying the role of those elements in the political system which ultimately presided over the transformation of these incipient options into the new orthodoxy of the state; therefore, the designation is used more in the neutral corporate or financial sense of the term (that is, the conversion of a floating debt into stock or shares) than as a judgment of the motivations of those actors involved (that is, the notion that certain parties took personal political advantage of the situation).

In gauging the influence of the Congress, we should naturally begin with the appropriations process. Given the legislative branch's coveted "power of the purse strings," "the defense budget represents the only consistent, regular, and systematic point of contact between Congress and the substantive issues of defense."[1] However, even before the recent atrophy in Congressional prerogative accentuated by the Southeast Asian conflict, scholars concerned with executive-legislative behavior had reached the conclusion that the Congress did not adequately come to terms with, nor ever seriously debate, national defense policy.[2] An important recent study, however, calls into question these previous assumptions. After a careful analysis of Congressional changes in administration military budget requests from FY 1960 through FY 1970, Arnold Kanter notes that while the dollar magnitudes of legislative modifications have not been large,

> the distribution of Congress's changes in the President's defense budget is consistent with the hypothesis that Congress has a programmatic as well as a fiscal orientation toward defense spending; that is, Congressional judgments regarding specific defense programs and their relation to national security rather than an exclusive concern with reducing spending and eliminating waste, explain Congress's scrutiny of the defense budget.[3]

Thus, Kanter maintains that Congressional influence over defense policy has been focused on certain areas of the budget (research and development, weapons systems procurement) which reflect the fact that the legislative branch does indeed seek shifts in appropriations to mirror its own conception of the needs of national security. Specifically, in regard to the period under investigation in this study, both chambers utilized the budgetary process to modify administration policy in both conventional and strategic weapons development, thus anticipating by no less than two years the official policy changes of President Kennedy. In 1959, for example, the House Appropriations Committee rejected the Eisenhower administration's policy toward limited war capabilities and increased the President's request for Army procurement by a full 20 per cent; by the following year, the House created a new budget line, "Airlift Modernization," and appropriated more than three hundred million dollars to increase the mobility of conventional war forces. Similarly, during the same years, the Senate Appropriations Committee, alarmed by the prospect of a missile gap, provided more funds for the new B-70 bomber than Eisenhower thought prudent.[4]

Yet the nature of the separation of powers in American government ultimately assures that even a Congress dominated by the opposition party can only push the President within severely confined limits—especially when Capitol Hill undertakes positive action on its own rather than merely placing checks upon the Chief Executive's actions.[5] For while the Congress may covet its Constitutional role to raise and dispense revenues to provide for the common defense, the President (and especially an esteemed military man) covets no less his Constitutional roles as Commander in Chief and coordinator of the nation's foreign relations. Indeed, Eisenhower's conception of the separation of powers doctrine led him not only to shun a dominant role in overseeing the affairs of the legislative branch, but at the same time to jealously guard executive prerogatives in the field of foreign and defense policy.[6] Moreover, he viewed the Congress as a whole (and especially the Senate) as a consistent pressure group for higher defense spending during the post-Sputnik years; in June of 1958 he would declare in exasperation at a Republican legislative meeting at the White House: "Congress seems to be going on the theory that we have to have all of everything everywhere all the time. . . . [N]ow everybody on the hill is being an expert."[7] Thus, the President could largely contain Congressional attempts to legislate defense policy by means of the appropriations process by simply impounding funds.[8]

But what President Eisenhower could not contain was the gradual shift in opinion throughout the Congress as well as the country as a whole regarding desirable and possible alternative defense measures. The influence of the Congress during the appropriations process cannot be inferred solely from the highly visible committee hearings and recommendations and floor votes—which, after all, the Chief Executive can circumvent—for of far more consequence, as Warner Schilling notes, is "the influence Congressmen exercise by virtue of their contribution to the general climate of opinion . . . [which] heavily conditions Executive and Congressional choices alike." Thus, it is "today's hearing which contributes to tomorrow's climate of opinion":

> a committee intent on influencing the high policy of the budget could undertake a serious review of the alternatives involved, not in the expectation that there would be any opportunity thereby to effect major changes in that budget, but in the knowledge that the effort would make possible some change in the control over opinions which would otherwise prevail at the time of the determination of the next budget and the ones thereafter.[9]

At several junctures in this study we have discussed the interaction between the Congress and both the innovators and the popularizers. Having approached the legislative capitalizers from these varying perspectives, we can now consider them in their own right. In this chapter, we will attempt to do the following: (1) note the general role of the Congress as a whole (and the Senate in particular) as a lobbyist for higher defense spending during the last Eisenhower years; (2) differentiate between the role perceptions and functions of the Senate and House Appropriations Committees on the one hand, and the divergence of views between the armed services and appropriations subcommittees within each chamber; (3) trace the intensification of partisanship within both legislative houses from the Sputnik launching of 1957 to the 1960 Presidential election campaigns; and, (4) consider the relationship between defense policy and the Presidential aspirations of two of the leading Eisenhower critics, Lyndon B. Johnson and Stuart S. Symington.

## II

In his definitive study of the self-defined roles of the Senate and House in the domestic appropriations process, Richard F. Fenno suggested that there was a significant divergence in the approaches of the two chambers; that is, while the House Appropriations Committee viewed itself primarily as the guardian of the national treasury, its counterpart in the upper house perceived its function predominantly as appellate in nature.[10] In his earlier attempt to study the House Appropriations Committee as a discrete unit of analysis, he maintained that the self-image of committee members as the protectors of public funds was so pervasive that there had developed the consensus that budget requests submitted by the executive should, on sheer principle, be reduced.[11] Yet while Fenno readily admitted that there was an important deference to specialization and minimal interference in subcommittee affairs, his emphasis on the problems of self-integration within the full Appropriations Committee may have led him to overlook significant variations among the several subcommittees. Indeed, an analysis of the behavior of the House and Senate defense appropriations subcommittees during the post-Sputnik period would seem to indicate that the differences in self-perception were ones of degree rather than kind, and that perhaps the two units concerned with military spending had as much in common with one another as they did with other appropriations subcommittees in their respective houses.

In the first series of hearings on the post-Sputnik budget for FY 1959, the Senate defense appropriations subcommittee reviewed the House version of the President's budget—a bill which was nearly a quarter of a billion dollars *more* than the Commander in Chief had requested. In his opening statement in June of 1958, chairman Dennis Chavez of New Mexico defined his committee's role neither in terms of economy nor even appropriations, but rather "to provide the American public with a full knowledge of the efforts the Congress and the Department of Defense are making to provide for our security and to keep America strong."[12] Similarly, the following year (quite significantly, perhaps, at an opening ceremony of the committee in which he accepted the four service flags from the Joint Chiefs of Staff), Chavez emphatically defined as the budgetary unit's first responsibility the provision of funds "to keep America strong." "In the years of international tension as we face today," he declared, "our security and our freedom itself may well depend on our military might. We of this committee intend to do all we can to provide the strength necessary to keep America free." Noting both the fact that economy in defense was of secondary importance and that events of the previous year had indicated that "the forces of oppression and aggression are ever on the march, seeking the weak links in our defense armor," he implicitly levelled an attack upon the Eisenhower policy of the long pull by warning that "we must not permit the continuing nature of this danger to dull our vigilance."[13] Moreover, at the same hearings, he suggested to Army Chief of Staff Lemnitzer that "I prefer your judgment over that of civilian personnel in the Pentagon," and criticized the Eisenhower administration for allowing budgetary considerations to take precedence over the needs of security.[14] In much the same manner for the remainder of the Republican era, Chavez consistently defined his committee's role in terms of providing adequate funding for the military services despite the administration's economy-mindedness. To the Chairman of the Joint Chiefs of Staff he would state his subcommittee's desire for a margin of safety and then ask General Twining to "tell us what you want" and the committee would not begrudge "one dime if it is necessary for our national security."[15]

If the chairman of the Senate Appropriations Committee's subcommittee on defense spending viewed his role largely in terms of protecting the country's security from being shortchanged by the administration, Chavez's counterpart in the House displayed much the same attitude. Heading the first unit of either house to investigate the state of American defenses in the wake of the Sputnik launching, George Mahon of Texas believed that the United States was witnessing "the most critical moment in several decades" and consistently took issue with the White House over the state of and needs for an acceptable security posture.[16] Two months later, having inserted large sections of the Rockefeller Fund report into his committee's record and having called upon Nelson Rockefeller himself to testify, he in effect treated the findings of this private group as a legitimate alternative defense budget, stating that he was "concerned as to whether or not this Committee on this bill should stay within the $40 billion program of the President for new obligational authority for 1959, or should we go above it and provide the $3 billion increase" urged by the report.[17] During the following year's battle of the budget, Mahon explicitly rejected the desirability of strategic parity between the United States and the Soviet Union and declared it the task of his subcommittee to discover how much money would be necessary to allow this country to keep abreast of the Soviets in ICBMs for the next several years. At the same time he charged Defense Secretary McElroy with tailoring intelligence estimates to fit the administration's conservative budget and severely took the executive branch to task for resigning itself to quantitative missile inferiority vis-a-vis the Russians. In regard to limited war capabilities, the chairman placed in his committee's record a lengthy speech by Maxwell Taylor dissenting from the President's policy and demanded an explanation of the executive branch's refusal to spend appropriated funds for the Army.[18] Displaying a consistently pro-defense attitude during the Presidential election year 1960, Mahon continued his anti-administration stance by charging that the Eisenhower administration was, by its policy of ignoring the prospect of a missile gap, dropping the United States' guard in its struggle with Communist Russia.[19]

Thus, during the last Eisenhower years there appears to have been little differentiation between the self-perceived roles of the Senate and House subcommittees; however, this might have been an aberration due to the general apprehension over the state of America's defenses caused by Sputnik and the resulting missile gap/limited war controversy. Given the limited time frame of this particular study, we would not be justified in claiming that the consonance in behavior displayed by the two legislative agencies during these years was necessarily indicative of general role patterns which transcended the crisis-like atmosphere surrounding the budgetary hearings treated in this chapter.[20]

If the defense appropriations subcommittees of both houses displayed a notable congruence of views regarding the primacy of increased defense spending over the administration's desires for fiscal restraint, the two armed services committees were even more outspoken. For while the appropriations committees, given their distinct perspective, were compelled to give at least passing lip-service to the traditional dictum that maximum security must be purchased at minimum cost,[21] those units of both chambers whose sole concern was with military preparedness lacked virtually any incentive to consider the economic and budgetary repercussions of their findings. As succinctly put by chairman Carl Vinson, the task of his House Armed Services Committee was simply to find the answer to one relevant question: "where do we stand in military power against Russia?" Moreover, as a chief guardian of the interests of the military services, the House committee viewed itself as largely responsible for preventing manpower and material cuts in the Army and Navy; declaring that his committee represented thirty-seven men "deeply concerned about the way the Army has been pushed about," he attacked the administration's policy of progressively diminishing the size of limited war forces and vowed that "we are going to make a fight to restore it."[22] The Senate Armed Services Committee (and especially its Preparedness Investigating Subcommittee) displayed a similarly monistic view of legislative policy. With his constant references to the Japanese attack upon the Hawaiian Islands in 1941, subcommittee chairman Lyndon Johnson defined the role of his group strictly in terms of maintaining superior military power in relation to the Soviet Union; indeed, at the height of the missile gap debate in 1960 he declared that the protection of United States retaliatory forces was "the Number One order of this Congress."[23]

## III

A careful analysis of the behavior of the rank-and-file members of the relevant Congressional committees concerned with military policy during this period indicates that the chief factor which accounted for patterns of behavior was party loyalty. Much as James Rosenau discovered in regard to the attitudes of individual Senators toward Secretary of State Dulles,[24] we find in our study that the position which legislators took regarding the issue of national defense was more a function of party identification than it was the product of personal preferences or self-perceived committee roles; that is, national security was a partisan issue. However, this point must be qualified in two ways. Firstly, one can discern two distinct legislative types: the partisans (for whom party loyalty took precedence over doctrinal preferences) and the dogmatists (those who maintained a remarkable consistency of opinion on behalf of a doctrinal cause). Secondly, though partisanship was by far the chief determinant of attitude on the defense issue, its intensity and importance varied in direct proportion to the proximity of the 1960 Presidential election; that is, the nearer one moves toward the great party clash for control of the White House, the more pronounced partisanship becomes.

Perhaps the easiest way of identifying the true dogmatist is to find a legislator who not only consistently adhered to a defense policy line, but did so in a way which conflicted with the dominant trend within his party. By such standards, Representative Jaimie L. Whitten (Democrat of Mississippi) in the House and Allen J. Ellender (Democrat of Louisiana) in the Senate readily qualify as "pro-economy" dogmatists.[25] Those who cannot be said to have bucked the "party-line" on the defense issue are ostensibly more difficult to identify; however, those who tenaciously held to a position of increased military spending before Sputnik—during the lean years when it was not yet in vogue to do so—as well as after, can justifiably be labelled "pro-defense" dogmatists. Legislators who may be placed in this category include Representative Daniel Flood (Democrat of Pennsylvania) and Senators Stuart Symington (Democrat of Missouri) and Henry M. Jackson (Democrat of Washington).

The lines between the two opposite dogmatists were drawn in the House defense appropriations subcommittee even before the tensions between economy and security became a (one is almost tempted to say *the*) national issue. In their deliberations on the Eisenhower budget for FY 1958, Whitten and Flood took up diametrically opposed positions—positions they would consistently occupy for the duration of the Republican interlude. Early in

1957, Flood was focusing on the Soviet strategic bomber and missile threat, citing the findings of the Symington "bomber gap" hearings of the year before and the Alsops in the press, while his colleague was preoccupied with fears that the American economy
was becoming irrevocably dependent on military procurement
contracts.[26] In the immediate aftermath of the Russian propaganda
coup later that year, Flood even more forcefully embraced a program of both strategic and conventional build-up, though his true
passion was for a limited war capability; indeed, he termed himself a "very noisy mouthpiece on limited war . . . for years. . . .
That is my baby." Attacking administration policy as well as its
personalities (for example, he deridingly referred to newly in-
stigated by the Kremlin; in his own inimitable style, he declared
"glorified bookkeeper"), he warned that in 1960 or 1961 the
United States would need a large, mobile, and versatile Army to
fight simultaneously numerous limited wars which would be in-
stigated by the Kremlin; in his own inimical style, he declared
that "anybody who thinks these 'Russkies' are dopes is crazy."[27]
Meanwhile, Whitten advised the Chairman of the Joint Chiefs of
Staff that,

> in spite of the fact that we would like to give everything to you
> and the Joint Chiefs of Staff and, under you, to the Army, Navy,
> and Air Force, so each of them could get everything which as
> military men they like to have, all of you are aware of the fact
> that spending must be consistent with maintaining a strong
> economy so that we can keep our country going rather than
> build it up and then bust it.

Pointing to "vested interests" in industry, the Pentagon, and the
Congress which pushed for excessive spending on the military,
he directed strong criticism toward committee witness Nelson
Rockefeller who was pressing for his alternative defense budget:

> I make this point which is so tragic in my opinion. Your report,
> as fine as it is as to where we need to give emphasis, admittedly
> without any study of the waste in the departments now in pro-
> curement, in contracting, in procedures, has seen fit to sell the

people on $3 billion more spending when you agree that you do not know and could not say how they are handling the money they now have. I think it is very serious.[28]

Both Whitten and Flood were so faithful to their respective opposing causes that even when the new Democratic administration took office they continued in much the same vein. Reviewing the first Kennedy budget (one which doubled the size of the counter-insurgency forces and produced a significant increase in airlift capacity), Flood complained in frustration to Secretary McNamara that "you have not scratched the surface of what must . . . be done in the budget for Army mobility and modernization," and reminded him that, "I have been manning the barricades about limited war around here since the memory of man runneth not to the contrary, getting nowhere rapidly." Critical of the notion held by his colleague Whitten that the country could not afford (both economically and socially) greatly increased defense expenditures, he retorted simply: "I would rather have red ink in the books than red blood on the streets of America."[29] Whitten, true to form, lamented that military spending was "almost a 100 per cent drain on the economy," but yet the new administration was building a false prosperity based upon the use of defense spending as "some kind of a pump-priming operation." Finally, he reiterated his counsel of the past years to the Democrats in power:

the big problem you are going to have is that we have . . . got ourselves all tied into this military complex; if we were to have peace with Russia for 5 or 6 years, we would have a terrific adjustment because so much of our . . . economy is tied to this military spending.[30]

Whitten's counterpart in the Senate was (with a slightly different emphasis) another loyal son of the old Confederacy—Ellender of Louisiana. As early as 1958, he warned his colleagues on the defense appropriations subcommittee that the United States had already "spread ourselves too thin" with its extensive global commitments, and that he could not reasonably conceive of the country planning to put out brush-fires without the assistance of the United Nations; that is, it was inconceivable to him that the American people be chosen to "carry the whole burden" in men and money of defending the whole world.[31] He later reminded his fellow committee members that America's allies—those who were supposed to be the targets of aggression, especially in Europe—were not shouldering a fair share of the defense burden. Not only was he apprehensive about the prospect of an over-extended American commitment abroad, but Ellender was also critical of the huge monetary requests of the Pentagon. Pointing out that the Navy alone had wanted 50 per cent more than the President's budget for FY 1961 provided, he declared that: "It just shows the extent to which the armed services proceed to get the Congress and the President to give them the maximum amount. I am wondering where this will take us."[32] But, for the most part, the pro-economy dogmatists (unlike their pro-defense foes) were voices crying in the wilderness during these years. Indeed, between those who embraced the program of a military build-up out of long-held conviction and those who did so out of party responsibility, Ellender was to remain a virtual one-man minority on the Committee and, at times, the Senate's Ralph Nader; for example, in considering the Pentagon budget for fiscal 1960, he raised what was for all intents and purposes the biggest economy measure considered by the committee—namely, the fact that high ranking men in uniform had used rented cars without the Senate's knowledge![33] In a much more serious vein, though, he was also the only member of the committee during the first appearance of Secretary McNamara to actually question the underlying assumptions of the new strategy of flexible response, arguing that a unilateral American commitment to defend the free world could lead only to economic ruin.[34]

If Ellender represented the quintessential pro-economy dogmatist in the Senate, then surely his colleague who most epitomized the opposite pole was Stuart Symington. Former Defense Secretary Clark Clifford (a long-time and intimate friend of Symington) once remarked of the former Secretary of the Air Force that "if he makes a decision after thinking the matter out, he goes to the very bitter end for it."[35] I can think of nothing which more aptly describes the long crusade of the Senator from Missouri.[36] Because we have discussed his views at length in previous chapters there is no need to re-state them here; however, a few words on his pre-Sputnik behavior should highlight the tenacity which is distinctly that of the dogmatist. Ever since taking office as the country's first Air Force Secretary in 1947, Symington was a force for greater investment in military hardware—arguing with Defense Secretary James Forrestal over the efficacy of airpower, warning of the growing Soviet military threat, fighting incessantly for a significant American build-up and getting deeply involved in the B-36 superbomber showdown with the Navy. Upon being elected to the Senate in 1952, he immediately charged that the new administration was allowing both a bomber- and missile-gap to develop.[37] By February of 1956, Symington's insistence had persuaded the Senate Armed Services Committee chairman, the late Richard B. Russell, to appoint a Subcommittee on the Air Force with Symington as chairman. With the espoused goal of "awaken[ing] the country to what the situation is,"[38] he and his collaborator Henry M. Jackson began a three-month series of highly publicized investigations on American defense posture, which resulted in an extremely pessimistic report and a nearly one billion dollar increase in the defense budget.[39] Thus, Symington's strongly pro-defense behavior during the late 1950's was merely the continuation of a long crusade.

In opposition to the unswerving doctrinal devotion of the dogmatist, one finds the loyal partisan—a legislator who approaches the defense debate with the structured outlook afforded by party allegiance. For this actor the nuances of the security landscape are so complex, and the facts so contradictory and confusing, that he feels safe and comfortable in falling back upon the interpretation of reality which is standardized by the norms of behavior fostered on his particular side of the aisle. Though we will deal at some length with the issue of partisanship in the next section, a brief example at this point will be enlightening. While their seniors on the defense appropriations subcommittee of the House Committee on Appropriations, Whitten and Flood, were locking horns in a doctrinal contest which would allow no quarter, Republicans Melvin Laird of Wisconsin (later to be Secretary of Defense under the next Republican President) and Gerald Ford of Michigan were staunchly supporting the administration line. Notice, for example, in comparing the following two passages, how Ford attempted to take the sting out of Flood's attack on the administration:

Mr. FLOOD. . . . We thought we gave you nine [Polaris submarines]. You did not get them. I heard the Director of the Bureau of the Budget say last week—and my mustache nearly dropped off on the floor—he said, 'I think that the national defense budget is adequate.' He thinks. Some glorified bookkeeper down there. We are going to give him a half dozen more stripes you know. We are talking about that, Admiral. The Director of the Bureau of the Budget is going to get three or four more of these stars up here. He thinks everything is all right. That's great.

    You did not get any part of the six [submarines] you asked for?

[Navy] Secretary GATES. In the supplemental budget request we made, we did not; that is correct.

Mr. FLOOD. Of course, you emphasize all through your testimony the manning levels of the operating fleet have never been this low before in percent; is that correct?

Admiral BURKE. Yes, sir.

Mr. FLOOD. 'Austere' and 'minimum.' That is great. Of course, we are all right. We never have been in this shape before, but we are all right.

      . . .

Mr. FORD. In the last month or so we have had a considerable amount of discussion, debate, many statements in the press and elsewhere about the adequacy of our deterrent and retaliatory power. . . . As Chief of Naval Operations . . . , as a member of the Joint Chiefs of Staff, are you convinced that at the present time our combined retaliatory forces are sufficient, with ample liberal safety factors, to hit and destroy all Soviet military targets?

Admiral BURKE. Yes, sir.

Mr. FORD. There is no question on your mind about that?
Admiral BURKE. . . . All the significant military targets, yes.
Mr. FORD. All the significant military targets in your judgment are amply covered by our existing forces today?
Admiral BURKE. Yes, sir.
Mr. FORD. And by those that are included within this budget?
Admiral BURKE. Yes, sir.[40]

## IV

The importance and intensity of partisanship as the organizing principle of the defense controversy in the Congress was rather muted in the immediate post-Sputnik period, but progressively increased with the approach of the 1960 Presidential election campaign. There can be little doubt that such events as the Soviet satellite launching and the virtually simultaneous publication of the contents of the Gaither and Rockefeller reports produced a genuine general concern with and confusion over the adequacy of United States defenses in the national legislature. Soon after the shock of the Soviet Sputnik, members of both parties called for Congressional investigation. In the Senate, there was overwhelming demand from both sides of the aisle for an immediate convening of the Armed Services Committee. On the Democratic side, Senators Symington, Johnson, majority whip Mike Mansfield, Sam Ervin, Estes Kefauver and George Smathers led the call upon Richard Russell for an emergency meeting of the committee; they were joined in their outcry by Minority Leader William F. Knowland, the two ranking Republicans on the Armed Services Committee (Styles Bridges and Leverett Saltonstall), Jacob Javits and Clifford Case.[41] As an omen of things to come, Case was the first major Republican legislator to openly criticize the administration. Originally a staunch supporter of Eisenhower budgetary policy, he now charged that such "dollar pinching" in defense had been "shortsighted" and "a dangerous gamble." Speaking for others in the Congress, he declared: "I have no doubt that . . . many of those who were most vocal, in demanding cuts, even in the defense budget, will be clamoring for far greater expenditures this coming year."[42]

As the House Armed Services took up the matter at the beginning of the new session of the Congress, Carl Vinson no less than ranking Republican Leslie Arends expressed concern over the state of military preparedness.[43] Questioning administration witnesses, committee members seemed generally perplexed and inquisitive rather than blatantly critical. F. Edward Hebert, ranking Democrat, nicely summed up the utter confusion of committee members as they were bombarded with conflicting views. To the Pentagon's civilian director of guided missiles who had just finished reassuring his listeners as to the propriety of current programs, he remarked: "As a matter of fact, less than an hour ago I was talking to a man who helped develop the [Army's] Jupiter C [IRBM] and he said had it not been for restrictions placed on him he would have had a Jupiter C that would have gone far further than 3000 miles. Now he may have been talking, I don't know. But you get so many of these propositions."[44] Yet though partisanship was muted during this period of initial disequilibrium, it was not altogether lacking, and a listener's propensity to believe the administration or its critics was closely related to party identification.[45]

If we return to the upper house, we can vividly trace the progressive intensification of partisanship as the trauma of Sputnik subsided. Party antagonisms were least evident during the Johnson Subcommittee hearings of late 1957 to early 1958. Finding themselves confronted with a well-orchestrated barrage of criticism from prestigious military men, scientists, and educators, the Republicans themselves apparently found the administration's reassurances a bit hard to accept. At the height of the subcommittee's deliberations, when the presentation of the Rockefeller report indicated that a sweeping revision of policy was in order, the disoriented Republicans (unlike the dogmatist Whitten in the House) could come up with no criticism of consequence either regarding the report's underlying premises or ramifications if adopted.[46] Indeed, the conclusions reached by the committee (which were generally quite critical of the President's policy) were unanimously accepted by the Republican members.

The following year's hearings before the Johnson committee,

however, witnessed a resurgence of party divisions, though still the minority members displayed a cautious ambivalence. That partisanship was now more pronounced is evidenced by the clash between the Democratic chairman and Republican Francis Case of South Dakota. When the latter sought to defend the incumbent President by placing the blame for an inadequate missile program on Harry Truman (a Democrat, naturally), Johnson abruptly injected: "I have no objection if he wants to go back as far as McKinley, as far as I'm concerned. This administration has had six years to do something about it and that is what we are trying to find out, what they have done about it."[47] Yet the clash of parties within the committee was still restricted at this point inasmuch as prestigious minority member Saltonstall was more concerned with the reservations which the military chieftains had regarding the President's budget than with defending administration decisions.[48]

If partisanship was muted (if not absent) in 1957-1958, growing but still ambivalent in 1959, it reached a climax with the opening of the Presidential election year 1960. And the Johnson committee investigations would break down with the constant thrusts and parries normally more indicative of a meeting of the United Nations Security Council than a Senate hearing. In the questioning of General Power (whose charges of a deterrent gap on the eve of a national election, it will be recalled, had severely undermined the reputation of the administration), the lines of inquiry were rigidly drawn between the two sides, and as one studies the fluctuations and oscillation of questioning back and forth between the two political parties (with the military man in the middle) one gets the distinct impression that one is following a sort of Congressional tennis match: Saltonstall (Republican) begins by demonstrating the General's parochialism; Stennis (Democrat) attempts to get Power to admit that the B-70 bomber is "essential" to American security; Wiley (Republican) succeeds in getting Power to admit that there are other elements in the United States retaliatory force besides SAC's bombers; Johnson (Democrat) trying to get a blanket statement to the effect that the entire budget as framed is simply "inadequate"; Martin (Republican) jumping into the fray to make Power acknowledge that fiscal constraints are necessary in military planning; Cannon (Democrat) citing the Alsop brothers to substantiate the Air Force's claims; Bridges (Republican) pointing out the limited nature of Power's distorted assessment; Jackson (Democrat) reminding his colleagues about what happened at Pearl Harbor; Saltonstall (Republican) jumping back into the game to demonstrate the error of the analogy; Weisl (Democratic counsel) citing a NATO report about one hundred missile bases in the Soviet Union; Wiley (Republican) saving the point for his team by pointing out that the report did not say one hundred *ICBM* bases; and so on, and on.[49] And as is to be expected in such a contentious atmosphere of partisan rivalry, the confrontation of different members' views often led to prolonged and rather emotional clashes between them —where debate between committeemen replaced the interrogation of witnesses. One such verbal battle occurred between Senators Wiley and Symington—only one in a series of such encounters—and began with the former's attempt to clarify a statement on the missile ratio between the two superpowers:

Senator WILEY. Does that include all the categories of missiles?
Senator SYMINGTON. We are talking about ICBMs.
Senator WILEY. I thought you were. . . .
Senator SYMINGTON. I am glad the Senator brought that up because if we include IRBMs, the ratio goes tremendously further against us.
Senator WILEY. What I have reference to—
Senator SYMINGTON. Do you understand that? You asked a question.
Senator WILEY. I am seeking to get the truth.
Senator SYMINGTON. Do you understand that? If we put in the IRBMs, . . . then the ratio is very much more in our disfavor. . . .
Senator WILEY. . . . I want to get a complete picture so that we don't go out and scare the American people. I think that is important.
Senator SYMINGTON. . . . I don't see why he is so worried

about scaring the American people to death. I think the American people can take. . . . But on the other hand, from the standpoint of democracy, you get down to questions of whether or not the people have a right to know the truth. . . .

. . .

Senator WILEY. On the other hand, it seems to be the important question, if we meet the Russians with the same number of missiles, have we added to our strength?

What have we done? Have we precipitated a race that will put both countries into bankruptcy? . . . .

. . .

May I ask the Senator a question? Suppose we do put on a crash program and get the equivalent in ICBMs that they have. Does that create a bigger deterrent?

Senator SYMINGTON. The premise of your question is a crash program. We don't need any crash program. . . . Thank you, Mr. Chairman.

Senator WILEY. You didn't answer my question. Leave the word 'crash' out. If we put on a program that you are talking about, will that be a deterrent?

Senator SYMINGTON. My answer to that is 'Yes.' . . .

Senator WILEY. Let me say if that is true, then we must consider it. Now, of course, the President doesn't make the appropriations. We make the appropriations and we cannot make it a political issue. . . .

Senator SYMINGTON. I thank the Senator.

Senator WILEY. We should do whatever is necessary but we do not want to go ahead and do it on the theory that someone is all right and the other fellow is all wrong.

Senator SYMINGTON. For the record, I thank the Senator for what he says. I agree with him that there should be more appropriations.

Let's not put on an emotional basis what I think is strictly reason. Thank you, Mr. Chairman.[50]

## V

The intensification of Congressional division over defense policy along partisan lines with the approach of the 1960 election can probably best be explained in terms of the unique interrelationship which existed between the Democratic party's nomination and its legislative leadership. It is quite apparent that the Congressional stake in the issues of the Presidential campaign was intimately affected by the fact that the four major contenders for the majority party's nomination (Johnson, Symington, Kennedy, Humphrey) were all United States Senators. Moreover, both Johnson and Symington had based much of their public reputations on the fact that they had helped make the defense policy of the incumbent administration a major campaign issue. Thus, the clash between Senators Wiley and Symington (as representative of the whole contest in the upper house between the two parties) was not simply an example of a loyal Republican legislator coming to the defense of his party's leader; it was significantly more than this, for while defending his own party's record he was at the same time rebuking a potential standard-bearer for the opposition.

Lyndon Johnson's claim to party leadership rested not simply on his innate persuasive talents, nor even on his elected position as Majority Leader in the Senate. Much of it stemmed from the peculiarities of the American system of government which allowed for the possibility of divided government and from the temperament of a President who, strictly interpreting the separation of powers doctrine, abstained from active intervention in the affairs of the legislature. Given a free hand in the Senate, Johnson was able to stake out a claim as the head of a shadow government, first based upon his position as leader of the majority party (which also made him chairman of the Democratic Conference, the Steering Committee and the Policy Committee)[51] and, secondly, founded on his status as chairman of both the Preparedness Investigating Subcommittee of the Armed Services Committee and the Committee on Aeronautical and Space Sciences.[52] By virtue of these several positions, he was able to successfully challenge the non-Congressional Democratic Advisory Council for the leadership of the party-out-of-power, and was able even to deliver addresses which were, in effect, his own state-of-the-union messages. In a party system which fails to allow for real leadership for the out-party, a premium is placed on the sheer appearance of rightful succession to power.

By the end of 1959, the issue of national defense was foremost in the minds of Democratic strategists. In its blueprint for the party's 1960 platform, the Democratic Advisory Council issued a statement in December of 1959 which declared that, "Nothing more clearly demonstrates the need for a Democratic President in 1961 than the decline in the military security of this country since 1953." Charging that the administration was pursuing a "second-best" defense policy which would give the Soviets a 3 to 1 ICBM advantage until well into 1963 and preclude the possibility of the United States fighting limited wars, the DAC called for the repudiation of a party which "believes money to be more important than the military security of our country."[53]

Within ten days of this statement, Johnson boldly announced that if the President did not decide "now once and for all" to close the defense and space gaps with the Soviet Union, the Congress would have to act on its own to prevent the "unilateral disarmament" of the nation which was leading to Communist domination of earth and space.[54] With the new session of the Congress and the final round of his joint committee hearings, the Majority Leader initiated his severest attack yet on the Eisenhower administration. Within weeks after beginning his investigation, he denounced the downward revision in the intelligence estimates as reported by the Defense Secretary and even threatened to hold up Gates' confirmation. "I cannot avoid the impression," he said, "that someone is leaping at straws to find an excuse for not going as far and as fast as we can to assure the security of this nation and the free world."[55] Making good on his pledge that the Democratic majority would legislate its own defense policy, he was instrumental in getting through the Senate a one billion dollar increase in military spending over the President's original request and followed this up with a broadside attack on the Republican administration delivered from the Senate floor.[56] By the time Lyndon Johnson's name had been placed in nomination at the Democratic National Convention in July, he had indeed established himself as a realistic alternative to the allegedly inept and complacent Eisenhower. The image which Johnson had sought to cultivate was aptly stated by his friend and colleague House Speaker Sam Rayburn in his nominating speech:

> The Administration now in power has been given every dollar that they have asked for to make the defense of this country safe and secure. But every American citizen today is humiliated by the fact that instead of the United States of America being first, it is second in the world today. If there had been imagination, if there had been coordination in Washington in taking the sinews that we have given this Administration, the American people would not be humiliated today by being second.[57]

Stuart Symington's bid for the Democratic Presidential nomination rested on a much narrower base of support. Unlike Johnson, he lacked the prestige and reputation for legislative leadership, as well as strong sectional support. Unlike Kennedy, he lacked the resources and popular appeal—which meant, quite simply, that he could not hope to compete in the primaries, but rather would have to await a draft in case of a deadlock between the two front-runners. Virtually the only asset which the Missouri Senator possessed (in addition to the support of former President Harry Truman) was his long renown as a defense advocate—an attribute which could prove to be quite attractive in a period when national leadership was constantly equated with national security. Thus, Symington became a one-issue candidate and surpassed even Lyndon Johnson in both his proposals for increased military spending and criticism of President Eisenhower. Symington consistently called for massive new appropriations for defense, and quoted various figures ranging from three to 4.2 billion dollars.[58] Citing intelligence estimates leaked from the Air Force, he claimed that the lower figures on Soviet missile capabilities used by the administration were designed purposefully to deceive the American people in order to buttress its antiquated argument against vigorous federal spending.[59] When he finally officially announced his candidacy for the nomination in March of 1960, it came as little surprise when he called for a new "decisive leadership" committed to a "first-rate, first-class, first-place" America.[60]

The impact of such defense advocates as Symington and Johnson, then, transcended the sphere of the legislative process and projected itself onto the arena of Presidential politics. And the issue which had come to dominate the deliberations of those committees of the Congress concerned with national security policy was now to make itself felt in the election campaign of 1960. While, of course, neither the Majority Leader nor the former Air Force Secretary were to have the opportunity to carry forth their party's Presidential banner, the man who was chosen in their stead would fulfill the hopes of all those who sought to discard the Eisenhower policy of the long pull.

1. Raymond H. Dawson, "Congressional Innovation and Intervention in Defense Policy: Legislative Authorization of Weapons Systems," *American Political Science Review* vol. 56, no. 1 (March, 1962), p. 46; also, Samuel P. Huntington, *The Soldier and The State: The Theory and Politics of Civil-Military Relations* (New York: Vintage, 1957), p. 407.

2. See, for example: Dawson, *op. cit.*; Lewis Anthony Dexter, "Congressmen and the Making of Military Policy," in Robert L. Peabody and Nelson W. Polsby, eds., *New Perspectives on the House of Representatives* (Chicago: Rand McNally & Company, 1963), pp. 305-324; Aaron Wildavsky, *The Politics of the Budgetary Process* (Boston: Little, Brown and Company, 1964); Richard F. Fenno, Jr., *The Power of the Purse: Appropriations Politics in Congress* (Boston: Little, Brown and Company, 1966).

3. Arnold Kanter, "Congress and the Defense Budget: 1960-1970," *American Political Science Review*, vol. 66, no. 1 (March, 1972), p. 130. (Emphasis in the original.)

4. U. S. House of Representatives, Committee on Appropriations, *Report on Department of Defense Appropriations Bill for Fiscal Year 1960*, 86th Congress, 1st Session, Report No. 408 (Washington, D. C.: Government Printing Office, 1959). (Cited in Kanter, *op. cit.*, p. 136.)

5. Burton M. Sapin, *The Making of United States Foreign Policy* (New York: Frederick A. Praeger, Publishers, 1966), p. 54.

6. See the text of a letter to the Defense Secretary dated 17 May 1954 in which Eisenhower invoked the doctrine of executive privilege vis-a-vis the Senate Committee on Governmental Operations which was at the time seeking information on administration discussions concerning military policy: Charles R. Dechert, "Availability of Information for Congressional Operations," in Alfred de Grazia, ed., *Congress, the First Branch of Government: Twelve Studies in the Organization of Congress* (Garden City: Doubleday

& Company, Publishers, 1967), pp. 181-182. See also Eisenhower's letter to the Johnson Subcommittee in January of 1958 in which he refused demands that he divulge the contents of the secret Gaither Committee report to the Congress: U. S. Senate, Preparedness Investigating Subcommittee of the Committee on Armed Services, *Inquiry into Satellite and Missile Programs*, part II, 85th Congress, 1st-2nd Sessions (Washington, D.C.: Government Printing Office, 1958), p. 2037. (Hereafter cited as *Senate: Inquiry.*)

7. Sherman Adams, *Firsthand Report: The Story of the Eisenhower Administration* (New York: Harper & Brothers, 1961), p. 420.

8. See, for example: the exchange between Dennis Chavez, the chairman of the Senate defense appropriations subcommittee, and Secretary of Defense McElroy over the administration's refusal to field an Army of 900,000 and a Marine Corps of 200,000 despite explicit Congressional authorization: U. S. Senate, Subcommittee of the Committee on Appropriations, *Department of Defense Appropriations for 1960*, 86th Congress, 1st Session (Washington, D.C.: Government Printing Office, 1959), pp. 20-21 (hereafter cited as *Senate: DOD FY1960*); Chavez's demands for an accounting of unspent funds by Defense Secretary Gates: U. S. Senate, Subcommittee of the Committee on Appropriations, *Department of Defense Appropriations for 1961*, part I, 86th Congress, 2nd Session (Washington, D. C.: Government Printing Office, 1960), pp. 1, 14-15 (hereafter cited as *Senate: DOD FY1961*).

9. Warner R. Schilling, "The Politics of National Defense: Fiscal 1950," in Warner R. Schilling, et al., *Strategy, Politics, and Defense Budgets* (New York: Columbia University Press, 1962), pp. 248-249.

10. Fenno, *op. cit.*, especially pp. 530-570.

11. In fact, an analysis of 443 separate bureau estimates submitted to the Committee between 1947 and 1959 indicated that over three-quarters had been cut before they reached the floor of the House. See, Richard F. Fenno, Jr., "The House Appropriations Committee as a Political System: The Problem of Integration," *American Political Science Review*, vol. 56, no. 2 (June, 1962), pp. 310-324.

12. U. S. Senate, Subcommittee of the Committee on Appropriations, *Department of Defense Appropriations for 1959*, 85th Congress, 2nd Session (Washington, D. C.: Government Printing Office, 1958), p. 2. (Hereafter cited as *Senate: DOD FY1959*).

13. *Senate: DOD FY1960*, pp. 1-3.

14. *Ibid.*, pp. 129, 184.

15. *Senate: DOD FY1961*, part I, pp. 1, 57.

16. U. S. House of Representatives, Committee on Appropriations, Subcommittee on Department of Defense Appropriations, *The Ballistic Missile Program*, 85th Congress, 1st Session (Washington, D. C.: Government Printing Office, 1958), p. 1.

17. U. S. House of Representatives, Committee on Appropriations, Subcommittee on Department of Defense Appropriations, *Department of Defense Appropriations for 1959*, 85th Congress, 2nd Session (Washington, D. C.: Government Printing Office, 1958), pp. 44 ff. (Hereafter cited as *House: DOD FY1959.*)

18. U. S. House of Representatives, Committee on Appropriations, Subcommittee on Department of Defense Appropriations, *Department of De-*

## American Defense Policy

*fense Appropriations for 1960,* part I, 86th Congress, 1st Session, (Washington, D.C.: Government Printing Office, 1959), pp. 2, 827, 41, 56, 97-101. (Hereafter cited as *House: DOD FY1960.)*

19. U. S. House of Representatives, Committee on Appropriations, Subcommittee on Department of Defense Appropriations, *Department of Defense Appropriations for 1961,* part I, 86th Congress, 2nd Session (Washington, D. C.: Government Printing Office, 1960), p. 21 (Hereafter cited as *House: DOD FY1961.)*

20. Indeed, as anxieties began to wane after the new Kennedy administration assumed power, Mahon began to display notably more concern with defense economy than did Chavez. While the latter declared that "no sacrifice is too great to insure our freedom and the freedom of other peoples," and emphasized the duty of the Congress to provide for the common defense, the former expressed to Secretary McNamara the concern that "our opponent would be glad to see us spend ourselves into bankruptcy." See, respectively: U. S. Senate, Subcommittee of the Committee on Appropriations, *Department of Defense Appropriations for 1962,* 87th Congress, 1st Session (Washington, D. C.: Government Printing Office, 1961), pp. 2 and 71 (hereafter cited as *Senate: DOD FY1962);* U. S. House of Representatives, Committee on Appropriations, Subcommittee on Department of Defense Appropriations, *Department of Defense Appropriations for 1962,* part 3, 87th Congress, 1st Session (Washington, D. C.: Government Printing Office, 1961), p. 56 (hereafter cited as *House: DOD FY1962).*

21. See, for example, the comments of Mahon and Chavez: *House: DOD FY1959,* p. 54; *Senate: DOD FY1960,* pp. 2-3; *Senate: DOD FY1961,* p. 1; *Senate: DOD FY1962,* p. 2.

22. U. S. House of Representatives, Committee on Armed Services, *Investigation of National Defense Missiles,* 85th Congress, 2nd Session (Washington, D. C.: Government Printing Office, 1958), pp. 3973 and 4329. (Hereafter cited as *House Armed Services: Missiles.)*

23. *Senate: Inquiry,* pp. 1-3; U. S. Senate, Investigating Subcommittee of the Committee on Armed Services and the Committee on Aeronautical and Space Sciences, *Military and Space Activities,* 86th Congress, 1st Session (Washington, D. C.: Government Printing Office, 1959), pp. 1-3 (hereafter cited as Senate: Joint Hearings 1959); U. S. Senate, Preparedness Investigating Subcommittee of the Committee on Armed Services in conjunction with the Committee on Aeronautical and Space Sciences, *Missiles, Space and Other Major Defense Matters,* 86th Congress, 2nd Session (Washington, D. C.: Government Printing Office, 1960), p. 133 (hereafter cited as *Senate: Joint Hearings 1960).*

24. In his analysis of senatorial behavior, Rosenau found that despite individual traits or committee assignments, Democratic Senators were more apt to be hostile toward John Foster Dulles than Republicans; similarly, the reverse was found to be the case regarding President Truman's Secretary of State, Dean Acheson. See James N. Rosenau, "Private Preferences and Political Responsibilities: the Relative Potency of Individual and Role variables in the Behavior of U. S. Senators," in J. David Singer, ed., *Quantitative International Politics: Insights and Evidence* (New York: The Free Press, 1968), pp. 17-50.

25.  That two of the best Representatives of the pro-economy dogmatists were Southern conservatives should come as little surprise. By now it should be evident that the issue of national security was not only a partisan issue but a philosophical one as well, with the liberals (who congregated in the Democratic party) aligning on the side of more federal expenditures for defense. The fiscal conservatives (that is, the proponents of minimal government spending, balanced budgets, no economic control or inflation)—of whom the President himself was the leading spokesman—tended to gravitate toward either the Republican party or the southern wing of the Congressional Democrats. Given the present vogue of placing those right-of-center in the "cold warrior" camp, the reader would do well to remember that during the 1950's and early 1960's, virtually everyone would fit the contemporary description of a hard-liner—both liberals and conservatives alike were engulfed by the cold war psychology. They differed merely on the means best suited to successfully wage the conflict.

26.  U. S. House of Representatives, Committee on Appropriations, Subcommittee on Department of Defense Appropriations, *Department of Defense Appropriations for 1958*, part I, 85th Congress, 1st Session (Washington, D.C.: Government Printing Office, 1957), pp. 50-53, 554-556, 655-657.

27.  *Ibid.*, pp. 71, 266, 544-547. It is interesting to note, in passing, that General Gavin (a principal innovator) was from Congressman Flood's home district and personally lobbied with the latter on behalf of the Army's cause.

28.  *Ibid.*, pp. 35, 86-87.

29.  *House: DOD FY1962*, pp. 57, 75.

30.  *Ibid.*, pp. 120-123.

31.  *Senate: DOD FY1959*, pp. 100-101.

32.  *Senate: DOD FY1961*, pp. 32-35, 77-78, 48-50.

33.  *Senate: DOD FY1960*, pp. 274-277.

34.  *Senate: DOD FY1962*, p. 80.

35.  Quoted in Paul I. Wellman, *Stuart Symington: Portrait of a Man With a Mission* (Garden City: Doubleday & Company, 1960), p. 14. This study was a most favorable political biography prepared for Symington's bid for the 1960 Democratic Presidential nomination, and as such grants the reader a useful insight into his campaign and image strategy—both of which revolved around the defense issue.

36.  During the early 1960's, of course, Symington performed a *volte face* on the issue of national security and suddenly became an outstanding critic of the defense establishment as a whole. Quite recently, for instance, Symington (now the second-ranking Democrat on the Armed Services Committee) declared at a party caucus which endorsed a resolution calling upon President Nixon to bring home many of the 600,000 United States servicemen stationed around the world: "No economy, not even the economy of the United States, can continue to police the world and babysit the world indefinitely." (*The New York Times*, 16 March 1973, p. 15.)

37.  In a much publicized speech delivered on the Senate floor in 1954 (unlike other freshman Senators, Symington was looked upon from the start as one of the house's leading defense experts), he warned that the Soviets would develop an ICBM capability well before the United States due to this country's meager investment in research and development, and prophesied:

"If we are attacked tomorrow, and do not have the capacity to retaliate with instant total devastation, we shall go down in defeat; and freedom will perish from the earth." (*The New York Times*, 22 July 1954, p. 3.)
38.  Wellman, *op. cit.*, p. 194.
39.  U. S. Senate, Committee on Armed Services, Subcommittee on the Air Force, *Study of Airpower*, 84th Congress, 2nd Session, Senate Document No. 29 (Washington, D. C.: Government Printing Office, 1956).
40.  *House: DOD FY1960*, pp. 578, 590-591. For other examples of Ford and Laird coming to the defense of the Eisenhower administration's military policy, see: *ibid.*, pp. 41-42, 184,400; *House: DOD FY1959*, p. 94; *House: DOD FY1961*, p. 126. True to the partisan role, with the change in administrations we find a reversal of roles; for example, reviewing the first Kennedy budget, Ford placed on record an article from the Chicago *Sun-Times* in which it was charged that "the Nation's military men are being edged out of crucial military decisions in the Kennedy administration"—a charge frequently levelled at its predecessor. (*House: DOD FY1962*, p. 33.)
41.  *The New York Times*, 6 October 1957 (pp. 1, 44), 8 October 1957 (p. 11), 9 October 1957 (p. 13), 10 October 1957 (pp. 1, 4, 16), 13 October 1957 (p. 36), 14 October 1957 (p. 1), 18 October 1957 (p. 2).
42.  *Ibid.*, 13 October 1957, p. 37.
43.  *House Armed Services: Missiles*, pp. 3973-3975.
44.  *Ibid.*, p. 4190.
45.  For example, compare Arend's rather critical interrogation of General Gavin with that by Mendel Rivers, *ibid.*, pp. 4349-4353.
46.  *Senate: Inquiry*, pp. 1005 ff.
47.  *Senate: Joint Hearings 1959*, pp. 221-222.
48.  *Ibid.*, p. 20.
49.  *Senate: Joint Hearings 1960*, pp. 19-50.
50.  *Ibid.*, pp. 103-105.
51.  For a discussion of Johnson's role as Majority Leader, see Ralph K. Huitt, "Democratic Party Leadership in the Senate," in Ralph K. Huitt and Robert L. Peabody, *Congress, Two Decades of Analysis* (New York: Harper & Row, Publishers, 1969), pp. 136-158.
52.  The Preparedness Investigating Subcommittee and the Committee on Aeronautical and Space Sciences were nearly identical in membership; however, the device of joint hearings added both credibility and prestige to the Johnson investigations of 1959 and 1960.
53.  *The New York Times*, 7 December 1959, p. 38. (Note that this statement was timed for release so as to coincide with Pearl Harbor Day.)
54.  *Ibid.*, 18 December 1959, p. 16.
55.  *Ibid.*, 24 January 1960 (pp. 1 ff.) and 26 January 1960 (p. 12).
56.  *Ibid.*, 20 February 1960 (pp. 1 ff.), 17 June 1960 (p. 1 ff.), 23 June 1960 (pp. 1 ff.).
57.  *Ibid.*, 14 July 1960, p. 16.
58.  In January of 1960, Symington proposed that the surplus in the Eisenhower budget for FY 1961 (estimated at 4.2 billion dollars) be spent on defense; during the U-2 affair and the resulting collapse of the Paris summit conference, he urged an immediate three billion dollar increase;

finally, the following month, he endorsed the figure quoted by the Rockefeller report—3.5 billion dollars. See, respectively: *The New York Times*, 11 January 1960 (p. 1), 27 May 1960 (p. 1), 10 June 1960 (p. 1).

59.  *Ibid.*, 22 January 1960 (p. 4), 2 February 1960 (p. 10), 15 February 1960 (p. 1), 20 February 1960 (p. 1).

60.  *Ibid.*, 24 March 1960, pp. 1 ff.

# 8

## THE CAPITALIZERS II: PRESIDENTIAL POLITICS

### I

THE AMERICAN PRESIDENTIAL ELECTION CAMpaign has been aptly characterized as "an emotional rather than a rational experience."[1] This was especially true for the 1960 contest where, in Theodore H. White's words, "specifics and issues had all but ceased to matter; only 'style' was important."[2] To be sure, all the major opinion polls indicated that foreign policy was the dominant issue in the minds of the voters, yet there failed to develop any concrete or tangible conflict of views between the two aspirants concerning the underlying assumptions and future course of American foreign policy.[3] The year 1960 was one of grave national concern, but a "vague, shapeless, unsettling, undefinable national concern,"[4] as the country became preoccupied, not with an immediate crisis, but with a search for identity in a world which was witnessing the decline of American power. Analyses of the mood of voters across the country indicated that concern with declining prestige abroad and the missile gap at home accounted for the uneasiness over the nation's future.[5]

Given the dominant American world view which approached the cold war as a zero-sum game—that is, as a confrontation between a monolithic Communist bloc emanating from the Kremlin and an equally mythical "free world" under the aegis of a benevolent American imperium—the relative decline in the United States' ability to affect the course of world politics (a decline already evident by the late 1950's) was taken to be synonymous with the accretion of Soviet power. The loss of American influence was, in reality, attributable to the evolution of the post-World War II international system; that is, the transformation of the brief and abnormal situation of bipolarity which existed after the defeat of Germany and Japan and the simultaneous exhaustion of Britain and France to one which would witness the gradual resurgence of these powers as well as the rise of nationalist movements in former colonial dependencies. However, viewing the world as rigidly bipolar—where the forces of "freedom" remained forever locked in mortal combat with the forces of "slavery"—many (if not most) Americans saw any deterioration in the relative position of the United States as a direct result of the machinations of Soviet leaders aided by the incompetency of the incumbent administration. As with the fall of the Nationalist regime on the mainland of China in the late 1940's, the realization of the waning omnipotence of the United States a decade later brought about charges of malfeasance at home.

Incapable of accepting the natural regeneration of independence abroad—refusing to believe that the era of unquestioned American predominance was a mere interlude in the history of world politics—it was probably inevitable that Americans would place the blame on the leadership (or lack of it) of Dwight Eisenhower. Yet inasmuch as no one (save a few on the fringe of the radical right) could dare to question the loyalty of the affable "Ike," the aging President was charged with complacency and ridiculed for being out of touch with the changing temper of the times. The dominant American perception of the world coupled with the mounting diversity in the international environment led, therefore, to a nebulous sense of frustration and confusion. And this crisis of self-confidence would make for the centrality of one issue in the 1960 Presidential election campaign: the loss of United States power and the changes in national leadership necessary to reverse the trend. Moreover, American power vis-a-vis the Communists would be equated with sheer quantitative military might.

## II

For the critics of the Republican administration (now, of course, termed the Eisenhower-Nixon administration), the fundamental issue in the campaign was, in the words of Arthur M. Schlesinger, Jr.,

> which candidate understands what the fundamental problem is of restoring American power and influence in the world? Which has the personal will and political authority required to persuade the American people to accept the measures essential for our survival as a great and free nation?[6]

And for individuals of such a suasion, John F. Kennedy was, naturally, the man of the hour. For Kennedy, the 1950's had been "an era of illusion" in which "we have failed . . . to build positions of long-term strength essential to successful negotiation." The "increasing deterioration of America's world position" and the "steady decrease in our relative strength" had "convinced [Khrushchev] that the balance of world power is shifting his way." Thus, the Democratic nominee called for a new coherent and purposeful strategy which would "restore our nation's relative strength." Warning that the "hour is late," he urged the reinforcement of United States retaliatory power and the expansion of its conventional war capabilities. Surveying the dramatic rise of Soviet military might since 1949, he noted that,

> [t]hey did more than merely make themselves the equal of the United States in the actual possession of nuclear bombs. Their startling advances in the techniques of rockets and missiles made them the superior of the United States in the power to deliver nuclear warheads onto a target. Thus they invalidated the original strategic conception of NATO, by outflanking its key element—the deterrent power of the U. S. Strategic Air Command. In this way, they also enlarged the military importance of Russia's vast conventionally equipped land army.

Given the fact that the Kremlin's assault on Europe had shifted to "the indirect route of winning the vast outlying raw materials region," this country "must regain the ability to intervene effectively and swiftly in *any* limited war *anywhere* in the world."[7] Though Kennedy failed to emerge as a major figure in the defense controversy until just before receiving his party's nomination, his views on national security as sporadically presented during the previous decade were consistent with the positions he would take in 1960. As early as 1949, he levelled a severe blow from the floor of the House against the Truman administration for its failure in preventing the fall of China to the Communists. Attacking the "Lattimores and the Fairbanks," he urged that the Congress "must now assume the responsibility of preventing the onrushing tide of communism from engulfing all of Asia."[8] Similarly, during the Korean War, he chided his own party for having "concentrated its attention too much on Western Europe," and warned that because the "tide of events has been moving against us," the Communists "have a chance of seizing all of Asia in the next five or six years."[9] Moreover, throughout his years in both houses of the Congress he consistently supported increased military spending all across the spectrum: in 1950 he called for the expansion of airlift capacity so as to allow the United States to make its power felt in all corners of the globe; the following year he reluctantly supported the dispatching of American ground troops to Europe, but only because he wanted larger forces there sooner; seeking to correct what he saw as "the most serious deficiency in our military strength" (i.e., "our weakness in the air"), he offered an amendment to the defense appropriations bill of 1952 which would have increased the Air Force budget by almost 1.5 billion dollars; from the Senate chamber, Kennedy joined with his colleague Stuart Symington as early as 1954 in an effort to prevent cuts in Army manpower, congratulated the latter on his fight on behalf of the defense effort, and (citing Army Chief of Staff Ridgway) criticized the underlying assumptions of the Eisenhower policy of the long pull.[10]

During his early years in public office, then, Kennedy had done little to ingratiate himself with the liberal wing of the Democratic party. Indeed, he was regarded by many liberals with suspicion when he captured the party's nomination in 1960 and was privately scornful himself of what he called the "real liberals." According to both Arthur Schlesinger and Theodore Sorensen, he knew and cared little about civil rights and civil liberties, and was hostile toward (or at least skeptical of) both the Americans for Democratic Action and the liberal American Veterans Committee. Also, his family's ties with Senator Joe McCarthy and the general distrust of the patriarch of the Kennedy clan by the liberal community tended to aggravate the young Senator's relations with an important segment of the Democratic coalition. As Sorensen recalls in regard to the Kennedys' relationship with McCarthy:

> No state had a higher percentage of McCarthy supporters than Massachusetts. No newspaper was more devoted to his every cause than the Boston Post. . . . McCarthy had Bob Kennedy on his committee staff in 1953. Earlier he had visited the Kennedy girls at Cape Cod, and for some time he had basked in the admiration of the Ambassador.[11]

Catapulted into the national arena with his bid for the Vice Presidential nomination in 1956, Kennedy was aware that in order to successfully aspire to the White House, he had to gain support in sections of the country other than the Northeast.[12]

Eclipsed in the defense field by such prestigious seniors as Symington and Johnson, Kennedy initially fell back upon domestic issues to build a wide base of support. The future candidate, who would eventually ride the post-Sputnik winds into the Executive Mansion, was conspicuously silent during the several months following the Russian scientific feat and did not deliver a major address on national defense until nearly a year later. In August of 1958 he delivered an address from the Senate floor which was a harbinger of things to come. Specifically citing the findings of defense advocates like James Gavin and Henry Kissinger, he warned of the consequences of a missile lag in the period 1960-1964—years during which the deterrent ratio "would in all likelihood be weighted very heavily against us." The first danger, as Kennedy saw it, was that Soviet superiority during the years of the gap might be so great as "to open to them a new shortcut to world domination"—i.e., a surprise attack upon the United States. But should they refrain from such a course of action,

> the Soviets may be expected to use their superior striking ability to achieve their objectives in ways which may not require launching an actual attack. Their missile power will be the shield from behind which they will slowly, but surely advance —through sputnik diplomacy, limited brushfire wars, indirect nonovert aggression, intimidation and subversion, internal revolution, increased prestige or influence, and the vicious blackmail of our allies. The periphery of the free world will slowly be nibbled away. The balance of power will gradually shift against us.

This, indeed, was the most likely threat. And the danger here stemmed from the fact that "we have extended our commitments around the world, without regard to the sufficiency of our military posture to fulfill those commitments." Having made this valid analysis of the incongruence between America's self-imposed responsibilities and the military means available, Kennedy failed to even consider the possibility of rectifying the situation by cutting back on the United States' far-flung commitments around the globe. Quite the contrary, he could see but one logical policy— namely, bringing commitments and capabilities into balance by simply increasing the means and options available to policymakers. Nor is this surprising, for the presumption of total conflict with an implacable and insatiable enemy leads inexorably to the conclusion that he must be opposed at all points along the periphery of freedom. The Eisenhower administration had, of course, the same perception of the nature of the conflict between the United States and the Soviet Union, but its policy had been tempered by its conservative fiscal policy which ranked the economic collapse and/or regimentation of American society on the same level with Communist victory in the struggle. Kennedy, however, explicitly rejected these restraints and criticized the President for his alleged "willingness to place fiscal security ahead of national security." Thus, he rose in the Senate to, in his words, "sound the alarm" that "time is running out" and urge major increases in spending for both strategic and limited warfare capabilities.[13]

But despite the first major plunge into the debate over national security, Senator Kennedy did not at this point follow through with a consistent and vigorous espousal of the cause. Seemingly content with leaving the issue to be kept alive by his colleagues Symington and Johnson, he lapsed back into the domestic field and, until 1960, would concentrate on labor legislation and the shoring up of his support on the union front.[14] With the opening up of the Presidential election year, however, Kennedy once again jumped onto the defense bandwagon. In mid-January he delivered an address before the National Press Club in which he rejected the Eisenhower conception of the Presidency and, in its stead, proposed a strong Commander in Chief capable of dealing with the "challenging and revolutionary '60's." Warning of the perils involved with an increasingly powerful and belligerent Soviet Union, he declared that "if a brushfire threatens some part of the globe—he [the President] alone can act, without waiting for the Congress."[15] With this opening volley (significantly, perhaps, rooted in his conception of executive prerogative), Kennedy embraced the issue made popular and appealing by others. Within a fortnight he charged that Eisenhower had brought the country, not an era of peace, but only "a period of stagnation, retreat, while America becomes second in missiles [and] second in space."[16] In February, he declared that the "very survival" of the United States was at stake in the upcoming election inasmuch as the victory of Richard Nixon would mean a continuation of Eisenhower's policies.[17] But unlike his senatorial opponents for the Democratic nomination, Kennedy's foray into the preference primaries necessitated that he stress local issues (for example, dairy farming in Wisconsin) much of the time; yet whenever focusing on a national audience he inevitably harked back to the theme of defense.[18]

In March, during an all day and night session of the Senate designed to break the Southern filibuster over the proposed civil rights bill of that year, Kennedy made his first major speech on defense since formally declaring his candidacy three months before. In it he charged the Eisenhower administration with "gambling with our national survival" and called for an upward revision of the military budget "to maintain the minimum conditions of our survival." Specifically, he endorsed a program of across-the-board increases in the service budgets, including General Power's proposed airborne alert for SAC, an acceleration of the missile programs, and a modernization of the Army and Navy "to prevent the brushfire wars that our capacity for nuclear retaliation is unable to deter."[19] As the Democratic national convention approached, the picture which Senator Kennedy painted of the country's future became grimmer and he began to express the conviction that world history would turn on the events and decisions of the early 1960's. With the gradual shift in the power relations between Moscow and Washington, the next administration would face both unprecedented peril and unheralded opportunity to forge the contours of the future of freedom in the world. The chief responsibility of the present administration, he charged, "has been that they have permitted the power and strength of the United States to decline in relation to the Communist world. And they have permitted that when we represent the only great hope for freedom around the world." The United States, he suggested, was the only force able to prevent the Sino-Soviet conquest of Eurasia: "We are the captains at the gate. If we fail, all fail." Thus, the American people—and their next President—had been vested with an historical mission—a "responsibility greater than any people have met since the time of ancient Athens." This challenge John Kennedy accepted with unmistakable zeal and the theme of the burden and the glory of national greatness would run through his entire campaign and Presidency as well.[20]

The historical mission which the Democratic contender so ardently manufactured and embraced was, however, fraught with pitfalls which he himself readily acknowledged. He became seriously distressed with the certainty that the next President, due to the failures of the current incumbent, "will find himself with far flung commitments without the strength to back them up." This, coupled with the fact that Khrushchev was firmly "convinced that the balance of power is shifting his way," would make the early sixties "the most critical period in our nation's history since the bleak winter at Valley Forge." With the realization that he himself might well be faced with the hard decisions to defend the integrity of the free world, his call for an immediate build-up in military power assumed a new sense of urgency. From the floor of the Senate he pleaded for a stepping up of missile production and the allocation of the resources necessary to give the next Commander in Chief "the ability to intervene effectively and swiftly in *any* limited war *anywhere* in the world." Whether or not such a build-up occurred under Eisenhower, his successor would confront a task of "unparalleled dimensions"—to test "whether our greatness is past." And for such an inevitable test of America's place in history, the new President must offer bold leadership and "demand sacrifices."[21] And when chided by former President Truman as to his youth and inexperience, Kennedy would retort that the failures of the old postwar leadership had brought the United States its present plight and that it was "time for a new generation of leadership to cope with new problems."[22]

With candidates Kennedy, Symington, and Johnson all agreed on the inadequacy of the administration's defense policy, the Democratic national convention met in Los Angeles unified on the issue of national security. Convinced that the balance of world power was being allowed to shift to the advantage of the Soviets, the Democrats anticipated numerous probes on the perimeter of the free world during the early 1960's. Making references to "world Communism" and the "Red empire," keynote speaker Frank Church of Idaho pointed to the overriding importance of the developing nations—

the 'no-man's-land' in which the fate of the human race will be determined. For if the continents of Asia and Africa are drawn behind the Iron and Bamboo Curtains, the economy of Western Europe is undermined. And if we yield to the Communists the continents of Africa, Asia, and Europe, the balance of power in the world fatally shifts against us thus assuring eventual Communist domination of the world.[23]

The platform adopted by the Democrats echoed the same theme:

> If America is to work effectively for . . . peace, we must first
> restore our national strength. . . .
> The new Democratic Administration will recast our military
> capacity in order to provide forces and weapons of a diversity,
> balance, and mobility in quantity and quality to deter both lim-
> ited and general aggressions.
> We pledge our will, energies and resources to oppose armed
> Communist aggression.
>
> . . .
>
> . . . we will use all the will, power, resources, and energy at our
> command to resist the further encroachments of communism on
> freedom—whether at Berlin, Formosa, or new points as yet un-
> disclosed.[24]

And after John F. Kennedy received the party's nod on the first
ballot, he rose to accept the nomination and warn the nation of
both the burden and the glory which awaited it:

> Abroad the balance of power is shifting. . . .
> The new frontier of which I speak is not a set of promises—
> it is a set of challenges. It sums up not what I intend to *offer*
> the American people, but what I intend to *ask* of them. . . .
> It holds out the promise of more sacrifice instead of more se-
> curity. . . .
> It would be easier to shrink back from that frontier, to look
> to the safe mediocrity of the past. . . . But I believe the times
> demand invention, innovation, imagination, decision. I am ask-
> ing each of you to be pioneers on that new frontier. . . .
> For the harsh facts of the matter are that we stand on this
> frontier at a turning point in history. . . .[25]

### III

If the Democrats were firmly united on the issue of national defense, the same matter would serve as a chief source of divisive-
ness for their Republican opponents. For just as the President
stood steadfastly behind his policy of the long pull, so did Gov-

ernor Rockefeller of New York exert powerful pressures in the opposite direction. And in between one finds Vice President Nixon pursuing an ambivalent line, seeking on the one hand not to alienate the prestigious Eisenhower, and on the other hoping to preserve the unity of the party and, hopefully, add to his chances of carrying New York State in November.

Nelson Rockefeller, leader of the liberal wing of the party, was an extreme hardliner[26] on security matters. As Theodore H. White describes his position at the time:

> Of all the nation's problems, . . . one had become an obsession with him: the interlocked perils of defense and foreign policy. He had come to believe so violently that America lived in imminent danger of destruction, that the security of America was being clipped to America's purse rather than the purse being stretched to provide security, that his position had become one of the far extreme. He was obsessed with the thought that the years 1961 through 1964, the years of the impending missile gap, were years of instant national emergency. And now, in May of 1960, the disarmament conference with the Russians was breaking down in Geneva; and from Africa through Asia, from Paris to Peking, America's position was crumbling.[27]

Disenchanted with administration policy, Rockefeller sought the repudiation of Eisenhower by both the national convention and the Presidential nominee. Ever since his impressive victory over Averill Harriman in 1958, he had used his national prominence to undermine the administration's position on military spending. In 1959, he fully endorsed a massive fallout shelter program for New York, urged the resumption of nuclear testing (halted since the summer of the previous year), called for a full 50 per cent increase in the defense budget, and remained conspicuously aloof from Nikita Khrushchev's visit to the United States and the resulting "spirit of Camp David." Indeed, he was so outspoken on behalf of national security that by the end of the year he was viewed by the Soviet press as the worst possible candidate and as "the chief opponent of improved Soviet-American relations."[28]

Having officially withdrawn from the field of Presidential aspirants before the end of 1959, Rockefeller remained a one-man lobbyist against administration policy. As chairman of a special committee on civil defense at the Governors' Conference in January of 1960, he called for more funds for a national shelter program. (Two months later, he was compelled to abandon his fight for mandatory shelters in public and private buildings in New York, substituting tax incentives to accomplish his goal.) He continually criticized the quality of White House leadership, attacked the American economic growth rate, and demanded an immediate 3.5 billion dollar increase in the defense budget to provide Washington with "a more flexible and balanced military establishment and doctrines to meet all contingencies including local aggression."[29] Attacking the equivocal stand of the Vice President, he incessantly prodded Nixon to make his position clear on national defense and flatly refused to pledge in advance his full and loyal support of Nixon should the latter be chosen the party's standard-bearer.[30] To the delight of the Democrats, he openly attacked Eisenhower's leadership before Senator Jackson's Subcommittee on National Policy Machinery and was applauded by Democrats at the Governor's Conference on the eve of their national convention for his criticism of the President's defense strategy. Indeed, he was so anti-administration and sounded so much like one of its Democratic critics that he had to deny reports that he was on the verge of bolting the Republican party.[31] As the Republican convention approached, he announced that he would accept a draft for the party's nomination and threatened a floor fight over the platform drafted by the White House and adopted by the platform committee.[32]

During all these months, Richard Nixon carefully watched and evaluated Rockefeller's moves. Aware that many Democrats (including Kennedy) believed the Governor to be the strongest candidate that the GOP could field, he wooed his Republican foe with the Vice Presidency only to be turned down publicly.[33] Unable to mollify Rockefeller with a place on the party's ticket, the Vice President endeavored instead to compromise over the wording in the convention platform, thus avoiding a divisive floor fight and assuring himself at least a chance of winning New York in the fall.

The result was the famed "Treaty of Fifth Avenue,"[34] the product of the secret meeting between the two adversaries in New York City while convention preliminaries were still going on in Chicago. The final draft of the defense planks contained four changes designed to satisfy Rockefeller (e.g., an "acceleration" rather than a "continuation" of the administration's missile program).[35] Instead, the Governor announced that he still was not satisfied and was especially displeased with the lack of a sense of urgency in the plank.[36] Meanwhile, President Eisenhower was furious over the joint communique which had, in effect, repudiated his policies.[37] Thus, neither Rockefeller nor Eisenhower was pleased: the President rankled by the Manhattan statement, the Governor thwarted by the actual platform entries.[38]

Eisenhower had begun his last year in office battling to preserve the policy of the long pull. The budget which he presented to the Congress for fiscal 1961 in mid-January was, in constant dollars, virtually the same level as that for the previous year; moreover, ever since Sputnik the President had actually managed to decrease the size of the defense budget.[39] In his last opportunity to hold the line on big spending, the Chief Executive began a counterattack against his Democratic (and, alas, Republican) critics. Just a few days before releasing the text of his budget message, he declared angrily at a news conference that "the people trying to make defense a partisan issue are doing a disservice to the United States," and two weeks later defended the downward revision of intelligence estimates on the Soviet missile threat. At the end of January, he delivered a surprisingly early television campaign speech in which he asserted that American military might was unassailable, discounted the significance of any transient missile gap, and sternly took to task his defense critics (whom he termed "political morticians") for irresponsibly playing politics with the national interest. Only a few days later, he declared at a press conference that United States prestige was not committed to the "race" for space exploration and restated his case for nuclear sufficiency: "A deterrent has no added power, once it has become completely adequate for compelling the respect of any potential enemy." As the tone of the detractors grew harsher, the President countered by calling "despicable" anyone who claimed that Eisenhower was misleading the people on the true dimensions of the Communist missile menace and used every opportunity which presented itself to assure the electorate that all was well with his tutelage; for example, on the eve of his departure for a Latin American good-will trip, he addressed the nation and reminded all that United States military power was "ample for today and constantly developing to meet the needs of tomorrow."[41]

As the national conventions of the two political parties approached, Eisenhower realized that there would be a tough fight over this defense policy in the fall election. On the one side he saw the Democratic front-runners—whom he scored as "ignorant" and "blind" ambitious men "hoping to scramble into the chair I shall soon vacate"—and on the other, Nelson Rockefeller seeking to undermine his leadership of the Republican party.[42] Thus, he pinned his hopes on the Vice President and constantly maneuvered to keep Nixon solidly within the Eisenhower fold. Hoping to hold tight reins on the party's convention, the President had his assistants Robert E. Merriam and Malcolm Moos draft the platform and dispatched a special assistant to the Defense Secretary to head a special unit for the Republican National Committee.[43] As Governor Rockefeller stepped up his pressure on the Vice President to endorse major increases in defense spending, Eisenhower conferred with Nixon at the White House and the next day issued a statement rejecting the view that "just more money" would provide more security.[44] When Nixon and Rockefeller concluded their rapprochement on the eve of the convention, the President saw to it that the new defense plank "incorporated my wording to the letter" as his aides remained in constant communication with the Nixon forces to prevent an unacceptable appeasement of Rockefeller.[45] And, finally, addressing the convention himself, Eisenhower specifically ridiculed the Rockefeller wing of the party by noting that: "we have a cult of professional pessimists who, taking counsel of their fears, continually mouth the allegation that America has become a second-rate military power."[46]

With both parties having selected their nominees, the President moved both to hold Nixon to the administration line and to blunt the edge of the Kennedy assault. The same day, for example, that Nixon (hoping to stake out an independent path of his own) announced that he had disagreed with certain administration decisions over the years upon which he would enumerate during the course of the campaign, Eisenhower issued a statement in which he maintained that his conversations with the Vice President indicated that Nixon was in total accord with the administration on defense policy.[47] Turning to the Democrats, the Commander in Chief emphasized once more that inasmuch as the risk of a garrison state was inherent in the cold war with Soviet Russia, that risk had to be kept minimal. The traditional Eisenhower sense of pathos was distinctly evident as he warned that "there has been an intrusion of defense matters into our national life on a scale never before approached except in time of war . . . [but] this condition will continue until powerful aggressors renounce their imperialistic aims of world conquest."[48] He believed the Kennedy challenge to be a fundamental assault upon his long-cherished approach of moderation and balance and informed Nixon in August that he "would do any honorable thing to avoid turning the country over to the 'big spending' type of Democrats."[49] The Democrats, he warned the people, were "counselling despair," "misguided people" who, while incorrectly lamenting the decline in American power, would bring the nation only inflation through inordinately huge defense expenditures. Calling for "fiscal responsibility" and a "balanced budget," Eisenhower advised the voters to choose a President who would not panic—a man who would remain deliberative and calm in the face of successive crises.[50]

Yet by the end of October it became evident to the outgoing President that an even more forceful partisan effort on behalf of the Nixon candidacy would be necessary to stem the Democrat advance as demonstrated by the public opinion polls. With the long pull hanging in the balance, Eisenhower briefly abandoned his usual monarchical detachment from the political arena and issued his strongest attacks yet on the Kennedy-Johnson alternative. Warning of the "cunning and facile tongue" that passes for "enlightened leadership," he charged that the Democrats were "talking carelessly and ignorantly about America's standing" and had "cruelly distorted the image of America" abroad. The United States must go forward (as the Democrats promised), he urged, but only "with maturity, with judgment, with balance." American defense policy "has been tuned to the continuity of the threat and to long-range goals, avoiding the wild fluctuations that too often follow upon the incidence of . . . panic." The final Eisenhower message was clear: the Nixon-Lodge team must triumph at the polls to continue his administration's "proven and prudent" economic politics. The rejection of the long pull by an irresponsible Democratic administration could bring the country nothing but deficit spending and inflation—in short, economic ruin which "could give Mr. Khrushchev the greatest victory he could hope for, and give it to him without firing a shot."[51]

Experiencing conflicting pressures from Rockefeller on the one side and Eisenhower on the other, Richard Nixon oscillated between the two managing to wholly embrace neither. While he ostensibly remained a loyal member of the administration, there were, in reality, two Nixons occupying the office of the Vice President:

> The first, the public Nixon, acclaimed Eisenhower as a savior of world peace, a statesman of rare acumen, and a national hero whom a thankful electorate would dare to slight by a vote for the Democratic party. The second, the private Nixon, patiently explained to visitors and journalists, in off-the-record conversations or over intimate dinners, his dismay with White House leadership, his dissent from decisions in the field of national defense and foreign policy, and his anxiety to offer the nation a more youthful, more vigorous, and more coherent presidency —in the person of himself.[52]

Long aware of the fact that he would have to run on the record of the incumbent administration, in which he had not been a major figure, Nixon had remained a force for greater emphasis on defense rather than fiscal economy and on dealing with unemployment rather than inflation.[53] During the campaign he remained extremely vague (and often contradictory) on what type of defense policy he would offer the American people if elected. On the one hand, he asserted that the United States was not a second-rate military power and consistently chided his Democratic rival for "selling America short"; he lavished praise on the President for giving the free world eight years of "peace without surrender," implying that the Democrats were the party of war and retreat; and, finally, he warned of the ills from massive federal spending which could be expected from a Kennedy administration.[54] At the same time he indicated that the balanced budget was not sacred to him; that security "must come first" even if it necessitated tax increases; that he anticipated rising defense spending for the next decade; and that, in an age of complex technology, the military budget "cannot be arbitrarily set."[55] At one point he implicitly rejected the assumptions of the long pull; at another juncture he explicitly endorsed the long pull.[56] Indeed, in the same speech he would attack his opponent for seeking to hitch his political bandwagon to the Sputnik star, and then pledge to best the Russians in a race for the moon—a contest which his mentor refused even to acknowledge.[57]

If Richard Nixon failed to articulate a coherent defense strategy (other than merely spending more for the military than Eisenhower), his Democratic opponent was anything but indecisive. As we have seen, Kennedy's prognostication regarding the plight of the next President was well developed even before he won his party's nomination. As the campaign moved into full swing in the late summer of 1960, he further developed these germinal themes. He declared early that the real issue confronting the American people was simply who could best restore the power of the United States in a time of peril. The stagnation of the fifties had brought about the relative decline in American vitality. The balance of power was shifting to the Communists. Kennedy knew it and Khrushchev knew it. The first task of a new administration would be to redress a waning security, and he pledged to ask the Congress for a sizable strategic and conventional build-up immediately upon taking office. It would be the responsibility of the next President to mobilize the resources and courage of the Amer-

ican nation for "the great struggle" with the Communist mono-
lith for the loyalties of the Third World—for here, ultimately, is
where the battle for freedom would be won in glory or irretriev-
ably lost in ignominy.[58] "The enemy is lean and hungry," warned
John Kennedy, "and the United States is the only strong sentinel
at the gate."[59] And he pledged this generation to "a rendezvous
with destiny"—"not the preservation of freedom here in the United
States. . . . It is the preservation of freedom around the world.
That is the responsibility and destiny of the United States in the
1960's."[60]

## IV

During his campaign for the Presidency, Kennedy had pledged
his new administration to an immediate increase of four billion
dollars a year in spending for strategic forces alone.[61] Upon taking
office, he immediately sought an upward revision of the Eisenhower military budget by two billion dollars and, with successive
increases, was spending six billion (or 15 per cent) more than his
predecessor had anticipated by the end of the year. The last annual spending level for the Department of Defense envisaged by
President Eisenhower was in the neighborhood of 42 billion dollars; within a thousand days, President Kennedy increased that
figure to a full 52 billion dollars, with outlays for strategic forces
peaking in fiscal 1962 at 11.2 billion dollars.[62] General Eisenhower
was extremely critical of such increases in spending for the military establishment, suggesting in 1963 that the new President's
proposed budget could be cut by at least 13 billion dollars (especially in the areas of defense and space); indeed, in responding to
the former President's charges, Kennedy was forced to acknowledge that greater increases in non-defense spending had taken
place during the last three years of the Republican administration than during the three years of his administration.[63] All in all,
the three years of the Kennedy interregnum witnessed, in the
words of Theodore Sorensen, "the largest and swiftest build-up in
this country's peacetime history" on behalf of a "radical change in
strategy."[64] And the overall result of abandoning the predeter-

mined spending ceilings which marked the Eisenhower approach was to increase the imbalance between defense expenditures and domestic priorities.[65]

On the verge of assuming the responsibilities of leading the nation through what he believed would be its greatest hour of peril, Kennedy took the oath of office of the Chief Executive greatly alarmed by the prospects of a newly envigored Communist thrust designed to overturn the existing international order. His Inaugural Address, devoted totally to foreign policy, echoed the theme which had run consistently through his campaign oratory: the sacrifices, on the one hand, and the glory, on the other, to which he intended to commit the American polity. The liberty of mankind, he suggested, was indivisible and the American people must be willing to shoulder the responsibility for its defense against Communist encroachment all across the globe: "Let every nation know, whether it wishes us well or ill, that we shall pay any price, bear any burden, meet any hardship, support any friend, oppose any foe to assure the survival and success of liberty." And the first sacrifice would be the expansion of military might for: "We dare not tempt them with weakness. For only when our arms are sufficient beyond doubt can we be certain beyond doubt that they will never be employed." This, then, was the call to a nation to embrace a quest for greatness—a quest which knew no limits, but which held out the prospects of fulfilling the American dream:

> Since this country was founded, each generation of Americans has been summoned to give testimony to its national loyalty. The graves of young Americans who answered the call surround the globe.
>
> Now the trumpet summons us again—not as a call to bear arms, though arms we need—not as a call to battle, though embattled we are—but a call to bear the burden of a long twilight struggle, year in and year out, 'rejoicing in hope, patient in tribulation'—a struggle against the common enemies of man: tyranny, poverty, disease and war itself.
>
> . . .

In the long history of the world, only a few generations have been granted the role of defending freedom in its hour of maximum danger. I do not shrink from this responsibility—I welcome it.

. . .

And so my fellow Americans: ask not what your country can do for you—ask what you can do for your country.[66]

Just a few weeks before his well-received address, Kennedy received news of Khrushchev's speech of 6 January in which the Soviet leader indicated his determination to support and encourage "wars of national liberation." Having read the works of Mao Tse-tung, his disciple Lin Piao, and Che Guevara on guerrilla warfare, the President believed he had come upon the essence of a new Russian attempt at universal dominion.[67] In his first State of the Union Message, delivered on Capitol Hill on the thirtieth of January, Kennedy sounded the alarm "in an hour of national peril." Citing the major asset of the United States—the willingness and determination of its people to meet danger without panic—he declared that:

No man entering upon this office, regardless of his party, regardless of his previous service in Washington, could fail to be staggered upon learning—even in this brief ten day period—the harsh enormity of the trials through which we must pass in the next four years. Each day the crises multiply. Each day the solution grows more difficult. Each day we draw nearer the hour of maximum danger, as weapons spread and hostile forces grow stronger. I feel I must inform the Congress that our analyses over the last ten days make it clear that—in each of the principal areas of crisis—the tide of events has been running out and time has not been our friend.

Alluding to Khrushchev's speech—which to Kennedy signalled the beginning of total conflict in the vital southern hemisphere—he reminded the nation that, "We must never be lulled into believing that either power [the Soviet Union or China] has yielded its ambitions for world domination—ambitions which they force-fully restated only a short time ago."[68] There could be little doubt that the President was alarmed. But what most legislators did not know was that he was becoming more agitated with the passing of every day. As he had reviewed each successive draft of the message, he constantly sought to "make more somber his warning to the country of the perils that lay ahead." In the original draft, for example, Kennedy read the following section approvingly: "Our problems are critical. The tide is unfavorable. The news will be worse before it is better. And while hoping and working for the best, we should prepare ourselves for the worst." As ominous as this passage already was, the President decided two days before delivery to insert the paragraph cited above: "Each day the crises multiply. . . ." And on the day before he was to address the joint session of the Congress, he added one more prediction: "There will be further setbacks before the tide is turned."[69]

The events of his first year tended to reinforce Kennedy's state of mind. During the first months, the crisis in Laos dominated the attention of the administration and crystallized for the President (in light of the Soviet Premier's recent speech) the problem of countering the new Kremlin tactic for expansion—that is, guerrilla warfare.[70] As the situation deteriorated, "long and agonizing" meetings were held in the Secretary of State's office among such figures as Dean Rusk, Robert McNamara, Chairman of the Joint Chiefs of Staff Lemnitzer, Paul Nitze, McGeorge Bundy, and Roger Hilsman. When proposals were advanced concerning the dispatch of anywhere from a division to sixty thousand Marines to the country, it became obvious that such an undertaking

would require more American ground forces than were available. The Eisenhower 'New Look' had reduced the ground forces in favor of air power, and it would have been impossible to put that many men into Laos without taking troops from the defense of Europe—right at a time when the Berlin crisis was daily becoming more acute.[71]

Shocked to discover that to send a mere ten thousand men to Southeast Asia would deplete the strategic reserve, President Kennedy immediately directed Defense Secretary McNamara "to begin the work of building a military establishment versatile enough to meet the full spectrum of possible threats from guerrilla infiltration to nuclear holocaust."[72] This, of course, was the beginning of a build-up in conventional and counterinsurgency forces which would eventually increase the manpower of the armed services by 200,000 men and the force level of the Army's Special Forces by sixfold.

But it was the Bay of Pigs fiasco which, in Sorensen's words, "altered Kennedy's entire approach."[73] Two days after the collapse of the ill-fated invasion of Castro's Cuba, the President made a surprise telephone call to retired Army Chief of Staff Maxwell Taylor, requesting that he serve as chairman of a committee (consisting of Arleigh Burke, Allen Dulles, and Robert Kennedy) to investigate the venture's failure. The charter of the Cuba Study Group as set forth by the President was, as Taylor interpreted it, "a broad invitation to make excursions into any aspect of limited and guerrilla warfare." In his letter to the committee, Kennedy noted that:

It is apparent that we need to take a close look at all our practices and programs in the areas of military and paramilitary, guerrilla and anti-guerrilla activities which fall short of outright war. I believe we need to strengthen our work in this area. In the course of your study, I hope you will give special attention to the lessons which can be learned from recent events in Cuba.[74]

As early as the first meeting of the National Security Council (1 February 1961), the President had indicated that he "took very seriously" Khrushchev's speech of the month before and had directed Secretary McNamara to consider means of placing more emphasis on the development of counterinsurgency techniques. A few months later, with a new sense of concern and urgency in light of the Bay of Pigs, he appointed General Taylor his Military Representative and placed him in the Executive Office Building alongside the White House to head a task force on "cold war planning," which turned out to be "primarily a matter of planning defenses against subversive insurgency . . . on the Sino-Soviet periphery."[75]

Kennedy was so impressed with the implications of the Bay of Pigs and Khrushchev's declaration of insurrectionary war that "he made anti-guerrilla instruction a personal project."[76] In the wake of his defeat ninety miles from the United States, he declared to the nation's newspaper editors:

Too long we have fixed our eyes on traditional military needs, on armies prepared to cross borders or missiles poised for flight. Now it should be clear that this is no longer enough, that our security may be lost piece by piece, country by country, without firing a single missile or the crossing of a single border.[77]

Shortly afterwards, he followed this up with a second State of the Union message in which he called for a third increase in the Eisenhower budget[78] and warned that while the Soviets

have fired no missiles, and their troops are seldom seen. They send arms, agitators, aid, technicians and propaganda to every troubled area. But where fighting is required, it is usually done by others, by guerrillas striking at night, by assassins striking alone. . . . Experience has taught us that . . . nuclear weapons cannot prevent subversion. . . .[79]

Enthralled with the euphoria which he himself had generated over the doctrine of counterinsurgency—and firmly believing that he had found the magic formula capable of stemming the new Communist advance—Kennedy assumed personal direction of the innovative concept. In fact, he became even so pedantic as to personally select the new equipment to be used by his Green Berets.[80] At one point, he was so impressed with the latest issue of the *Marine Corps Gazette* (which was devoted entirely to guerrilla warfare) that he summoned the State Department's chief of Intelligence and Research, Roger Hilsman, to the White House. (Hilsman, who had led an OSS guerrilla group behind enemy lines in Burma during the Second World War, had been a major contributor to the journal.) For nearly three-quarters of an hour, Kennedy led a spirited conversation:

> the President firing questions about my wartime experiences, exchanging arguments with me on the theory of fighting and meeting guerrilla wars, and repeating his own conviction that the most likely and immediate threat from the Communists was neither nuclear war nor large-scale conventional wars, as in Korea, but the more subtle, ambiguous threat of the guerrilla. To meet this threat, new military tactics had to be developed, which he hoped the Special Forces would do.[81]

Given Kennedy's belief that the Kremlin was committed to the domination of the developing nations (and, thus, the entire world) through the manipulation of local Communist parties, he decided to confront Khrushchev personally with his determination to thwart the perversion of the process of modernization in the Third World. On the eve of his departure for the superpower summit conference in early June, 1961, the President specifically cited the Russian Premier's January enunciation of the doctrine of wars of national liberation and stated that he was going to Vienna to prevent "serious miscalculations" about the intentions of the United States so as to preclude the possibility of war.[82] At his meeting with Khrushchev, Kennedy set forth as the major issue between the two powers the problem of the Soviet desire to disrupt the existing equilibrium of power by means of local Communist insurrections. For his part, Khrushchev disclaimed any control over foreign Communist movements and pointed out the danger of the United States' regarding revolution everywhere as the result of Soviet machinations. He maintained that the development of Communist regimes outside the borders of the Soviet Union was a natural stage of historical development which could not be prevented by American intervention and neo-colonialism. Both had inevitably run up against the stone walls of each other's dogma. Each viewing the world through his respective ideological lens, neither could comprehend the position which the other so doggedly held. For the American President, world peace and stability could be assured simply by the Soviet Union's abandoning its goal of instigating turmoil and upheaval in the developing nations. In the eyes of the Russian leader, it was natural for the status quo to be challenged and supplanted, and peace could be attained if only the Americans would refrain from pursuing a reactionary rear-guard policy against internal revolution.[83] It is little wonder, then, that Kennedy came away "deeply disturbed" by his inability to communicate with Khrushchev.[84] Rather than leading to an improvement in their mutual perception of each other's motives, the encounter probably served merely to reinforce their respective suspicions. Reporting to the nation on his return from Europe, the President expressed his conviction that his adversary "was certain that the tide was moving his way, that the revolution of rising peoples would eventually be a Communist revolution, and that the so-called wars of liberation, supported by the Kremlin, would replace the old methods of direct aggression and invasion." Surveying the change in Soviet tactics to achieve world domination, he reiterated his view that it was now the device of the war of national liberation under the umbrella of the thermonuclear stalemate which would serve as the "continuing crisis of this decade."[85]

Within six weeks after sitting down and attempting to thrash things out with Khrushchev, Berlin once more became the focal point of crisis in the cold war. For Kennedy, the Soviet probe in Europe was but one example of the Communist attempt to challenge American commitments all along the defacto truce lines of the world struggle.[86] Once again he sought supplementary defense appropriations from the Congress—this time in the order of three and a quarter billion dollars, bringing his increase in the military budget to six billion since taking the oath of office in January. In a televised address to the American people, he warned that:

> The immediate threat is in West Berlin. But that isolated outpost is not an isolated problem. The threat is worldwide. Our effort must be equally wide and strong, and not obsessed by any

single manufactured crisis. We face a challenge in Berlin, but there is also a challenge in Southeast Asia. . . .

Announcing a 25 per cent increase in military strength, the President proceeded to call reserve units to active duty and reinforce the beleaguered American garrison in Berlin. The current crisis was a lesson, he suggested, that

> we need the capability of placing in any critical area at the appropriate time a force which . . . is large enough to defend our rights at all costs—and to meet all levels of aggressive pressure with whatever levels of force are required. We intend to have a wider choice than humiliation or all our nuclear action.[87]

The mere fact that reserve forces had to be called up confirmed the administration's predisposition for an expansion of general-purpose capabilities.[88]

## V

The men around John Kennedy held much the same view of the world. W. W. Rostow, an important member of the White House staff in 1961 and later chairman of the Policy Planning Council of the State Department (whose function it would be to develop an overall world view for American foreign policy), had long meditated on both the Communist proclivity for "salami tactics" in overturning the balance of power and the primordial significance of the developing world.[89] Rostow fervently believed that the great task of the Kennedy administration was "the turning back of the great post-Sputnik Communist offensive"—a tide brought to "a virtual halt" by the time of the Cuban missile crisis of October, 1962. The turn-around effort was, he believed, accomplished by

> a radical strengthening of the American military posture: a 50 percent increase in the Polaris submarine program; a very significant increase in the number of Minuteman missiles; a 50 percent increase in the number of strategic bombers on fifteen

minute ground alert; an increase in the combat-ready Army divisions from eleven to sixteen; a very substantial increase in the size of our airlift and sealift; a very new and major effort on behalf of both the civil and military techniques of subversion, insurrection, and guerrilla warfare. But no amount of additional military hardware would have helped us if the Communists were not convinced that we would use American military force to defend vital interests of the free world.[90]

Adhering to the position that the national interest of the United States required a pluralist world in which American values could be protected, he viewed with horror the Soviet support of wars of national liberation as a means of communizing underdeveloped areas. Rostow believed that the Soviet Union would systematically avoid confrontation with the United States at points of real strength, but instead would endeavor to conquer by subterfuge the vulnerable underbelly of the non-Communist world. Thus, Communism was seen as "a disease of the transitional process" of modernization as the Soviet scavengers would seek to exploit to their advantage the political turbulence and upheaval which was endemic to that area of the globe. The task of the United States, therefore, was "to protect the independence of the revolutionary process." Equating North Vietnam's complicity in the revolution in the South with North Korea's blatant aggression of a decade before, he saw the maintenance of a non-Communist government in Saigon as the testcase for the containment of this new form of Soviet aggression. Here, in the jungles and rice paddies of Vietnam, the issue was being met head-on: "the backslide has been halted, forward movement has begun, and can be sustained if we face and surmount the problems posed for us in Southeast Asia. . . ."[91]

Maxwell Taylor, the great proponent of the doctrine of "flexible response" in the late 1950's, broadened his strategy to include guerrilla as well as conventional warfare under the Kennedy administration. He argued that the United States had "to find a way to cope with [the war of national liberation] and expose the myth of its invincibility" and urged that American forces stay in

Southeast Asia until the Kremlin relented and abandoned this new tactic "as a way of 'crawling under' the conventional defense of the Free World." To fail in a test of will in Vietnam, he maintained, "would inevitably set in train a disastrous series of events, starting perhaps among the neighboring countries of Southeast Asia, but surely extending over much of the underdeveloped world."[92]

The President's brother and Attorney General—later to be a vociferous critic of Lyndon Johnson's handling of the Kennedy commitment—adhered to a world view consistent with that of Taylor and Rostow. Robert Kennedy firmly believed that the Kremlin's purpose was "now as in 1917 to remake the world in the Communist image." Convinced "that history will sweep all other forms of society, democracy included, into obscurity," the Soviet Union sought at this juncture in history "to undermine and capture free governments and free peoples" by means of guerrilla warfare and subversion.[93] American interests, in the younger Kennedy's mind, necessitated the maintenance of a diversity of states, free from control by the international Communist movement orchestrated from Moscow. He saw the 1960's as one long "unending battle between diversity and dogmatism" and pledged the power of the United States to the defense of non-Communist development "by affirmation, by argument and if necessary . . . by arms."[94] Referring to the national liberation wars in Indochina, he promised as late as 1964: "This kind of war can be long-drawn-out and costly, but if Communism is to be stopped, it is necessary. And we mean to see this job through to the finish."[95]

The Kennedy administration, and its foreign policy advisors whom Lyndon Johnson would inherit, steadfastly maintained the "conviction that the United States did indeed face a hostile, coordinated power bent on world conquest; moreover, that the U. S. must be ready to fight at nearly every level of armed conflict to defend interests that had no apparent geographical limit."[96] In addition to this rationale for intervention, the Johnson administration also came into possession—by means of the Kennedy build-up —of the readily available means to sustain (indeed, elicit) such a course of action.[97] This is not to suggest that the Johnson administration had been irrevocably committed to the policy it pursued by the acts of its predecessor. Neither is it to be assumed that John F. Kennedy, had he lived, would have further escalated the conflict and the American commitment.[98] But leaving motives aside and considering only consequences, the fact remains that the decisions made during the Kennedy years physically committed the United States to a role for which it had been primed by the cold war oratory during the Eisenhower administration. And with the constraints fostered by Dwight Eisenhower's fiscal philosophy torn asunder, the American military machine was left to develop its own momentum.

1.  Wilfred E. Binkley, *The Man in the White House: His Powers and Duties*, rev. ed. (New York: Harper & Row, Publishers, 1964), p. 79.
2.  Theodore H. White, *The Making of the President 1960* (New York: Atheneum Publishers, 1961), p. 364.
3.  Stanley Kelley, Jr., "The Presidential Campaign," in Paul T. David, ed., *The Presidential Election and Transition, 1960-1961* (Washington, D.C.: The Brookings Institute, 1961), pp. 57-87.
4.  White, *op. cit.*, p. 377.
5.  *Ibid.*, pp. 319-320; also, James L. Sundquist, *Politics and Policy* (Washington, D. C.: The Brookings Institute, 1968), pp. 466-467.
6.  Arthur M. Schlesinger, Jr., *Kennedy or Nixon: Does It Make Any Difference?* (New York: The Macmillan Company, 1960), pp. 32-33.
7.  John F. Kennedy, *The Strategy of Peace*, edited by Allan Nevins (New York: Harper & Row, Publishers, 1960), pp. 1-5. (Emphasis added.)
8.  John F. Kennedy, *John Fitzgerald Kennedy: A Compilation of Statements and Speeches Made During His Service in the United States Senate and House of Representatives*, 88th Congress, 2nd Session, Senate Document No. 79 (Washington, D. C.: Government Printing Office, 1964), pp. 41-42. (Hereafter cited as *Kennedy: House and Senate Speeches*.)
9.  *Ibid.*, pp. 120-121.
10.  *Ibid.*, pp. 66, 77-78, 112-114, 320-323, 366.
11.  Theodore C. Sorensen, *Kennedy* (New York: Harper & Row, Publishers, 1965), pp. 17, 45-46; also, Arthur M. Schlesinger, Jr., *A Thousand Days: John F. Kennedy in the White House* (Boston: Houghton-Mifflin Company, 1965), pp. 11-12. It is interesting to note, in passing, that Kennedy did quite well in McCarthy country in the Wisconsin Presidential primary in April of 1960; see White, *op. cit.*, p. 94.
12.  Sorensen, *op. cit.*, p. 102.
13.  *Kennedy: House and Senate Speeches*, 14 August 1958, pp. 705-715.

14.  See, for example, *The New York Times*: 5 February 1959, p. 1; 23 April 1959, p. 1; 7 June 1959, p. 51; 20 September 1959, p. 1; 11 October, 1959, p. 66.

15.  *Ibid.*, 15 January 1960, text p. 15.

16.  *Ibid.*, 24 January 1960, p. 1.

17.  *Ibid.*, 14 February 1960, p. 1.

18.  *Ibid.*, 22 February 1960, p. 5; also, White *op. cit.*, pp. 107-108.

19.  *Ibid.*, 1 March 1960, p. 4.

20.  The titles of two collections of Kennedy's speeches and addresses as President aptly illustrate for the moment the themes and preoccupations of his regency: John F. Kennedy, *To Turn the Tide*, edited by John W. Gardner (New York: Harper & Brothers, Publishers, 1962); also, *The Burden and the Glory*, edited by Allan Nevins (New York: Harper & Row, Publishers, 1964).

21.  *Kennedy: House and Senate Speeches*, 14 June 1960, pp. 926-935. (Emphasis added.)

22.  *The New York Times*, 5 July 1960, text p. 20.

23.  *Ibid.*, 12 July 1960, p. 21.

24.  *Ibid.*, 13 July 1960, p. 20.

25.  *Ibid.*, 16 July 1960, text p. 7. (Emphasis in the original.) It should also be noted that of the individuals considered by Kennedy to be his running mate, two names high on the list were those of Symington and Jackson—two renowned defense partisans. (See Schlesinger, *op. cit.*, pp. 40-42).

26.  See the discussion by columnist Arthur Krock, *The New York Times*, 1 November 1959, section 4, p. 3.

27.  White, *op. cit.*, p. 183.

28.  *The New York Times*, 1 July 1959, p. 1; 26 October 1959, p. 1; 1 November 1959, p. 1; 15 November 1959, section 4, p. 1; 27 December 1959, p. 59.

29.  *Ibid.*, 26 January 1960, p. 1; 24 March 1960, p. 1; 23 April 1960, p. 1; 2 June 1960, p. 17; 9 June 1960, pp. 1, 16.

30.  *Ibid.*, 22 June 1960, p. 1; 26 June 1960, p. 1; 27 June 1960, p. 1.

31.  *Ibid.*, 29 June 1960, text p. 5; 11 July 1960, p. 17; 30 June 1960, p. 10.

32.  *Ibid.*, 26 May 1960, p. 1; 10 July 1960, p. 54; 20 July 1960, p. 1; 23 July 1960, p. 1.

33.  *Ibid.*, 14 April 1959, p. 8; 5 May 1960, p. 1; 15 May 1960, p. 1. Also, Richard M. Nixon, *Six Crises* (New York: Pocket Books, 1962), pp. 326-328.

34.  The joint statement issued by Rockefeller and Nixon contained the following on national defense policy:

In national defense, the swiftness of the technological revolution—and the warning signs of Soviet aggressiveness—makes clear that new efforts are necessary, for the facts of our survival in the 1950's give no assurance of such survival, in the same military .posture, in the 1960's. The two imperatives of national security in the 1960's are:

a.  A powerful second-strike capacity . . . , and

b.  A modern, flexible and balanced military establishment capable of deterring or meeting any logical aggression.

These imperatives require: more and improved bombers, airborne alert, speeded production of missiles and Polaris submarines, accelerated dispersal and hardening of bases, full modernization of the equipment of our ground forces, and an intensified program for civil defense.

The United States can afford and must provide the increased expenditures to implement fully this necessary program for strengthening our defense posture. There must be no price ceiling on America's security. (*The New York Times*, 24 July 1960, text p. 38.)

35.  The final draft of the defense plank included the following pledge for a: "Continuation of the 'long pull' preparedness policies which, as inaugurated under the Eisenhower-Nixon Administration, have avoided the perilous peaks and slumps of defense spending and planning which marked earlier Administrations." (*Ibid.*, 25 July 1960, text p. 14.)

36.  *Ibid.*, 25 July 1960, p. 1; 26 July 1960, p. 1.

37.  Dwight D. Eisenhower, *Waging Peace: The White House Years, 1956-1961* (Garden City: Doubleday & Company, 1965), pp. 593-597; White, *op. cit.*, chapter 7.

38.  The conservative wing of the party, led by Senator Barry Goldwater, was also incensed, in this case over what it believed to be a sell-out to the "ultra-liberal" Eastern establishment. See *The New York Times*, 24 July 1960, p. 38; also, White, *op. cit.*, chapter 7.

39.  *The New York Times*, 19 January 1960, pp. 17-22; Richard J. Whalen, "The Shifting Equation of Nuclear Defense," *Fortune*, 1 June 1967, pp. 85 ff.

40.  *The New York Times*, 14 January 1960, p. 1; 26 January 1960, p. 14. Eisenhower, who on the basis of previous experience with intelligence estimates of Soviet capabilities and intentions had not really been worried about the Russian missile threat, became convinced that the missile gap was a fiction as a result of the highly secret U-2 program. See David Wise and Thomas B. Ross, *The U-2 Affair* (New York: Random House, 1962), p. 263.

41.  *The New York Times*, 28 January 1960, p. 18; 4 February 1960, p. 12; 18 February 1960, p. 12; 22 February 1960, p. 2.

42.  *Ibid.*, 5 April 1960, p. 20.

43.  *Ibid.*, 23 June 1960, p. 13; Paul Tillett, "The National Conventions," in David *op. cit.*, pp. 31-56; Eisenhower, *op. cit.*, chapter 25.

44.  *The New York Times*, 7 July 1960, p. 1.

45.  Eisenhower, *op. cit.*, chapter 27; White *op. cit.*, chapter 7.

46.  *The New York Times*, 27 July 1960, p. 27.

47.  *Ibid.*, 14 August 1960, section 4, p. 12.

48.  *Ibid.*, 7 September 1960, p. 9.

49.  Eisenhower, *op. cit.*, p. 597.

50.  *The New York Times*, 11 October 1960, p. 35; 21 October 1960, p. 1; Eisenhower, *op. cit.*, p. 600.

51.  *Ibid.*, 26 October 1960, p. 30; 28 October 1960, p. 18; 29 October 1960, p. 14; 2 November 1960, p. 25; 3 November 1960, p. 24; 5 November 1960, p. 10.

52.  Emmet John Hughes, *The Ordeal of Power: A Political Memoir of the Eisenhower Years* (New York: Atheneum Publishers, 1963), p. 316.

53.  Earl Mazo, *Richard Nixon: A Political and Personal Portrait* (New

*The Capitalizers II*

York: Harper & Brothers, Publishers, 1963), pp. 6-7, 201, 268-275; Steward Alsop, *Nixon and Rockefeller: A Double Portrait* (Garden City: Doubleday & Company, 1960), pp. 177-178.

54. *The New York Times*, 28 January 1960, p. 19; 22 September 1960, p. 1; 1 October 1960, p. 9; 2 October 1960, p. 1; 30 October 1960, p. 44. Also: U. S. Senate, Committee on Commerce, Subcommittee on Communications, *Freedom of Communications*, part I, 87th, 1st Session, Senate Report No. 994 (Washington, D. C.: Government Printing Office, 1961), pp. 1120-1124 (1 August 1960), 1169-1178 (4 August), 24-32 (24 August), 62-66 (12 September), 81-90 (13 September), 94-102 (14 September), 156-164 (17 September), 178-179 (19 September), 223-229 (21 September), 306-313 (27 September), 328-340 (28 September), 360-366 (30 September), 373-380 (1 October), 557-564 (14 October), 632-635 (17 October), 736-741 (25 October), 797-800 (27 October), 962-965 (2 November). (This Senate document, hereafter cited as *Freedom of Communications*, represents a complete record of the 1960 campaign speeches and statements of the two candidates.)

55. *The New York Times*, 25 August 1960, p. 1; 8 October 1960, pp. 10-11; 30 October 1960, p. 56. Also, Freedom of Communications, part II, pp. 94-102 (14 August 1960), 663-669 (18 October), 692-694 (20 October). See also, Richard M. Nixon, *The Challenges We Face: Selected Speeches and Papers of Richard M. Nixon* (New York: McGraw-Hill, 1960).

56. *Freedom of Communications*, part II, pp. 1152-1169 (3 August 1960); part III, p. 36 (2 November 1960).

57. *New York Times*, 26 October 1960, p. 1.

58. *Freedom of Communications*, part I, pp. 41-46 (24 August 1960), 50-55 (26 August), 78-82 (2 September), 985-989 (5 September), 125-129, 992-994 (6 September), 998-1000 (7 September), 230-234 (14 September), 249-254 (15 September), 256-262 (16 September), 403-406 (29 September), 649-654 (18 October), 699-702 (22 October), 934-936 (24 October), 894-898 (4 November), 953-955 (7 November).

59. *Ibid.*, pp. 295-298 (20 September 1960).

60. *Ibid.*, pp. 426-430 (1 October 1960).

61. Richard J. Barnet, *The Economy of Death* (New York: Atheneum, 1970), pp. 124-125.

62. Whalen, *op. cit.*, p. 86; Jack Raymond, *Power at the Pentagon* (New York: Harper & Row, Publishers, 1964), p. 294; Raymond Aron, *The Great Debate: Theories of Nuclear Strategy*, translated by Ernest Pawel (Garden City: Doubleday & Company, 1965), p. 117; Walter LaFeber, *America, Russia and the Cold War, 1945-1966* (New York: John Wiley & Sons, Inc., 1967), pp. 218-219.

63. Sorensen, *op. cit.*, chapter 22. Also see Kennedy's responses at press conferences on 27 June 1962 and 3 April 1963 in: John F. Kennedy, *Kennedy and the Press: The News Conferences*, edited by H. W. Chase and A. H. Lerman (New York: Thomas Y. Crowell Company, 1965), pp. 273-279 and 413-419. (Hereafter cited as *Kennedy and the Press*.)

64. Sorensen, *op. cit.*, pp. 608-609, 626.

65. See the discussion by Adam Yarmolinsky, *The Military Establishment: Its Impacts on American Society* (New York: Harper & Row, Publishers, 1971), chapter 7.

66. "Inaugural Address, 20 January 1961," in U. S. President, *Public Papers of the Presidents of the United States: John F. Kennedy*, vol. I (Washington, D. C.: Government Printing Office, 1962-1964), pp. 1-3. (Hereafter cited as *Public Papers: Kennedy.*)

67. As Schlesinger notes: "Kennedy, reading the speech, accepted Khrushchev's rejection of nuclear war as honest enough. . . . But the bellicose confidence which surged through the rest of the speech and especially the declared faith in victory through rebellion, subversion and guerrilla warfare alarmed Kennedy more than Moscow's amiable signals assuaged him." (*Op. cit.*, p. 303.)

68. "Annual Message to the Congress on the State of the Union, 30 January 1961," *ibid.*, pp. 19-28.

69. Sorensen, *op. cit.*, p. 292.

70. Schlesinger, *op. cit.*, p. 340.

71. Roger Hilsman, *To Move a Nation: The Politics of Foreign Policy in the Administration of John F. Kennedy* (Garden City: Doubleday & Company, 1967), pp. 127-128.

72. Schlesinger, *op. cit.*, pp. 315-317.

73. Sorensen, *op. cit.*, p. 631.

74. Maxwell D. Taylor, *Swords and Ploughshares* (New York: W. W. Norton & Company, Inc., 1972), p. 184.

75. *Ibid.*, p. 200. By the end of the year, Kennedy's dissatisfaction with progress in the field caused him to establish a Special Group Counterinsurgency (CI)—an inter-departmental committee chaired by Taylor the purpose of which was to assure recognition throughout the Government of the overriding importance of the project. To ensure this reorientation of military strategy, Taylor was later (October 1962) appointed Chairman of the Joint Chiefs of Staff.

76. Schlesinger, *op. cit.*, p. 340.

77. "Address Before the American Society of Newspaper Editors, 20 April 1961," *Public Papers: Kennedy*, vol. I, pp. 304-306.

78. In March, the President followed up the call for more funds for the military in his State of the Union message with a request for an additional 650 million dollar increase. See "Special Message to Congress on the Defense Budget, 29 March 1961," *ibid.*, pp. 229-240.

79. "Special Message to Congress on Urgent National Needs, 25 May 1961," *ibid.*, pp. 396-406.

80. As Sorensen notes: "He personally supervised the selection of new equipment—the replacement of heavy, noisy combat boots with sneakers, for example, and when the sneakers proved vulnerable to bamboo spikes, their reinforcement with flexible steel inner soles. He ordered more helicopters, lighter field radios and—for use by the smaller Vietnamese—a shorter, lighter rifle, with a less powerful kick, which still provided all the range jungle warfare required." (*Op. cit.*, p. 633.)

81. Hilsman, *op. cit.*, pp. 52-53. The President's enthusiasm eventually caused the *Gazette* to expand its issue into a book with Kennedy writing the preface. In his introduction, he indicated that he had read the work "from cover to cover" and was "most impressed" with such an "outstanding presentation of a vital subject." Urging military officers to digest its sub-

stance, he warned that "this is the kind of circumstance we may be called upon to face in many parts of the world." See, T. N. Greene, ed., *The Guerrilla—And How to Fight Him* (New York: Frederick A. Praeger, Publisher, 1962).

82. "Remarks at the President's Birthday Dinner in Boston, 29 May 1961," and "Transcript of Interview by the B. B. C., 5 June 1961," in *Public Papers: Kennedy*, vol. I, pp. 416-418 and 430. Also, "Remarks at a Paris Press Luncheon, 2 June 1961," *Kennedy and the Press*, pp. 80-85.

83. See the excellent summary of the Kennedy-Khrushchev confrontation in Vienna in Schlesinger, *op. cit.*, pp. 358-374.

84. *Ibid.*, p. 374.

85. "Radio and Television Report to the American People on Returning from Europe, 6 June 1961," *Public Papers: Kennedy*, vol. I, pp. 441-446.

86. "News Conference, 19 July 1961," *Kennedy and the Press*, pp. 99-100.

87. "Radio and Television Report to the American People on the Crisis in Berlin, 25 July 1961," *Public Papers: Kennedy*, vol. I, pp. 533-535.

88. Robert S. McNamara, *The Essence of Security: Reflections in Office* (New York: Harper & Row, Publishers, 1968), p. 79.

89. See, for example, the following by Rostow: *The United States in the World Arena: An Essay in Recent History* (New York: Harper & Row, Publishers, 1960); *The Stages of Economic Growth: A Non-Communist Manifesto* (London: Cambridge University Press, 1960).

90. W. W. Rostow, *View From the Seventh Floor* (New York: Harper & Row, Publishers, 1964), pp. 3 and 11.

91. *Ibid.*, pp. 18, 85, 116, 120, 160-161.

92. Maxwell D. Taylor, *Responsibility and Response* (New York: Harper & Row, Publishers, 1967), pp. 2-10. It will be recalled that it was Taylor, along with Rostow, who urged an "expanded commitment" on the part of the United States in South Vietnam after their fact-finding visit to Southeast Asia in the fall of 1961. For Taylor's recollection of their report and its reception by the administration, see his *Swords and Ploughshares*, chapters 18 and 10.

93. Robert F. Kennedy, *The Pursuit of Justice* (New York: Harper & Row, Publishers, 1964), p. 129. The President's brother was a leading force in the counterinsurgency movement within the administration.

94. Robert F. Kennedy, *Just Friends and Brave Enemies* (New York: Harper & Row, Publishers, 1962), pp. 56-57.

95. Robert Kennedy, *The Pursuit of Justice*, p. 132.

96. Townshend Hoopes, *The Limits of Intervention* (New York: David McKay Company, Inc., 1970), p. 13. (Hoopes, who had been executive secretary to the Military Panel of the Rockefeller Brothers Special Study Project in 1957-1958, was later Deputy Assistant Secretary of Defense for International Security Affairs and then Undersecretary of the Air Force under President Johnson.)

97. For a detailed consideration of the actual nature of the massive military build-up under the Kennedy administration, see: McNamara, *op. cit.*; William W. Kaufmann, *The McNamara Strategy* (New York: Harper & Row, Publishers, 1964); Robert N. Ginsburgh, *U. S. Military Strategy in the Sixties*

(New York: W. W. Norton & Company, Inc., 1965); U. S. House of Representatives, Committee on Appropriations, Subcommittee on Department of Defense Appropriations, *Department of Defense Appropriations for 1962*, part 3, 87th Congress, 1st Session (Washington, D. C.: Government Printing Office, 1961), testimony of Robert S. McNamara, pp. 4-20; U. S. Senate, Subcommittee of the Committee on Appropriations, *Department of Defense Appropriations for 1962*, 87th Congress, 1st Session (Washington, D. C.: Government Printing Office, 1961), pp. 2-27.

98. For the argument that President Kennedy had, indeed, planned to withdraw all American troops from South Vietnam by the end of 1965, but intended to delay such an announcement until after his re-election, see John Galloway, ed., *The Kennedys and Vietnam* (New York: Facts-on-File, 1971), pp. 49-51.

# 9

## CONCLUSIONS

### I

JOHN F. KENNEDY'S "NEW FRONTIER"—THE RUBRIC under which he framed an interventionist policy designed to preserve the world in the image of the United States—hardly received an unqualified mandate in the 1960 elections. In fact, the Presidential election which brought the Democrats back to power was the closest in percentage terms since 1824. Failing to receive an actual majority of the popular votes cast (the winning margin was so slight that Vice President Nixon seriously considered contesting the results[1]), the Kennedy quest for the burden and the glory of world leadership was, in reality, a mission imposed upon the nation from above. The President and his advisors adopted the soldier's outlook on international events, but (unlike the Soldier-President Dwight Eisenhower) failed to develop the military man's sense of caution and restraint.[2] Moreover, unlike the prestigious Eisenhower, who was never awed by his uniformed advisors and remained skeptical of military solutions to foreign policy problems, the Kennedy team became more heavily reliant upon military options. As one observer puts it: "It takes a confident and courageous civilian official in the DOD, in Congress, or in the White House to face up to a roomful of hard-faced, well-decorated generals and admirals and either to stare them down or talk them down."[3] And as Arthur M. Schlesinger, Jr., recalls in regard to the Kennedy administration:

> It is one thing for a Special Assistant to talk frankly in private to a President at his request and another for a college professor, fresh to government, to interpose his unassisted judgment in open meeting against that of such august figures as . . . the Joint Chiefs of Staff, each speaking with the full weight of his institution behind him. Moreover, the advocates of the adventure [in this case, the Bay of Pigs invasion] had a rhetorical advantage. They could strike virile poses and talk tangible things—fire power, air strikes, landing crafts and so on. . . . I could not help feeling that the desire to prove to the C. I. A. and the Joint Chiefs that they were not soft-headed idealists but were really tough guys, too influenced State's representatives at the cabinet table.[4]

In light of the fact that the hysteria surrounding the Russian Sputnik of 1957 found the Eisenhower administration in the midst of one of its economy drives in the Defense Department and still it failed to shift policy (coupled with the fact that despite the off-year elections of 1958 bringing the heaviest Democratic majorities to the Congress since the Roosevelt landslide of 1936, the President proceeded to impound hundreds of millions of dollars slated for the military), leads one to reject an explanation of shifting American defense policy which looks solely to the international environment. The formulation of national security policy lies at the juncture of the domestic and international systems, and while stimuli from the external environment tend to elicit responses from national systems, many outcomes are consistent with initial conditions. The initial input from the environment (in our case study, the shock of the Soviet space satellite and the resulting fears of a deterrent gap) will be transformed into specific policy outputs by the peculiar nature of the domestic decision-making process. In general, one can say that the broad contours of foreign policy (such as America's postwar containment of Soviet influence) are largely a function of external factors—that is, national interest and power considerations. But specific decisions on the

Conclusions

disposition of the defense effort (such as the strategic and conventional build-up which occurred under the Kennedy and Johnson administrations) are conditioned by the internal political process.

The outcome of military planning, which is a social rather than an intellective process, tends to be a reflection of the constellation of domestic forces and the nature of the governmental process. In the American political system, the Constitutional dispersion of authority over defense policy leads inexorably to the involvement of the Congress (more as a pressure group or appellate division than a prime mover) in the fashioning of military posture. The divergence of perspectives and institutional interests within the mammoth executive bureaucracy assures dissension over White House decisions on resource allocation and the involvement of the military establishment in the appropriations process. Outside the confines of government proper, one finds both the press and the academic worlds as the managers of dominant elite opinions, the former setting the parameters of national debate and the latter granting the aura of intellectual legitimacy to those doctrines opposed to official administration policy. Finally, there is the peculiarly American procedure for the "changing of the guard"—the quadrennial Presidential election—which caps the whole process, allowing the innovating arguments (already given a sense of propriety by other actors in the controversy) to become a new orthodoxy of the state.

## II

The original set of defense doctrines—that which would be supplanted by the new administration in 1961—was largely a reflection of the exigencies of Dwight Eisenhower's political philosophy. Holding a zero-sum game view of the cold war much in the same manner as did his successor, Eisenhower nonetheless sought a security program which would balance two supreme values—the external security of the United States in a hostile world and the preservation of the core values of American society during an indefinite period of semi-mobilization. Believing the Soviet

265

threat to be a given for the foreseeable future, he endeavored to direct the country's defense policy in such a way so as to maintain a constant, minimal, and sustained effort which would prevent the dislocation of an inherently precarious and unplanned domestic economic system. Inordinately huge defense expenditures would, in the eyes of President Eisenhower and his advisors, lead to inflation (which would undermine the faith in the free economy so necessary to its beneficial operation) or to economic controls (which would destroy the spontaneity of individual decision seen as the irreducible minimum of liberty in a free society). Furthermore, the psychological and physical mobilization for war during an extended period of peace could bring only the attrition of individual autonomy and the domination of a consumer-oriented economy by defense related industries. Any way the matter was approached, it seemed obvious to the Eisenhower administration that the result of massive military spending could be only the disruption of the free economic system and the values which it nurtured. The specter which loomed ominously in the background of budget deliberations was that of the garrison state.

An important—and, until recent years, a little appreciated—byproduct of this fiscal conservatism was the necessity for minimal intervention abroad with either American dollars or United States combat forces. Planning for the long pull meant a New Look in defense policy which precluded reliance upon conventional forces for either frequent or prolonged deployment overseas. The two major examples of direct involvement in the internal affairs of foreign states—Guatemala in 1954 and Lebanon in 1958—aptly illustrate the limits of intervention compatible with Eisenhower's notion of the national interest.

In Central America, a traditional American sphere of influence, the Eisenhower administration mounted an "indirect 'therapeutic' intervention" to thwart the attempt by a relatively small group of native Communists to undermine the pro-American alignment of the tiny republic of Guatemala.[5] The decade of social upheaval in that country which followed the dictatorship of Jorge Ubico witnessed the mounting rise of Communist influence, first under the progressive regime of Juan José Arévalo who permitted

Conclusions

the Communists to obtain a solid base of support within the labor movement and among students. Under his successor, Jacobo Arbenz (who assumed office in 1951), Communist influence was consciously permitted to pervade the government. In 1952, Arbenz legalized the Communist party and soon called upon its members to serve in the government coalition. Though not a Communist himself, Arbenz relied heavily upon party elements for the supervision of his agrarian reform program and ultimately presided over their infiltration among workers, peasants, students and the educational system. Thus, within a mere decade, "Communism was born and grew until it exerted greater influence than in any country outside the Iron Curtain."[6] And by late 1953, Eisenhower decided that the leftist regime would have to be deposed. But the method employed for ridding the hemisphere of potential Soviet influence is instructive. The United States, through agents of the Central Intelligence Agency in Honduras, invested the sum total of seven million dollars to finance an invasion by some 150 men (supported by a handful of P-47 World War II vintage fighter bombers) under the leadership of Colonel Carlos Castillo Armas—a rival leader opposed to the regime for a number of years.[7] Not only did the United States refrain from overt or costly intervention, but the administration carefully isolated the Arbenz government from regional institutions, getting through the Tenth Inter-American Conference at Caracas three months before the invasion a virtually unanimous resolution (Guatemala, naturally, being the lone dissenter) condemning Communist infiltration of the Western Hemisphere. When the venture was completed, Castillo Armas was in Guatemala City—and the United States was out seven million dollars.

The Eisenhower administration's dispatch of troops to the Middle East several years later similarly serves as an indication of the restrained and cautious nature of American ventures abroad in the 1950's.[8] Much as was the case with Central America, the national interests of the United States were unmistakably entwined with the turn of events in this vital area. The cold war having been, in effect, initiated in the Eastern Mediterranean with the enunciation of the Truman Doctrine in 1947, the United States had long been aware of the disastrous consequences which would ensue from Soviet domination of the Middle East; that is, Kremlin control of the Moslem world would have meant control over the geographical crossroads of three continents, the vital oil resources of the area (with the resulting capability of disrupting the free world economy) and the psychological outflanking of the North Atlantic alliance. Moreover, fears of Soviet designs in the area were by no stretch of the imagination illusory. Indeed, the Russian goals of controlling the Black Sea, dominating the Straits, and obtaining a sphere of influence in the Persian Gulf long preceded the Bolshevik Revolution. And the continuity of Russian foreign policy had been vividly illustrated by Stalin's blatant demands on Turkey and Iran during the immediate postwar years. Thus, when Secretary of State John Foster Dulles supported the creation of the Baghdad Pact beginning in 1953, he merely followed the lead of his predecessor who had pushed various Middle East defense proposals to be built around Great Britain and the Commonwealth. The organization of the "Northern Tier" into what is now the Central Treaty Organization (CENTO) served to buttress the position of those states which felt most threatened by the Soviet Union and which were most receptive to the idea of an alliance. Allowing the initiative for such a pact to come from the regional powers, the United States refused to formally join despite the urging of all four local participants as well as the United Kingdom. While participating in the consultative arrangements of the organization and yet remaining formally aloof, this country became "a participant for all practical purposes but without the legal commitments."[9] The Eisenhower administration thus believed it had secured a vital area of American interest while only indirectly intervening.

With the Suez crisis of 1956, however, the Soviets increased their pressure on and influence in the area while the British had all but lost their traditional role as a Great Power in the Middle East. Fearing a power vacuum, President Eisenhower sought to restore stability in the region and prevent the expansion of Soviet influence by associating the Congress with a solemn declaration of intent. Given the long objective of the United States to block Communist domination of the Middle East, the resulting Eisenhower Doctrine represented merely "a new public posture rather than . . . new aims and policies."[10] Careful to obtain legislative authorization to employ American armed forces in the area in order to protect the independence of the several states,—a power which many contemporary observers believed the President already had by virtue of his role as Commander in Chief—Eisenhower also requested a mere two hundred million dollars in aid to the area (in fact, funds which had already been appropriated by the Congress) free from existing legislative restrictions. Having formulated a declaratory policy of intent, the administration was able to preserve the Jordanian government of King Hussein a few months later with the investment of ten million dollars and a redeployment of the Sixth Fleet. The following year, with civil war in Lebanon and the continuing threat to neighboring Jordan, the United States did indeed intervene directly with military forces in the area, as the British dispatched paratroops to Jordan. The American intervention in Lebanon was a peculiar affair, consisting of but a few thousand Marines for a period of a few months with the force being involved in no hostilities (and consequently neither receiving nor inflicting casualties). And as soon as the Arab states introduced a resolution at the United Nations pledging to respect each other's systems of government in the future, and the Lebanese factions formed a government of "national conciliation" to be neutral in inter-Arab and the East-West conflicts, the troops were withdrawn. As one observer aptly sums up the whole episode:

The brief visit of U. S. troops to Lebanon was indeed a strange kind of intervention. They came fully equipped for battle but under instructions not to shoot unless shot at, and they were not. They were not used to impose the Lebanese Government's will on its rebellious citizens, but served rather as part of the scenery while the warring factions worked out a compromise. They had no sooner arrived when how to get them out again became the diplomatic question of the day. The United States, from the beginning, stated its willingness to withdraw the troops if and when the United Nations would take over the task they were performing or the Lebanese Government should

269

request that they leave. After the passage of the Arab resolution by the United Nations and the political compromise in Lebanon the Lebanese Government did so request and the troops were withdrawn.[11]

The Eisenhower strategy of intervention, then, moderated and conditioned by its fiscal conservatism, was of a specific nature —preferring covert operations to overt involvement, multilateral commitments to going it alone, Congressional authorization to Executive initiation, surgical strikes to bottomless entanglements. Foreign relations during the 1950's resembled more the game of the grand chessmaster than the crusade of the true believer.

## III

The Eisenhower policy of the long pull—which was less a pure military policy founded upon solely military considerations than part of a larger social philosophy—did not at all sit well with many factions within the defense establishment. Given the divergent perspectives and institutional interests among the armed services (as well as within each service) coupled with the fixed nature of the defense budget, a struggle for the allocation of funds and the serving of differing versions of the national interest was bound to arise. This was especially true of the late 1950's, when the President's doctrine of nuclear sufficiency and the avoidance of limited war would conflict with the official views of all three services— the Army and the Navy seeking a significant conventional war capability, the Air Force hoping to retain a superiority in strategic striking power. Some of the more recent critiques of the military, it would seem, have, in their valid attempts to circumscribe the impact of the cold war on American society, beclouded the actual nature of the soldier's role in the policy process. Military involvement in the budgetary process—both within the executive branch and at the other end of Pennsylvania Avenue—has come to be accepted as legitimate. The rules of the game of our system of government have drawn the profession of arms off the battlefield and into the committee rooms of the Capitol.

While the military profession as a whole is subject by the very nature of its environment to political temptations, the sources of non-professionalism (in the sense of the proclivity for active involvement in the political process) have also been systemic in nature; that is, the fact that high-ranking members of the officer corps dissent so vigorously from administration policy and carry their case through non-executive channels is more a function of the changing nature of the military establishment and the setting for the formulation of strategic policy than it is a result of the personality quirks or ambitious motivations of individuals in the Pentagon. In regard to internally generated stimuli for dissension, we have noted both the tendency of officers of innovating perspectives and unconventional backgrounds—less hampered by the rigidities of the professional ethic—to rise to the top of the military hierarchy as well as the dramatic transformation of the military establishment itself since the Second World War. This second factor concerns the change in the internal structure of a small, isolated, cloister-like warrior class to that of a vast and permanent bureaucracy and technocracy where the management of organizations and an increasingly complex technology have taken precedence over Clausewitzian field tactics. As for the external sources of dissension, one finds a political system which has purposefully failed to identify the powers to which the military elite is ultimately accountable—that is, at what stage in the policy process it must accept the verdict of civilian authorities as final. In addition, the attempt by the Eisenhower administration to bypass its military advisors in the formulation of doctrine served to further undermine the professional ethic.

Though the Eisenhower New Look served primarily to maintain a ceiling on defense expenditures during the post-Sputnik period, the President had previously found it at times necessary to protect the external security of the country against an overemphasis on economy. During these "lean years," when the Congress was apt to consider the administration overly generous toward the defense establishment, the services as a whole demonstrated remarkable loyalty to the President's budget (minimal as it may have been considered by the military) and, while nonetheless asserting the particular roles and missions of their respec-

271

tive services, the Chiefs of Staff and the Chief of Naval Operations (as well as the service Secretaries) tended to mute their traditional rivalries. With the fears over the adequacy of security posture precipitated by the Russian satellite, however, the military chieftains were quick to abandon their marriage-of-convenience and align themselves with the legislative branch against the Chief Executive. The need for simply minimizing losses having been eclipsed by the "Pearl Harbor" psychology which swept the Congress, the several services now vociferously pressed their particular versions of the general welfare. In effect, the military elite split into two opposing doctrinal camps: the Air Force, on the one side, arguing for the paramountcy of air and missile power and the cardinal importance of preserving and expanding a position of strategic superiority; and, on the opposite side, the Army and Navy urging the acceptance of nuclear sufficiency and stalemate and the redistribution of resources away from airpower and toward limited war capabilities. The Congress, during this period, was to be a natural ally for all the services, for while it failed to develop a consistent doctrinal line of its own, it remained receptive to everyone's pleas for more funds. The administration, rejecting both the Air Force's demands for assured superiority and her sister services' pleas for an expansion of conventional capabilities, was compelled to wage alone what was to be a rear-guard action against an upward revision of the budget.

President Eisenhower's desire to circumvent the parochialism of the military hierarchy led him to politicize the professional soldiery by eliciting from the Joint Chiefs of Staff their formal acquiescence to what was, in reality, a treaty of the budget. These highly vulnerable statements of support for the executive level and allocation of expenditures (submitted to the respective appropriations subcommittees of both houses of the legislature along with the several individual reservations) merely served as an impetus for Congressional critics to breach this façade. Seeking to exploit the fissures between the administration and the military, members of both houses attempted to exploit the inconsistencies between the treaty and the reservations by enticing service witnesses with the prospect of a *carte blanche*, reminding them of the appellate function of the Congress, and lauding the military's expertise while attacking the civilian leadership of the Defense Department and the Bureau of the Budget.

The very nature of the appropriations process, then, served to draw even the most reluctant general or admiral into the political arena. Those innovators solidly committed to their particular causes rather than that of the administration needed little in the way of temptation to spring into the thick of things. And, again, the political system was such that there were several readily available and effective instruments at their disposal to affect the course of policy formulation. The convenience of the Congressional forum afforded certain able activists (like Taylor and Gavin) an excellent opportunity to air their views; the information "leak," skillfully employed by the intelligence arms of all the services (especially the Air Force) during the missile gap controversy, called into question the very foundations of the administration's stand on Soviet capabilities; addresses (e.g., Power in 1960) and interviews (e.g., Gavin in 1958) allowed the dissenters to set the tone for Congressional debate and hearings; publications from retirement (most notably, Ridgway, Gavin, Taylor, and Medaris) permitted the innovators to cast aside the remnants of professional loyalty to the Commander in Chief and severely take the administration to task; and, finally, the very act of retirement itself (especially in the midst of confrontation with the administration) served as the supreme manifestation of politicization.

In short, then, out of the perennial internecine struggle among the military services there emerged an incipient set of alternative doctrines.

## IV

Innovating doctrines having been spawned by military politics, it remained for the press to popularize the alternative policies and for academia to afford them with an intellectual justification.

The press, not notably successful in dictating its views to the general population, is influential in setting the focus of attention of the foreign and defense policy elite. News in the nation's capital being largely defined by the incestuous Washington press corps and disseminated to the newspapers of the country at large, the press has, in effect, been granted the ill-defined role of setting the parameters of acceptable policy. Moreover, the Congress (for the most part deprived of an independent source of intelligence and expertise) remains highly dependent upon the prestige press (for example, the *New York Times*) for both the definition and analysis of news. During the post-Sputnik period, the communications media presented individual legislators with general information on the substance of the national security debate (especially the activities and views of the innovators), intelligence on divisions within the executive branch, and authoritative analyses of complex policy alternatives. Given the President's sources of expertise and information-gathering and analysis, the press' influence on the Chief Executive was of a different variety. The adversary environment of the Presidential news conference forced Eisenhower to come to terms with his critics publicly—to popularize by sheer repetition an issue which he would rather have ignored.

The *New York Times*, during this period, was representative of the general cold war psychology and rhetoric which had engulfed the nation for a decade. Assuming Communism to be a monolithical menace bent on world conquest, its editorials identified any increase in the power of the Soviet Union with a correlative deterioration of American security abroad. Highly critical of the Republican administration for accepting temporary quantitative inferiority in missiles and long-run strategic parity, the *Times* argued consistently for greater allocations for space exploration, the Strategic Air Command, and the armed services whose primary responsibility it was to wage conventional war. Aside from its overall desire to increase defense spending, the press was no more able to coalesce around a specific strategic doctrine than was the Congress. Indeed, on the one hand there were nationally syndicated columnists like the Alsop brothers who had consistently argued for an expansion of general war capabilities while, at the same time, there existed an extremely articulate and constant partisan of finite deterrence and the strategy of limited war like Hanson Baldwin.

274

## Conclusions

It would remain the task of strategic experts from the academic world to bridge the gap between the two opposing camps—that is, the general war vs. the limited war groups. To be sure, initially academia itself was divided over the priorities of national defense. Ever since John Foster Dulles' elaboration upon the strategy of massive retaliation—which we have suggested was, in actuality, a threat of *selective* retaliation—scholars (like W. W. Kaufman, Robert Osgood, and Henry Kissinger) had criticized a policy which they contended would lead only to the paralysis of national resolve in an era which would experience the progressive undermining of the world balance of power through termite tactics. With the shock of Sputnik, a new school came into the foreground claiming that not only had there not been an overemphasis on nuclear retaliatory might, but that the United States was in mortal danger of missile blackmail at best or a preventive Soviet attack at worst. The transition of Henry Kissinger from a strictly limited war advocate to a theorist on the dangers of falling behind in both thermonuclear and conventional capabilities marks the intellectual's synthesis of the two themes which previously had remained inalterably opposed. Therefore, by the time of the 1960 Presidential contest, an alternative to the Eisenhower doctrine of finite deterrence/no conventional war had evolved. A strategy of assured superiority/limited war was now a legitimate policy substitute.

### V

Whatever influence the innovators and the popularizers had over the shift in American defense policy between the Eisenhower and Kennedy administrations, they simply did not have the power to make the ultimate decisions. It was the capitalizers who presided over the transformation of a legitimate alternative into official policy. The innovators may have devised new alternatives and the popularizers may have propagated them, but it was the capitalizers who, in the final scene of our drama, had the choice of either accepting or rejecting the new strategy.

The Congress was a consistent force for high defense spending during the months and years after Sputnik. While this branch appropriated more money for the military establishment than the President requested, the Chief Executive simply impounded funds despite Congressional intent. But the incessant clamoring for high defense spending was indicative of an influence which Eisenhower could not contain—namely, the structuring of a new climate of opinion. This was to be especially significant inasmuch as it was the Senate which would not only forge the contours of the campaign debate of 1960, but also spawn the next President and Vice President of the United States.

Several discernible patterns of behavior are evident from examining Congressional hearings and debates during the 1957-1960 period. Firstly, contrary to what should have been the case given the findings of Richard Fenno, no significant differences were found in the self-perceived roles of the House and Senate defense appropriations subcommittees. Both legislative units appear to have been more concerned with defense than with economy; furthermore, the respective armed services committees and subcommittees, though perhaps more onesided given the absence of any self-perceived role in guarding the Treasury, did not differ in kind from their sister agencies. Defense, not economy, was the preoccupation of the legislative branch during the last Eisenhower years. Differences among committees were muted. Secondly, two distinct legislative types were prevalent; the dogmatists and the partisans. Though party loyalty would appear to have been the chief factor accounting for legislative behavior on the issue of defense, deviants like the pro-economy Whitten in the House and Ellender in the Senate, as well as the tenacious pro-defense Flood in the lower house and Symington in the upper, demonstrated a consistent adherence to a philosophical imperative. The most common type, however, was the partisan (Laird and Ford, for example) and the extent to which party identification coincided with the line-up on military policy intensified with the approach of the Presidential election of 1960.

The major issue which marked the election year was the general uneasiness over the loss of American power abroad. This was unavoidable given the predominant zero-sum game view of the cold war and the beginning of the break-up in the postwar bipolar international system. With the United States losing its grasp on the course of world events due to the resurgence of other power centers, many Americans equated such a condition with the machinations of the Soviet Union. A latecomer to the forefront of the critics of the Eisenhower policy of the long pull (though a long-time friend of the military establishment), John Kennedy declared it the paramount task of a new administration to restore America's declining military might and stem the Communist advance across the developing world. Enraptured with the prospect of leading the nation out of its greatest hour of peril and into the pages of history, the Democratic standard-bearer saw the United States on the edge of a New Frontier—one which demanded the sacrifices of active world leadership and held out the promise of historical greatness and national glory.

President Kennedy's first year in office was a year of recurring crises. Alarmed by Khrushchev's fateful rhetoric concerning Soviet support for "wars of national liberation," the new Commander in Chief initiated the largest and swiftest military build-up in America's peacetime history, substituting the strategy of "flexible response" for that of massive retaliation and assured superiority for nuclear sufficiency. Confronting crises in Cuba, Laos, Vietnam, Berlin, and the Congo, Kennedy viewed them all as part of the final climactic Communist assault upon world freedom. Ultimately, he saw the world balance of power at stake in an insurgency conflict in a far-off exotic corner of the globe.[12] It is true, of course, that Kennedy's commitment to South Vietnam at the time of his death did not entail a large-scale deployment of American troops. Nor did his enlargement of Eisenhower's commitment make inevitable the further escalation of the war under his successor. Yet unlike Dwight Eisenhower, whose version of American intervention abroad was defined implicitly by the nature of his philosophy of balance and moderation, John Kennedy failed to define the limits of the United States' commitments and responsibilities. And thus he bequeathed Lyndon Johnson a commitment limited neither by his own conception of the nature of the cold war nor by the versatility of the military establishment.

1. Emmet John Hughes, "The Politics of the Sixties: From the New Frontier to the New Revolution," *The New York Times Magazine*, 4 April 1971, p. 46.

2. For a discussion of the professional military ethic of caution and restraint in resorting to force of arms, see Samuel P. Huntington, *The Soldier and The State: The Theory and Practice of Civil-Military Relations* (New York: Vintage Books, 1957), chapter 3. For example, former Army Chief of Staff Matthew B. Ridgway cautioned civilian policy-makers a decade after retiring that they ought to recognize that many foreign policy problems "do not lend themselves to purely military solutions," and that American resources, "not endless," must be conserved and not squandered "in the persuit of vague and unreachable objectives." See his *The Korean War* (Garden City: Doubleday & Company, 1967), chapter 10; see also his discussion of his opposition to American intervention in Indochina in 1954 in his *Soldier: The Memoirs of Matthew B. Ridgway* (New York: Harper & Row, Publishers, 1956), chapter 32.

3. James A. Donovan, *Militarism, U. S. A.* (New York: Charles Scribner's Sons, 1970), p. 194.

4. Arthur M. Schlesinger, Jr., *A Thousand Days: John F. Kennedy in the White House* (Boston: Houghton-Mifflin Company, 1965), pp. 355-356.

5. Ronald M. Schneider, "Guatemala: An Aborted Communist Takeover," in *Studies in the Soviet Union: The Anatomy of Communist Takeovers* (Munich, Germany: Institute for the Study of the U. S. S. R., 1971), p. 516. The analysis of the turn of events in Guatemala up to the American supported revolution of 1954 referred to in this section is drawn from this article as well as Schneider's *Communism in Guatemala, 1944-1954* (New York: Frederick A. Praeger, Publishers, 1959). For the opposite view, which discounts the actual threat of Communist subversion and points instead to the machinations of the United Fruit Company, see William Everett Kane, *Civil Strife in Latin America: A Legal History of U. S. Involvement* (Baltimore: The Johns Hopkins Press, 1972).

6. Schneider, *Communism in Guatemala*, p. 1.

7. For a discussion of the C. I. A.'s role in the Guatemalan affair, see David Wise and Thomas B. Ross, *The Invisible Government* (New York: Bantam Books, 1965), chapter 11.

8. The discussion of the Eisenhower Doctrine and American intervention in Lebanon presented here is drawn largely from John C. Campbell's excellent contemporary account in his *Defense of the Middle East: Problems of American Policy*, rev. ed. (New York: Harper & Brothers, Publishers, 1960). Another example of the administration's covert intervention in the area would be the C. I. A.'s supervision of the riots which led to the ouster of Mossadegh and the restoration of the Shah in Iran in August of 1953. See, in this regard, the discussion by Miles Copeland, *The Game of Nations: The Amorality of Power Politics* (New York: Simon and Schuster, 1969).

9. *Ibid.*, p. 61.

10. *Ibid.*, pp. 121-122.

11. *Ibid.*, p. 144.

# Conclusions

12. As Arthur Schlesinger writes in regard to Kennedy and Vietnam: "the President unquestionably felt that an American retreat in Asia might upset the whole world balance." (*Op. cit.*, p. 548.)

# APPENDIX

## TABLE 1
### MANPOWER LEVELS OF THE ARMED FORCES, FISCAL YEARS 1953-1962
(Millions of Men)

| Fiscal Year | | Army | Navy | Marines | Air Force | Total |
|---|---|---|---|---|---|---|
| 1953 | Regular | 1.53 | .79 | .25 | .98 | 3.55 |
| | Reserves* | .13 | .13 | .01 | .02 | .29 |
| 1954 | Regular | 1.40 | .74 | .26 | .96 | 3.36 |
| | Reserves* | .14 | .14 | .03 | .02 | .33 |
| 1955 | Regular | 1.11 | .66 | .22 | .96 | 2.95 |
| | Reserves* | .16 | .14 | .04 | .05 | .37 |
| 1956 | Regular | 1.02 | .67 | .20 | .91 | 2.80 |
| | Reserves* | .20 | .15 | .04 | .05 | .42 |
| 1957 | Regular | 1.00 | .68 | .20 | .92 | 2.80 |
| | Reserves* | .27 | .15 | .05 | .07 | .54 |
| 1958 | Regular | .90 | .64 | .19 | .87 | 2.60 |
| | Reserves* | .32 | .14 | .05 | .05 | .56 |
| 1959 | Regular | .86 | .63 | .18 | .84 | 2.51 |
| | Reserves* | .35 | .13 | .05 | .07 | .60 |
| 1960 | Regular | .87 | .62 | .17 | .81 | 2.47 |
| | Reserves* | .36 | .13 | .05 | .07 | .61 |
| 1961 | Regular | .86 | .63 | .18 | .82 | 2.49 |
| | Reserves* | .32 | .13 | .04 | .14 | .63 |
| 1962 | Regular | 1.07 | .67 | .19 | .88 | 2.81 |
| | Reserves* | .31 | .12 | .05 | .07 | .55 |

* Does Not Include Army and Air National Guards
Source: *Budget of the U. S. Government* (Washington, D.C.: Government Printing Office, 1954-1965).

*Appendix*

## TABLE 2
### PRESIDENTIAL BUDGET REQUESTS FOR THE DEPARTMENT OF DEFENSE, FISCAL YEARS, 1957-1960
(Billions of Dollars)

| Fiscal Year | Army | Navy* | Air Force | Misc.** | Total |
|---|---|---|---|---|---|
| 1957 | 8.58 | 9.57 | 16.54 | .67 | 36.36 |
| 1958 | 9.13 | 10.35 | 17.47 | .73 | 37.68 |
| 1959 | 8.66 | 10.72 | 18.00 | .81 | 38.19 |
| 1960 | 9.26 | 11.60 | 18.68 | 1.41 | 40.95 |

\* Includes Marine Corps
\*\* Includes Secretary of Defense and Revolving and Management Funds
Source: *Budget of the U. S. Government* (Washington, D.C.: Government Printing Office, 1957-1960).


## TABLE 3
### ACTUAL EXPENDITURES FOR THE DEPARTMENT OF DEFENSE, FISCAL YEARS 1953-1963
(Billions of Dollars)

| Fiscal Year | Army | Navy | Marines | Air Force | Misc.* | Total |
|---|---|---|---|---|---|---|
| 1953 | 13.30 | 10.59 | 1.15 | 15.30 | 7.22 | 47.56 |
| 1954 | 14.49 | 10.11 | 1.33 | 15.54 | .45 | 41.92 |
| 1955 | 10.59 | 8.80 | 1.07 | 16.54 | .49 | 37.49 |
| 1956 | 9.33 | 8.85 | 1.09 | 16.85 | .61 | 36.72 |
| 1957 | 9.06 | 9.39 | 1.01 | 18.36 | .62 | 38.44 |
| 1958 | 9.05 | 10.91** | — | 18.44 | .67 | 39.06 |
| 1959 | 9.47 | 11.73** | — | 19.08 | .95 | 41.23 |
| 1960 | 9.39 | 11.64** | — | 19.07 | 2.72 | 42.82 |
| 1961 | 10.40 | 11.26 | .97 | 19.80 | 2.25 | 44.68 |
| 1962 | 11.41 | 11.18 | 1.10 | 20.70 | 2.52 | 46.82 |
| 1963 | 11.95 | 13.67 | 1.08 | 20.60 | 1.72 | 49.97 |

\* Includes Secretary of Defense and Revolving and Management Funds
\*\* Includes Expenditures for Marine Corps
Source: *Budget of the U. S. Government* (Washington, D.C.: Government Printing Office, 1955-1965).

# BIBLIOGRAPHY

## I. PRIMARY SOURCES:
## NEWSPAPERS AND PUBLIC DOCUMENTS

*New York Times.* 1 October 1957 to 31 December 1961.

U. S. Congress. House. Committee on Appropriations. *The Ballistic Missile Program. Hearings* before the Subcommittee on Department of Defense Appropriations, House of Representatives, 85th Cong., 1st sess., 1957.

———. ———. ———. *Department of Defense Appropriations for 1958. Hearings* before the Subcommittee on Department of Defense Appropriations of the Committee on Appropriations, House of Representatives, 85th Cong., 1st sess., 1957.

———. ———. ———. *Department of Defense Appropriations for 1959. Hearings* before the Subcommittee on Department of Defense Appropriations of the Committee on Appropriations, House of Representatives, 85th Cong., 2nd sess., 1958.

———. ———. ———. *Department of Defense Appropriations for 1960. Hearings* before the Subcommittee on Department of Defense Appropriations of the Committee on Appropriations, House of Representatives, 86th Cong., 1st sess., 1959.

———. ———. ———. *Department of Defense Appropriations for 1961. Hearings* before the Subcommittee on Department of Defense Appropriations of the Committee on Appropriations, House of Representatives, 86th Cong., 2nd sess., 1960.

———. ———. ———. *Department of Defense Appropriations for 1962. Hearings* before the Subcommittee on Department of Defense Appropriations of the Committee on Appropriations, House of Representatives, 87th Cong., 1st sess., 1961.

———. ———. ———. *Department of Navy Appropriations for 1958. Hearings* before the Subcommittee on Department of Navy Appropriations of the Committee on Appropriations, House of Representatives, 85th Cong., 1st sess., 1957.

———. ———. ———. Committee on Armed Services. *Investigation of National Defense Missiles. Hearings* before the Committee on Armed Services, House of Representatives, 85th Cong., 2nd sess., 1958.

———. Senate. *John Fitzgerald Kennedy: A Compilation of Statements and Speeches Made During His Service in the United States Senate and House of Representatives,* S. Doc. 79, 88th Cong., 2nd sess., 1964.

———. ———. Committee on Appropriations. *Department of Defense Appropriations for 1958. Hearings* before the Subcommittee of the Committee on Appropriations, Senate, 85th Cong., 1st sess., 1957.

———. ———. ———. *Supplemental Defense Appropriations Bill, 1958. Hearings* before the Subcommittee of the Committee on Appropriations, Senate, 85th Cong., 2nd sess., 1958.

———. ———. ———. *Department of Defense Appropriations for 1959. Hearings* before the Subcommittee of the Committee on Appropriations, Senate, 85th Cong., 2nd sess., 1958.

———. ———. ———. *Department of Defense Appropriations for 1960. Hearings* before the Subcommittee of the Committee on Appropriations, Senate, 86th Cong., 1st sess., 1959.

———. ———. ———. *Department of Defense Appropriations for 1961. Hearings* before the Subcommittee of the Committee on Appropriations, Senate, 86th Cong., 2nd sess., 1960.

———. ———. ———. *Department of Defense Appropriations for 1962. Hearings* before the Subcommittee of the Committee on Appropriations, Senate, 87th Cong., 1st sess., 1961.

———. ———. ———. Committee on Armed Services. *Study of Airpower. Hearings* before the Subcommittee on the Air Force of the Committee on Armed Services, Senate, 84th Cong., 2nd sess., 1956.

———. ———. ———. *Inquiry into Satellite and Missile Programs. Hearings* before the Preparedness Investigating Subcommittee of the Committee on Armed Services, Senate, 85th Cong., 1st-2nd Sess., 1957-58.

———. ———. ———. *Missile and Space Activities. Hearings* before the Preparedness Investigating Subcommittee of the Committee on Armed Services in conjunction with the Committee on Aeronautical and Space Sciences, Senate, 86th Cong., 1st sess., 1959.

———. ———. ———. *Missiles. Space and Other Major Defense Matters. Hearings* before the Preparedness Investigating Subcommittee of the Committee on Armed Services in conjunction with the Committee on Aeronautical and Space Sciences, Senate, 86th Cong., 2nd sess., 1960.

———. ———. Committee on Commerce. Subcommittee of the Subcommittee on Communication. *Freedom of Communications.* S. Rept. 994, 87th Cong., 1st sess., 1964.

U. S. National Archives and Records Service. John F. Kennedy Library, *Oral Histories.*

U. S. President. *Public Papers of the Presidents of the United States.* Washington, D. C.: Office of the *Federal Register*, National Archives and Records Service, 1960-61. Dwight D. Eisenhower, 1953-1961.

——. *Public Papers of the Presidents of the United States.* Washington, D. C.: Office of the *Federal Register*, National Archives and Records Service, 1962-64. John F. Kennedy, 1961-1963.

## II. PRIMARY SOURCES:
## PERIOD MONOGRAPHS, RECOLLECTIONS AND MEMOIRS

Acheson, Dean. *Power and Diplomacy.* Cambridge, Mass.: Harvard University Press, 1958.

Adams, Sherman. *Firsthand Report: The Story of the Eisenhower Administration.* New York: Harper & Brothers, 1961.

Alsop, Joseph and Stewart. *The Reporter's Trade.* New York, Regnal & Co., 1958.

Alsop, Stewart. *Nixon and Rockefeller: A Double Portrait.* Garden City, N. Y.: Doubleday & Co., 1960.

——. *The Center: People and Power in Political Washington.* New York: Harper & Row, 1968.

Aron, Raymond. *The Great Debate: Theories of Nuclear Strategy.* Garden City, N. Y.: Doubleday & Co., 1965.

Baldwin, Hanson W. *The Great Arms Race: A Comparison in U. S. and Soviet Power Today.* New York: Frederick A. Praeger, 1958.

Barclay, Brigadier C. N. *The New Warfare.* New York: Philosophical Library, 1954.

Brennan, Donald G., ed. *Arms Control, Disarmament and National Security.* New York: George Braziller, 1961.

Brodie, Bernard. *Strategy in the Missile Age.* Princeton, N. J.: Princeton University Press, 1959.

——. *Sea Power in the Machine Age.* Princeton, N. J.: Princeton University Press, 1941.

——. *A Layman's Guide to Naval Strategy.* Princeton, N. J.: Princeton University Press, 1942.

——, ed. *The Absolute Weapon: Atomic Power and World Order.* New York: Harcourt, Brace and Co., 1946.

——. *The Atomic Bomb and American Security.* Memorandum No. 18. New Haven, Conn.: Yale Institute of International Studies, 1947.

——. *The Atomic Bomb and the Armed Services.* Public Affairs Bulletin No. 55. Washington, D. C.: Government Printing Office, 1947.

Burns, Arthur F. *Prosperity Without Inflation.* Garden City, N. Y.: Doubleday & Co., 1958.

Bush, Vannevar. *Modern Arms and Free Men: A Discussion of the Role of*

# Bibliography

*Science in Preserving Democracy.* New York: Simon and Schuster, 1949.

Dietchman, Seymour. *Limited War and American Defense Policy.* Cambridge, Mass.: M. I. T. Press, 1964.

Dinerstein, H. S. *War and the Soviet Union: Nuclear Weapons and the Revolution in Soviet Military and Political Thinking,* rev. ed. New York: Frederick A. Praeger, 1962.

Dulles, Allen W. *The Craft of Intelligence.* New York: The New American Library, 1965.

Dulles, John Foster. *War, Peace and Change.* New York: Harper & Brothers, 1939.

———. *War or Peace.* New York: The Macmillan Co., 1950.

Eisenhower, Dwight D. *Crusade in Europe.* Garden City, N. Y.: Doubleday & Co., 1948.

———. *Mandate for Change: The White House Years, 1953-1956.* Garden City, N. Y.: Doubleday & Co., 1963.

———. *Peace with Justice: Selected Addresses.* Edited by Grayson Kirk. New York: Columbia University Press, 1961.

———. *Waging Peace: The White House Years, 1956-1961.* Garden City, N. Y.: Doubleday & Co., 1965.

Finletter, Thomas F. *Power and Policy.* New York: Harcourt, Brace and Co., 1954.

Fryklund, Richard. *One Hundred Million Lives: Maximum Survival in a Nuclear War.* New York: The Macmillan Co., 1962.

Garthoff, Raymond L. *Soviet Military Doctrine.* Glencoe, Ill.: The Free Press, 1953.

———. *The Soviet Image of Future War.* Washington, D. C.: Public Affairs Press, 1959.

———. *Soviet Strategy in the Nuclear Age,* rev. ed. New York: Frederick A. Praeger, 1962.

Gavin, James M. *War and Peace in the Space Age.* New York: Harper & Brothers, 1958.

———. *Crisis Now.* New York: Random House, 1968.

Goldwin, Robert A., ed. *America Armed: Essays on United States Military Policy.* Chicago: Rand McNally & Co., 1963.

Hahn, Walter F., and John C. Neff, eds. *American Strategy for the Nuclear Age.* New York: Doubleday & Co., 1960.

Halperin, Morton H. *Limited War in the Nuclear Age.* New York: John Wiley and Sons, Inc., 1960.

Hilsman, Roger, and Robert C. Good, eds. *Foreign Policy in the Sixties: The Issues and Instruments.* Baltimore: The Johns Hopkins Press, 1965.

Hilsman, Roger. *To Move a Nation: The Politics of Foreign Policy in the*

*Administration of John F. Kennedy.* Garden City, N. Y.: Doubleday & Co., 1967.

Hoopes, Townshend. *The Limits of Intervention.* New York: David McKay Co., 1970.

Hughes, Emmet John. *America the Vincible.* Garden City, N. Y.: Doubleday & Co., 1959.

———. *The Ordeal of Power: A Political Memoir of the Eisenhower Years.* New York: Atheneum, 1963.

Huszar, George B. de, ed. *National Strategy in an Age of Revolutions: Addresses and Panel Discussions of the Fourth National Military-Industrial Conference.* New York: Frederick A. Praeger, 1959.

Institute for Strategic Studies. *The Communist Bloc and the Western Alliance: The Military Balance, 1962-1963.* London: Institute for Strategic Studies, 1963.

Jordan, Amos A., Jr., ed. *Issues of National Security in the 1970's: Essays Presented to Colonel George A. Lincoln on His Sixtieth Birthday.* New York: Frederick A. Praeger, 1967.

Kaufmann, William W. *The Requirements of Deterrence.* Memorandum No. 7. Princeton, N. J.: Center for International Studies, 1954.

———, ed. *Military Policy and National Security.* Princeton, N. J.: Princeton University Press, 1956.

Kennedy, John F. *Kennedy and the Press.* Edited by A. H. Lerman. New York: Thomas Y. Crowell Co., 1965.

———. *The Burden and the Glory.* Edited by Allan Nevins. New York: Harper & Row, 1964.

———. *The Strategy of Peace.* Edited by Allan Nevins. New York: Harper & Row, 1960.

———. *To Turn the Tide.* Edited by John W. Gardner. New York: Harper & Brothers, 1962.

Kissinger, Henry A. *A World Restored: The Politics of Conservatism in a Revolutionary Age.* New York: Universal Library, 1964.

———. *Nuclear Weapons and Foreign Policy.* New York: Harper & Brothers, 1957.

———. *The Necessity for Choice: Prospects of American Foreign Policy.* Garden City, N. Y.: Anchor Books, 1962.

Knorr, Klaus, and Thornton Read. *Limited Strategic War.* New York: Frederick A. Praeger, 1962.

Lincoln, George A. *Economics of National Security: Managing America's Resources for Defense,* 2nd ed. Englewood Cliffs, N. J.: Prentice-Hall, Inc., 1954.

McNamara, Robert S. *The Essence of Security: Reflections in Office.* New York: Harper & Row, 1968.

Mager, N. H., and J. Katel, eds. *Conquest Without War: An Analytical*

# Bibliography

*Anthology of the Speeches, Interviews, and Remarks of Nikita S. Khrushchev.* New York: Simon and Schuster, 1961.

Medaris, John B. *Countdown for Decision.* New York: G. P. Putnam's Sons, 1960.

Millis, Walter, ed. *American Military Thought.* New York: Bobbs-Merrill Co., 1966.

Mitchell, William. *Winged Defense.* New York: G. P. Putnam Sons, 1925.

Morgenstern, Oskar. *The Question of National Defense.* New York: Random House, 1959.

Murphy, Robert. *Diplomat Among Warriors.* Garden City, N. Y.: Doubleday & Co., 1964.

New York Times. *The Pentagon Papers.* Written by Neil Sheehan, Hedrick Smith, E. W. Kenworthy, and Fox Butterfield. Articles and documents edited by Gerald Gold, A. M. Siegal, and Samuel Abt. New York: Bantam Books, 1971.

Nixon, Richard M. *The Challenges We Face.* New York: Popular Library, 1961.

————. *Six Crises.* New York: Pocket Books, 1962.

————. *United States Foreign Policy for the 1970's: A New Strategy for Peace.* New York: Bantam Books, 1970.

Osgood, Robert E. *Ideals and Self-Interest in America's Foreign Relations: The Great Transformation of the 20th Century.* Chicago: University of Chicago Press, 1953.

————. *Limited War: The Challenge to American Security.* Chicago: University of Chicago Press, 1957.

————, and Robert W. Tucker. *Force, Order, and Justice.* Baltimore: The Johns Hopkins Press, 1971.

Padelford, Norman J., and George A. Lincoln. *The Dynamics of International Politics.* New York: The Macmillan Co., 1962.

Pearson, Drew, and Jack Anderson. *U. S. A.—Second-Class Power?* New York: Simon and Schuster, 1958.

Power, Thomas S. *Design for Survival.* New York: Coward-McCann, Inc., 1965.

Quade, E. S., ed. *Analysis for Military Decisions: The RAND Lectures on Systems Analysis.* Chicago: Rand McNally & Co., 1964.

Raymond, Jack. *Power at the Pentagon.* New York: Harper & Row, 1964.

Ridgway, Matthew B. *Soldier: The Memoirs of Matthew B. Ridgway.* New York: Harper & Brothers, 1956.

————. *The Korean War.* Garden City, N. Y.: Doubleday & Co., 1967.

Rockefeller Brothers Fund. *Prospects for America: The Rockefeller Panel Reports.* Garden City, N. Y.: Doubleday & Co., 1961.

Rostow, W. W. *The Stages of Economic Growth: A Non-Communist Manifesto.* New York: Cambridge University Press, 1960.

——. *The United States in the World Arena: An Essay in Recent History.* New York: Harper & Row, 1960.

——. *View From the Seventh Floor.* New York: Harper & Row, 1964.

Schelling, Thomas C., and Morton H. Halperin. *Strategy and Arms Control.* New Haven, Conn.: The Twentieth Century Fund, 1961.

Schelling, Thomas C. *Arms and Influence.* New Haven, Conn.: Yale University Press, 1966.

Schlesinger, Arthur M., Jr. *Kennedy or Nixon: Does It Make Any Difference?* New York: The Macmillan Co., 1960.

——. *A Thousand Days: John F. Kennedy in the White House.* Boston: Houghton-Mifflin Co., 1965.

Schwartz, Harry. *The Red Phoenix: Russia Since World War II.* New York: Frederick A. Praeger, 1961.

Seversky, Alexander P. de. *Air Power: Key to Survival.* New York: Simon and Schuster, 1950.

Slessor, Sir John. *Strategy for the West.* New York: William Morrow & Co., 1954.

——. *The Great Deterrent.* New York: Frederick A. Praeger, 1957.

Snyder, Glenn H. *Deterrence and Defense: Toward a Strategy of National Security.* Princeton, N. J.: Princeton University Press, 1961.

Sokolovsky, V. D. *Military Strategy: Soviet Concepts and Doctrines.* New York: Frederick A. Praeger, 1963.

Sorensen, Theodore C. *Decision Making in the White House: The Olive Branch and the Arrows.* New York: Columbia University Press, 1964.

——. *Kennedy.* New York: Harper & Row, 1965.

Taylor, Maxwell D. *The Uncertain Trumpet.* New York: Harper & Brothers, 1959.

——. *Responsibility and Response.* New York: Harper & Row, 1967.

——. *Swords and Ploughshares.* New York: W. W. Norton & Co., 1972.

Toledano, Ralph de, ed. *The Conservative Papers.* Garden City, N. Y.: Doubleday & Co., 1964.

Turner, Gordon B., and Richard D. Challenger, eds. *National Security in the Nuclear Age: Basic Facts and Theories.* New York: Frederick A. Praeger, 1960.

Twining, Nathan F. *Neither Liberty Nor Safety: A Hard Look at United States Military Policy and Strategy.* New York: Holt, Rinehart and Winston, 1966.

Wallich, Henry C. *The Cost of Freedom: Conservatism and Modern Capitalism.* New York: Collier Books, 1962.

Witkin, Richard, ed. *The Challenge of Sputnik.* Garden City, N. Y.: Doubleday & Co., 1958.

## III.  SECONDARY SOURCES: BOOKS

Albertson, Dean. *Eisenhower as President.* New York: Hill and Wang, 1963.

# Bibliography

Almond, Gabriel. *The American People and Foreign Policy*. New York: Harcourt, Brace and World, Inc., 1950.

Alperovitz, Gar. *Atomic Diplomacy: Hiroshima and Potsdam*. New York: Simon and Schuster, 1965.

Art, Robert J., and Kenneth N. Waltz, eds. *The Use of Force: International Politics and Foreign Policy*. Boston: Little, Brown and Co., 1971.

Barnet, Richard J. *Intervention and Revolution*. New York: The World Publishing Co., 1968.

———. *The Economy of Death*. New York: Atheneum, 1970.

Beal, John Robinson. *John Foster Dulles, 1888-1959*. New York: Harper & Row, 1959.

Beaufre, Andre. *An Introduction to Strategy: With Particular Reference to Problems of Defense, Politics, Economics, and Diplomacy in the Nuclear Age*. New York: Frederick A. Praeger, 1965.

Berding, Andrew H. *Dulles on Diplomacy*. Princeton, N. J.: D. Van Nostrand Co., 1965.

Binkley, Wilfred E. *The Man in the White House: His Powers and Duties*, rev. ed. New York: Harper & Row, 1964.

Bottome, Edgar M. *The Missile Gap: A Study of the Formulation of Military and Political Policy*. Rutherford, N. J.: Fairleigh Dickenson University Press, 1971.

Boulding, Kenneth E. *Conflict and Defense: A General Theory*. New York: Harper & Row, 1963.

Braybrooke, David, and Charles E. Lindbloom. *A Strategy of Decision: Policy Evaluation as a Social Process*. Glencoe, Ill.: The Free Press, 1963.

Brown, Seyom. *The Faces of Power: Constancy and Change in United States Foreign Policy*. New York: Columbia University Press, 1968.

Bull, Hedley. *The Control of the Arms Race*. New York: Frederick A. Praeger, 1961.

Campbell, Angus, and others. *The American Voter*. New York: John Wiley and Sons, 1964.

Campbell, John C. *Defense of the Middle East: Problems of American Policy*, rev. ed. New York: Harper & Brothers, 1960.

Caraley, Demetrios. *The Politics of Military Unification: A Study of Conflict and the Policy Process*. New York: Columbia University Press, 1966.

Cater, Douglass. *Power in Washington*. New York: Vintage Books, 1964.

Catton, Bruce. *The Warlords of Washington*. New York: Harcourt, Brace and Co., 1948.

Childs, Marquis William. *Eisenhower: Captive Hero*. New York: Harcourt, Brace and World, 1958.

Clayton, James L., ed. *The Economic Impact of the Cold War*. New York: Harcourt, Brace & World, 1970.

Coffin, Tristam. *The Armed Society: Militarism in Modern America*. Baltimore: Penguin Books, 1964.

Cohen, Bernard C. *The Press and Foreign Policy*. Princeton, N. J.: Princeton University Press, 1963.

Copeland, Miles. *The Game of Nations: The Amorality of Power Politics*. New York: Simon and Schuster, 1969.

Cook, Fred J. *The Warfare State*. New York: The Macmillan Co., 1962.

Crozier, Michel. *The Bureaucratic Phenomenon*. Chicago: University of Chicago Press, 1964.

David, Paul T. ed. *The Presidential Election and Transition, 1960-1961*. Washington, D. C.: The Brookings Institute, 1961.

Davidson, Roger H. *The Role of the Congressman*. New York: Pegasus, 1969.

De Grazia, Alfred, ed. *Congress—The First Branch of Government: Twelve Studies in The Organization of Congress*. Garden City, N. Y.: Doubleday & Co., 1967.

Domhoff, G. William. *Who Rules America?* Englewood Cliffs, N. J.: Prentice-Hall, Inc., 1967.

———, and Hoyt B. Ballard, eds. *C. Wright Mills and the Power Elite*. Boston: Beacon Press, 1969.

Donovan, James A. *Militarism, U. S. A.* New York: Charles Scribner's Sons, 1970.

Drummond, Roscoe, and Gaston Coblentz. *Duel at the Brink: John Foster Dulles' Command of American Power*. Garden City, N. Y.: Doubleday & Co., 1960.

Dulles, Eleanor Lansing. *John Foster Dulles: The Last Year*. New York: Harcourt, Brace & World, 1963.

Duscha, Julius. *Arms, Money and Politics*. New York: Ives Washburn, Inc., 1964.

Ellul, Jacques. *Propaganda: The Formation of Men's Attitudes*. New York: Alfred A. Knopf, 1965.

Etzioni, Amitai. *A Comparative Analysis of Complex Organizations: On Power, Involvement and Their Correlates*. New York: The Free Press, 1961.

———. *The Moon-Doggle: Domestic and International Implications of the Space Race*. Garden City, N. Y.: Doubleday & Co., 1964.

Farrell, John C., and Asa P. Smith, eds. *Image and Reality in World Politics*. New York: Columbia University Press, 1967.

Fleming, Denna F. *The Cold War and Its Origins, 1917-1960*, 2 vols. New York: Doubleday & Co., 1961.

Ginsburgh, Robert N. *United States Military Strategy in the Sixties*. New York: W. W. Norton & Co., 1965.

Goold-Adams, Richard. *John Foster Dulles: A Reappraisal*. New York: Appleton-Century-Crofts, Inc., 1962.

Green, Philip. *Deadly Logic: The Theory of Nuclear Deterrence*. Ohio State University: Mershon Center for Education in National Security, 1966.

# Bibliography

Gross, Bertram M. *The Legislative Struggle*. New York: McGraw-Hill, 1953.

Guhin, Michael A. *John Foster Dulles: A Statesman and His Times*. New York: Columbia University Press, 1972.

Halperin, Morton H. *Defense Strategies for the Seventies*. Boston: Little, Brown and Co., 1971.

Hammond, Paul Y. *Organizing for Defense: The American Military Establishment in the Twentieth Century*. Princeton, N. J.: Princeton University Press, 1961.

———. *The Cold War Years: American Foreign Policy Since 1945*. New York: Harcourt, Brace & World, Inc., 1969.

Heilbroner, Robert L. *Between Capitalism and Socialism: Essays in Political Economy*. New York: Vintage Books, 1968.

Herring, Pendleton. *The Impact of War: Our American Democracy Under Arms*. New York: Farrar and Rinehart, 1941.

Herz, John H. *International Politics in the Atomic Age*. New York: Columbia University Press, 1959.

Hoffman, Stanley, ed. *Contemporary Theory in International Relations*. Englewood Cliffs, N. J.: Prentice-Hall, Inc., 1960.

Horelick, Arnold, and Myron Rush. *Strategic Power and Soviet Foreign Policy*. Chicago: University of Chicago Press, 1965.

Horowitz, David. *Free World Colossus*. New York: Hill and Wang, 1965.

———, ed. *Containment and Revolution*. Boston: Beacon Press, 1968.

Huitt, Ralph K., and Robert L. Peabody, eds. *Congress: Two Decades of Analysis*. New York: Harper & Row, 1969.

Huntington, Samuel P. *The Common Defense: Strategic Programs in National Politics*. New York: Columbia University Press, 1961.

———. *The Soldier and The State: The Theory and Politics of Civil-Military Relations*. New York: Vintage Books, 1957.

———, ed. *Changing Patterns of Military Politics*. New York: The Free Press, 1962.

Ickes, Harold L. *America's House of Lords: An Inquiry into the Freedom of the Press*. New York: Harcourt, Brace and Co., 1939.

Janowitz, Morris. *The Professional Soldier: A Social and Political Portrait*. New York: The Free Press, 1960.

———, ed. *The New Military: Changing Patterns of Organization*. New York: W. W. Norton & Co., 1969.

———, and Roger Little. *Sociology and the Military Establishment*, rev. ed. New York: Russell Sage Foundation, 1965.

Kane, William Everett. *Civil Strife in Latin America: A Legal History of U. S. Involvement*. Baltimore: The Johns Hopkins Press, 1972.

Kaplan, Morton. *System and Process in International Politics*. New York: John Wiley & Sons, Inc., 1957.

Kaufmann, William W. *The McNamara Strategy*. New York: Harper & Row, 1964.

Key, V. O., Jr. *Public Opinion and American Democracy.* New York: Alfred A. Knopf, 1961.

Knoll, Erwin, and J. N. McFadden, eds. *American Militarism, 1970: A Dialogue on the Distortion of Our National Priorities and the Need to Reassert Control Over the Defense Establishment.* New York: The Viking Press, 1969.

Kolkowicz, Roman. *The Soviet Military and the Communist Party.* Princeton, N. J.: Princeton University Press, 1967.

LeFeber, Walter. *America, Russia, and the Cold War, 1945-1966.* New York: John Wiley and Sons, Inc., 1967.

Lane, Robert E. *Political Ideology: Why the American Common Man Believes What He Does.* New York: The Free Press, 1967.

Lapp, Ralph E. *Kill and Overkill: The Strategy of Annihilation.* New York: Basic Books, Inc., 1962.

———. *Man and Space: The Next Decade.* New York: Harper & Brothers, 1961.

———. *The Weapons Culture.* Baltimore: Penguin Books, 1969.

Larson, Arthur. *Eisenhower: The President Nobody Knew.* New York: Charles Scribner's Sons, 1968.

Lens, Sidney. *The Military-Industrial Complex.* Philadelphia: Pilgrim Press & The National Catholic Reporter, 1970.

Levine, Robert A. *The Arms Debate.* Cambridge, Mass.: Harvard University Press, 1963.

Lindbloom, Charles E. *The Intelligence of Democracy: Decision Making Through Mutual Adjustment.* New York: The Free Press, 1965.

Lynn, Kenneth S., ed. *The Professions in America.* Boston: Houghton-Mifflin Co., 1965.

Masland, John W., and Laurence I. Radway. *Soldiers and Scholars: Military Education and National Policy.* Princeton, N. J.: Princeton University Press, 1957.

Mazo, Earl. *Richard Nixon: A Political and Personal Portrait.* New York: Harper & Brothers, 1959.

McClelland, Charles A. *Theory and the International System.* New York: The Macmillan Co., 1966.

McWilliams, Wilson C., ed. *Garrisons and Governments: Politics and the Military in New States.* San Francisco: Chandler Publishing Co., 1967.

Melman, Seymour. *Our Depleted Society.* New York: Holt, Rinehart and Winston, Inc., 1965.

Miksche, F. O. *The Failure of Atomic Strategy—and a New Proposal for the Defense of the West.* New York: Frederick A. Praeger, 1958.

Mills, C. Wright. *Power, Politics and People: The Collected Essays of C. Wright Mills,* ed. by I. L. Horowitz. New York: Ballantine Books, 1963.

———. *The Power Elite.* New York: Oxford University Press, 1959.

Morgenthau, Hans J. *Politics Among Nations: The Struggle for Power and Peace,* 4th ed. New York: Alfred A. Knopf, 1966.

# Bibliography

Mosely, Philip E., and Marshall Schulman. *The Changing Soviet Challenge.* Racine, Wis.: The Johnson Foundation, 1964.

Nelson, Donald M. *Arsenal of Democracy: The Story of American War Protection.* New York: Harcourt, Brace and Co., 1946.

Niebuhr, Reinhold. *Christianity and Power Politics.* New York: Charles Scribner's Sons, 1940.

———. *Moral Man and Immoral Society: A Study in Ethics and Politics.* New York: Charles Scribner's Sons, 1952.

Nieburg, H. L. *In the Name of Science,* rev. ed. Chicago: Quadrangle Books, 1970.

Parmet, Herbert S. *Eisenhower and the American Crusades.* New York: The Macmillan Co., 1972.

Parry, Albert. *Russia's Rockets and Missiles.* Garden City, N. Y.: Doubleday & Co., 1960.

Peabody, Robert L., and Nelson W. Polsby, eds. *New Perspectives on the House of Representatives.* Chicago: Rand McNally & Co., 1963.

Penkovskiy, Oleg. *The Penkovskiy Papers,* trans. by Peter Neriabin and ed. by Frank Gibney. Garden City, N. Y.: Doubleday & Co., 1965.

Pennington, L. A., and others. *The Psychology of Military Leadership.* New York: Prentice-Hall, Inc., 1943.

Price, Don K. *The Scientific Estate.* Cambridge, Mass.: Harvard University Press, 1967.

Rathjens, George W. *The Future of the Strategic Arms Race: Options for the 1970's.* New York: Carnegie Endowment for International Peace, 1969.

Reston, James. *The Artillery of the Press: Its Influence on American Foreign Policy.* New York: Harper & Row, 1966.

Rivers, William L. *The Opinionmakers.* Boston: Beacon Press, 1965.

Roherty, James M. *Decisions of Robert S. McNamara: A Study of the Role of the Secretary of Defense.* Coral Gables, Fla.: University of Miami Press, 1970.

Rosenau, James N., ed. *Domestic Sources of Foreign Policy.* New York: The Free Press, 1967.

———, ed. *International Politics and Foreign Policy.* New York: The Free Press, 1961.

———, ed. *Linkage Politics: Essays on the Convergence of National and International Systems.* New York: The Free Press, 1969.

Rosten, Leo C., *The Washington Correspondents.* New York: Harcourt, Brace and Co., 1937.

Sapin, Burton M. *The Making of United States Foreign Policy.* New York: Frederick A. Praeger, 1966.

Schattschneider, E. E. *The Semi-Sovereign People: A Realist's View of Democracy in America.* New York: Holt, Rinehart and Winston, 1960.

Schilling, Warner R., and others. *Strategy, Politics, and Defense Budgets.* New York: Columbia University Press, 1962.

Schneider, Ronald M. *Communism in Guatemala, 1944-1954.* New York: Frederick A. Praeger, 1959.

Seabury, Paul A., ed. *Balance of Power.* San Francisco: The Chandler Publishing Co., 1965.

Skolnick, J. H., and E. Currie, eds. *Crisis in American Institutions.* Boston: Little, Brown and Co., 1970.

Smith, A. Merriam. *A Presidential Odyssey.* New York: Harper & Row, 1961.

Stanley, David, and others. *Men Who Govern.* Washington, D. C.: The Brookings Institute, 1967.

Stoessinger, John G. *Nations in Darkness: China, Russia and America.* New York: Random House, 1971.

Swomley, John M., Jr. *The Military Establishment.* Boston: Beacon Press, 1964.

Tyrrell, C. Merton. *Pentagon Partners: The New Nobility.* New York: Grossman Publishers, 1970.

Ulam, Adam B. *Expansion and Coexistence: Soviet Foreign Policy, 1917-1967.* New York: Frederick A. Praeger, 1968.

———. *The Rivals: America and Russia Since World War II.* New York: The Viking Press, 1971.

Vagts, Alfred. *A History of Militarism: Civilian and Military,* rev. ed. New York: The Free Press, 1959.

Van Dusen, Henry P., ed. *The Spiritual Legacy of John Foster Dulles: Selections from his Articles and Addresses.* Philadelphia: Westminster Press, 1960.

Van Dyke, Vernon. *Pride and Power: The Rationale of the Space Program.* Urbana, Ill.: University of Illinois Press, 1964.

Walton, Richard J. *Cold War and Counterrevolution: The Foreign Policy of John F. Kennedy.* New York: The Viking Press, 1972.

Warner, W. Lloyd, and others. *The American Federal Executive: A Study of the Social and Personal Characteristics of the Civilian and Military Leaders of the United States Federal Government.* New Haven, Conn.: Yale University Press, 1963.

Wellman, Paul I. *Stuart Symington: Portrait of a Man With a Mission.* Garden City, N. Y.: Doubleday & Co., 1960.

White, Theodore H. *The Making of the President 1960.* New York: Atheneum, 1961.

Wildavsky, Aaron. *The Politics of the Budgetary Process.* Boston: Little, Brown & Co., 1964.

Wise, David, and Thomas B. Ross. *The U-2 Affair.* New York: Random House, 1962.

———. *The Invisible Government.* New York: Random House, 1964.

Wolfe, Thomas W. *Soviet Strategy of the Crossroads.* Cambridge, Mass.: Harvard University Press, 1964.

# Bibliography

———. *Soviet Power and Europe, 1945-1970.* Baltimore: The Johns Hopkins Press, 1970.

Yarmolinsky, Adam. *The Military Establishment: Its Impact on American Society.* New York: Harper & Row, 1971.

## IV.  SECONDARY SOURCES: PERIODICALS

Aliano, Richard A. "The American Military: A Reappraisal." *Military Review,* LII, (January, 1972), 51-57.

Allison, Graham T. "Conceptual Models and the Cuban Missile Crisis." *The American Political Science Review,* LXIII (September, 1969), 689-718.

Aron, Raymond. "A Half-Century of Limited War." *Bulletin of the Atomic Scientists,* XII (April, 1956), 99-104.

Asparurian, Vernon V. "The Soviet Military-Industrial Complex—Does It Exist?" *Journal of International Affairs,* XXVI, 1 (1972), 1-28.

Ball, George W. "The Lessons of Vietnam: Have We Learned or Only Failed?" *New York Times Magazine,* 1 April 1973, pp. 12 ff.

Brodie, Bernard. "Navy Department Thinking of the Atomic Bomb." *Bulletin of the Atomic Scientists,* III (July, 1947), 177 ff.

———. "Strategic Bombing: What It Can Do." *The Reporter,* 15 August 1950, pp. 28-31.

———. "Some Notes on the Evolution of Air Doctrine." *World Politics,* VII (April, 1955), 349-370.

———. "More About Limited War." *World Politics,* X (October, 1957), 121 ff.

———. "Strategy Hits a Dead End." *Harper's Magazine,* October, 1955, pp. 32 ff.

———. "Unlimited Weapons and Limited War." *The Reporter,* 18 November 1954, pp. 16 ff.

Buchanan, James. "The Pure Theory of Government Finance: A Suggested Approach." *Journal of Political Economy,* LVII (December, 1949), 496-505.

Bundy, McGeorge. "To Cap the Volcano." *Foreign Affairs,* XLVIII (October, 1969), 1-20.

Burns, Arthur Lee. "From Balance to Deterrence." *World Politics,* IX (July, 1957), 494-529.

Cimbala, Stephen J. "New Myths and Old Realities: Defense and Its Critics." *World Politics,* XXIV (October, 1971), 127-157.

Dallin, Alexander. "Soviet Foreign Policy and Domestic Politics: A Framework for Analysis." *Journal of International Affairs,* XIII, 2 (1969), 250-264.

Dawson, Raymond H. "Congressional Innovation and Intervention in Defense Policy: Legislative Authorization of Weapons Systems." *American Political Science Review,* LVI (March, 1962), 42-57.

# American Defense Policy

Dulles, John Foster. "Challenge and Response in U. S. Foreign Policy." *Foreign Affairs*, XXXVI (October, 1957), 29-42.

———. "Policy for Security and Peace." *Foreign Affairs*, XXXII (April, 1954), 353-364.

———. "A Policy of Boldness." *Life*, XXXII (19 May 1952), 51 ff.

Ferrell, Robert H. "The Merchants of Death, Then and Now." *Journal of International Affairs*, XXVI, 1 (1972), 29-39.

Foster, William G. "Prospects for Arms Control." *Foreign Affairs*, XLVII (April, 1969), 413-419.

Gray, Colin S. " 'Gap' Predictions and America's Defense: Arms Race Behavior in the Eisenhower Years." *Orbis*, XVI (Spring, 1972), 257-274.

Grodzins, Morton. "American Political Parties and the American System," *The Western Political Science Quarterly*, XIII (Fall, 1960), 974-998.

Guhin, Michael A. "Dulles' Thoughts on International Politics: Myth and Reality." *Orbis*, XIII (Fall, 1969), 865-889.

Halle, Louis J. "Lessons of the Nuclear Age." *Encounter*, XXX (March, 1968), 17-26.

Halperin, Morton H. "Why Bureaucrats Play Games." *Foreign Policy*, II (Spring, 1971), 70-90.

Hart, Philip A. "Militarism in America." *The Center Magazine*, III (January, 1970), 16 ff.

Hess, Stephen. "Foreign Policy and Presidential Campaigns." *Foreign Policy*, VIII (Fall, 1972), 3-22.

Hoag, Malcolm W. "What New Look in Defense?" *World Politics*, XXII (October, 1969), 1-28.

Holsti, Ole, and others. "The Management of International Crisis: Affect and Action in American-Soviet Relations." *Journal of Peace Research*, III (1964), 170-190.

Horelick, Arnold. "The Cuban Missile Crisis: An Analysis of Soviet Calculations and Behavior." *World Politics*, XVII (April, 1964), 66-85.

Hughes, Emmet John. "The Politics of the Sixties: From the New Frontier to the New Revolution." *New York Times Magazine*, 4 April 1971, pp. 24 ff.

Huntington, Samuel P. "Political Modernization: America vs. Europe." *World Politics*, XVIII (April, 1966), 378-414.

Jacobs, Walter Darnell. "Soviet Strategic Effectiveness." *Journal of International Affairs*, XXVI, 1 (1972), 60-72.

Janowitz, Morris. "Volunteer Armed Forces and Military Purpose." *Foreign Affairs*, L (April, 1972), 427-443.

Jervis, Robert. "Hypotheses on Misperception." *World Politics*, XX (April, 1968), 454-479.

Jones, Stephen B. "Global Strategic Views." *The Geographical Review*, XLV (October, 1955), 492-508.

# Bibliography

Kanter, Arnold. "Congress and the Defense Budget, 1960-1970." *The American Political Science Review*, LXVI (March, 1972), 129-143.

Kaufmann, William W. "The Crisis in Military Affairs." *World Politics*, X (July, 1958), 579-603.

King, James E., Jr. "Deterrence and Limited War." *Army*, VIII (August, 1957), 21-26.

———. "Nuclear Plenty and Limited War." *Foreign Affairs*, XXXV (January, 1957), 238-256.

Kissinger, Henry A. "Military Policy and Defense of the 'Grey Areas.'" *Foreign Affairs*, XXXIII (April, 1955), 416-428.

———. "Force and Diplomacy in the Nuclear Age." *Foreign Affairs*, XXXIV (April, 1956), 349-366.

———. "Reflections on American Diplomacy." *Foreign Affairs*, XXXV (October, 1956), 37-56.

———. "Strategy and Organization." *Foreign Affairs*, XXXV (April, 1957), 378-394.

———. "Missiles and the Western Alliance." *Foreign Affairs*, XXXVI, (April, 1958), 383-400.

———. "Nuclear Testing and the Problems of Peace." *Foreign Affairs*, XXXVII (October, 1958), 1-18.

———. "The Search for Stability." *Foreign Affairs*, XXXVII (July, 1959), 537-560.

———. "Domestic Structure and Foreign Policy." *Daedalus*, XCV (Spring, 1966), 503-529.

Kohler, Foy D. and M. L. Harvey. "Soviet Science and Technology: Some Implications for United States Policy." *Orbis*, XIII (Fall, 1969), 658-708.

Kolkowicz, Roman. "Strategic Elites and Politics of Superpowers." *Journal of International Affairs*, XXVI, 1 (1972), 40-59.

———. "Strategic Parity and Beyond: Soviet Perspectives." *World Politics*, XXIII (April, 1971), 431-451.

———. "The Impact of Modern Technology on the Soviet Officer Corp." *Orbis*, XI (Summer, 1967), 378-393.

Lake, Anthony. "Lying Around Washington." *Foreign Policy*, II (Spring, 1971), 91-113.

Lee, William T. "The 'Politico-Military-Industrial Complex' of the U. S. S. R." *Journal Of International Affairs*, XXVI, 1 (1972), 73-86.

Levine, Robert A. "Facts and Morals in the Arms Debate." *World Politics*, XIV (January, 1962), 239-258.

Lindbloom, Charles E. "The Science of 'Muddling Through.'" *Public Opinion Review*, XIX (Fall, 1959), 79-88.

McClelland, Charles A. "General Systems Theory in International Relations." *Main Currents in Modern Thought*, XII (November, 1955), 27-34.

Morse, Edward L. "The Transformation of Foreign Policies: Moderniza-

## American Defense Policy

tion, Interdependence, and Externalization." *World Politics,* XXII (April, 1970), 371-392.

Raymond, Jack. "The Growing Threats of Our Military-Industrial Complex." *Harvard Business Review,* LI (May-June, 1968), 56-64.

Singer, J. David. "Threat Perception and the Armament-Tension Dilemma." *Journal of Conflict Resolution,* II (1958), 90-105.

Roche, John P. "Can a Free Society Fight a Limited War?" *The New Leader,* 21 October 1968, pp. 6-11.

Rusk, Dean. "The President." *Foreign Affairs,* XXXVII (April, 1960), 353-369.

Schlesinger, Arthur M. "Our Presidents: A Rating by Seventy-Five Historians." *New York Times Magazine,* 29 July 1962, pp. 12 ff.

Schneider, Ronald M. "Guatemala: An Aborted Communist Takeover." *Studies on the Soviet Union: The Anatomy of Communist Takeovers,* XI (1971), 516-535.

Scowcroft, Brent. "Deterrence and Strategic Superiority." *Orbis,* XIII (Summer, 1969), 435-454.

Schulman, Marshall D. "Recent Soviet Foreign Policy: Some Patterns in Retrospect." *Journal of International Affairs,* XXII, 1 (1968), 26-47.

Shoup, David M., and James Donovan. "The New American Militarism." *Atlantic,* April, 1969, pp. 51-56.

Snyder, Glenn H. "Balance of Power in the Missile Age." *Journal of International Affairs,* XIV, 1 (1960), 21-34.

Symington, Stuart. "Where the Missile Gap Went." *The Reporter,* 15 February 1962, pp. 21-23.

Whalen, Richard J. "The Shifting Equation of Nuclear Defense." *Fortune,* 1 June 1967, pp. 85 ff.

Wohlstetter, Albert. "The Delicate Balance of Terror." *Foreign Affairs,* XXXVII (January, 1959), 209-234.

Wolfers, Arnold. "The Pole of Power and the Pole of Indifference. *World Politics,* IV (October, 1951), 39-63.

Yarmolinsky, Adam. "Bureaucratic Structures and Political Outcomes." *Journal of International Affairs,* XXIII (1969), 225-235.

———. "The Military Establishment (or How Political Problems Became Military Problems)." *Foreign Policy,* I (Winter, 1970-71), 78-97.

# INDEX

Adams, Sherman: on the policy of the "long pull," 33-34, 37; on Eisenhower's contribution as President, 59-60

Air Force, U. S.: plans for nuclear war under Truman administration, 33; successfully tests Thor IRBM, 51; and Sputnik, 56; War College of, 85; Academy of, 87; missile program of, 51, 113-114; and general war capabilities, 119-120, 217; B-70 bomber, 125-126, 202, 216; and "bomber gap" controversy, 127, 212; and intelligence "leaks" to press, 136, 273; intelligence on Soviet missile capabilities, 136, 273; B-36 bomber controversy with Navy, 212; Kennedy seeks increase in 1952 budget for, 231

Almond, Gabriel: 148

Alsop, Joseph and Stewart: as "popularizers," 17, 167, 274; on the "herd instinct" of Washington Press corps, 146-148; as defense advocates, 159-162; cited in Congressional debate, 217; as proponents of general war capabilities, 174

American Federation of Labor-Congress of Industrial Organizations (AFL-CIO): and Sputnik, 59

Americans for Democratic Action (ADA): and Kennedy, 232

Anderson, Jack: as critic of Eisenhower defense policies, 127, 162

Arends, Leslie: 215

Arms race behavior: threat perceptions and, 4; interlocking nature of, 4-6; uncertainties concerning enemy capabilities and intentions, 4-6; "action-reaction syndrome" and, 5, 7, 8; counterforce and counterinsurgency,

8; and "flexible response" doctrine, 16

Army, U. S.: Congressional pressure to maintain 900,000-man force level floor, 7, 207; budget allowances for under Truman administration, 33; and Jupiter IRBM, 51, 215; fares worst of three services under "long pull," 54ff.; satellite and missile program of, 54, 114; and doctrine of "massive retaliation," 55, 116; frustrations over share of Sputnik budgetary dividend, 55; recent image of, 70; War College of, 85; U. S. Military Academy (West Point), 86-87, 88, 89; Nike-Zeus missile defense system of, 112; and doctrine of limited war, 118, 137-139; manpower level of, 119; Symington and, 131-132; research and development program of, 133; and news "leaks" to press, 135-136

Baldwin, Hansen W.: on limited war and the "missile gap," 164-165, 167, 274

Barnet, Richard J.: 72, 76

Boulding, Kenneth: on "reaction processes" and international politics, 4

Bradley, Omar N.: 36

Bridges, Styles: 214

Brodie, Bernard: as a "popularizer," 17, 179-182

Bruckner, Wilber: 106, 112, 118, 123

Bundy, McGeorge: on the foreign policy making process, 4; cited for militarism, 76; as advisor to President Kennedy, 248

# Index

Bureaucracy: reciprocal relationship with legislative branch, 13; process of "legislating" defense policy, 14; conflicts within spill over into field of executive-legislative relations, 15; parochialism of, 15; and inflation, 29; and the press, 152

Burke, Arleigh M.: admits parochialism, 23; on limited war, 56, 108, 114-115, 119, 120, 128, 213-214; appointment to Cuba Study Group, 249

Burns, Arthur F.: as economic advisor to Eisenhower, 30

Bush, Vannevar: 110

Case, Clifford: 214

Case, Francis: 216

Central Intelligence Agency (CIA): intelligence estimate of Soviet missile capabilities, 136; and overthrow of Arbenz regime in Guatemala, 267

Chavez, Dennis: as chairman of Senate Defense Appropriations Subcommittee, 131, 167, 204-205, note 224

Church, Frank: makes keynote speech at 1960 Democratic National Convention, 236

Clifford, Clark: and Symington, 211-212

Cohen, Bernard C.: quoted on the influence of the communications media, 146

Cold war: America's conception of, 2, 228, 277; Eisenhower's perception of, 44; U. S. impatience with, 71; ascendancy of national security policy during, 77; and the 1960 election, 228-229

Communism: mythical nature of bloc, 2; as threat to U. S., 27; indirect threat to U. S. economic system, 33; threat of internalized by U. S., 36; threat of to periphery of "free world," 39; and "massive retaliation," 41; machinations of, 44-45; containment of, 103; balance of power with, 160-161, 229, 244; and Leninist concept of "relations of forces," 185-186; and Asia, 231; missile menace of, 241; as threat to Third World, 245, 252ff.; Kennedy perception of upon taking office, 246ff.;

proclivity for "salami tactics," 253; post-Sputnik offensive of, 253; and Guatemala, 266-267

Congress, U. S.: and civilian control of the military, 13; power of appropriations and defense policy, 15, 94, 129, 132, 201ff., 265, 271-173, 275-276; appellate function of, 15, 129ff., 272-273, 275-276; as opponent of the executive, 18, 93, 128, 156, 201-203, 275; viewed by Eisenhower as force for the "garrison state," 36; and Sputnik, 58-59, 109; and military professionalism, 90; budgetary process and, 101, 102ff., 129, 132, 204, 271ff., 275-276; and defense economy, 105, 109; alternative defense policies of, 116, 200-202, 272-273; exploits differences between President and Pentagon, 129ff., 272-273; testimony of military chieftains before as a weapon of influence, 133ff., 273; dependence upon the press, 148-149, 274; and strategic theorists, 176; influence of the press upon, 162, 166ff.; general influence on defense policy considered, 201ff.; interaction with "innovators" and "popularizers," 203ff.; as a lobbyist for higher defense spending, 203ff., 205, 275-276; intensification of partisanship within, 203, 205, 207ff.; divergence of perspective among the committees of, 203ff.; partisan vs. dogmatist roles in, 208ff.; inexorably drawn into defense policy debate, 265

Constitution, U. S.: and defense policy, 13-14, 83, 93, 265

Conventional war: Kennedy administration decisions concerning, 1; and the ability to wage war in Southeast Asia, 2-3; increase in capabilities for under Kennedy administration, 3; and technological determinism, 7; Congressional policy toward, 7-8; Eisenhower and, 7-8, 37-40, 118; reallocation of military expenditures away from under Eisenhower administration, 37; Dulles on, 40; Army position on, 55, 118-119, 134-135; Gavin on, 106, 137-138; Taylor on, 108; strategic build-up and, 137-138, 275; Hanson Baldwin on, 164-165; theorists on, 176ff., 275; House Appropriations Committee and airlift capacity for, 202; and House Armed

# Index

Laird, Melvin R.: as defense partisan, 213

LeMay, Curtis: 114, 131

Lemnitzer, Lyman L.: attacks "massive retaliation," 55; as Army Chief of Staff, 132, 205; as Chairman of JCS under Kennedy, 248

Lens, Sidney: 72

Limited war: lack of U. S. preparedness for and non-intervention, 3; build-up in capabilities for and Vietnam, 3; counterinsurgency and counterforce, 8; lessons of Korea for Eisenhower, 34, 168; Army pressures and, 55-56; Navy and, 114-115; and Flood, 116; underlying assumptions of, 117-118; and policy of deterrence, 119, 137-138, 275; Gavin and, 137-138; strategic build-up and, 137-138, 206, 275; Hanson Baldwin on, 164-165; theorists on, 176ff., 275; House Appropriations Committee rejects Eisenhower policy toward, 202; and "missile gap," 206; Senate Defense Appropriations Subcommittee rejects Eisenhower policy toward, 206; President Kennedy on, 247ff.; and assured superiority, 275

Lincoln, George A.: affects military education system, 86-88; views on defense policy, 87-88

Lincoln Summer Study Group: 160

McCarthy, Joseph R.: and the Kennedys, 232

McClelland, Charles A.: and open systems approach to international politics, 10-11

McElroy, Neil H.: announces effort to expedite missile program in wake of Sputnik, 51; desires to accelerate missile program within budgetary limits, 110, 111, 114; endorses policy of strategic parity, 116; presents signed approval of JCS to Congress, 128; charged by Mahon with tailoring intelligence estimates to policy, 206; attacked by Flood, 209; defends "long pull," note 223

McNamara, Robert S.: quoted on causes of U. S. strategic build-up, 5-6; admits mythical nature of "missile gap," 8; cited for militarism by

Shoup, 76; as Defense Secretary, 176, 177, 178, 200, 249; criticized by Ellender on implications of "flexible response," 211

McWilliams, Wilson C.: quoted on military intervention in democratic political systems, 81

Macmillan, Harold: 52

Madariaga, Salvador de: 102

Mahon, George H.: 166, 205, note 224

Mansfield, Mike: 214

Marine Corps, U. S.: Congressional pressure to maintain force level floor at 200,000, 7-8

Massive retaliation: shift away from under Kennedy administration, 1; announced by Dulles, 40; criticized, 41; as selective retaliation, 41-42; and deterrence, 46; affect of Sputnik on, 53

Medaris, John B.: as an "innovator," 17, 91, 273; and Sputnik, 55, 113; and the education variable in military dissention, 89; critical of the Eisenhower administration, 127

Militarism: consideration and critique of the concept, 79ff.

Military establishment: differences in educational experience within, 18, 84-88; professionalism and careerism, 18, 81, 89, 91, 92, 94, 271; contingency plans for under Truman administration, 33; Dulles on foreign policy and, 42-43; part of larger coalition dissatisfied with administration policy, 54; thirst for funds, 56-57; recent image of, 70ff., 82-83; divisions within, 75-76, 83-84, 93, 165, 175; domination by civilians, 77; intervention in budgetary process, 81-82, 100ff., 270; causes of dissention within, 83ff., 100, 270-271; changes in the nature of the profession, 85, 90, 92-93, 271; as a technical bureaucracy, 92-93, 122, 271; Eisenhower policy toward, 93-94, 100-101, 270; behavior of during "lean years" as opposed to the "Pearl Harbor syndrome," 101; inter-service rivalries, 101ff., 114, 121-122, 272, 273; alliances with executive and legislative branches, 101ff., 271-273; Congress fails to adopt coherent policy to-

# Index

# Index

Kennedy, 250; as advisor to President Kennedy, 254-255

Teller, Edward: 110

Thomas, Charles S.: 108

Tocqueville, Alexis de: on the military spirit of a people, 72

Truman, Harry S.: projected deficit for FY1954, 31; and Eisenhower policy of the "long pull," 33; defense policies of, 36-37, 38; quoted on ideal of political neutrality for military, 84; supports Symington for President, 221; attacked by Kennedy on China policy, 231; and the Middle East, 267-268

Twining, Nathan F.: on the "bomber gap," 107; as chairman of the JCS, 117; as proponent of airpower, note 142; differences in perspective as Air Force Chief of Staff and JCS Chairman, 125-126; and Chavez, 205

Tyrrell, C. Merton: 72

Union of Soviet Socialist Republics (U. S. S. R.): and Sputnik, 1, 47-48, 272; and cold war confrontation with the U. S., 2; strategic build-up in, 2, 136, 154; arms race rivalry with the U. S., 4, 110, 111, 114, 136, 154, 163, 206; capacity and intentions concerning strategic weapons deployment, 5-6, 136, 137-139, 154; perceived missile threat of, 7, 105, 154, 157-158, 160-161, 162-163, 164-165, 177ff.; Kennedy and, 8; domestic influences on foreign policy of, 12; question of use of nuclear weapons against, 33; mutual security against, 40; and "massive retaliation," 41-42; non-military nature of challenge posed by, 42; thrusts burden of arms on U. S., 52; deterrence against, 46, 105, 114, 137-139, 177ff., 206; ICBM capability of, 48-49, 50, 105, 114, 136, 137-139, 154, 161; space feat humiliates U. S., 52; and the Middle East, 52, 151, 154, 269; recent image of, 71; as long term threat, 104; anticipated liberalization within, 103; U. S. intelligence estimates on capabilities of, 136; U. S. tendency to underrate,

160; quest for absolute security, 189; machinations of and decline of U. S. power, 229; rise in power of since 1949, 230; assault of on periphery of free world, 230-231, 152ff.; Kennedy perception of upon taking office, 247ff.

United Automobile Workers (UAW): and Sputnik, 58

United Nations: 40, 269

U. S. Chamber of Commerce: and Sputnik, 58

Vagts, Alfred: quoted on militarism, 77

Vietnam: Kennedy administration escalation of Eisenhower commitment to, 2-3; Kennedy and, 2-4, 255-256, 277; U. S. involvement in as the fruition of dynamic leadership, 25; disillusionment over U. S. intervention in and historical revisionism, 71; large-scale commitment to, 71

Vinson, Carl: 207, 215

Von Braun, Wernher: 113, 162

Wallich, Henry C.: as Eisenhower economic advisor, 30

Warner, Lloyd: quoted on the backgrounds of military and civilian bureaucrats, 92

White, Theodore H.: quoted on the nature of American presidential election campaigns, 228

White, Thomas D.: as Air Force Chief of Staff, 56, 113, 120, 123-124, 128-129, 130

Whitten, Jamie L.: as pre-economy dogmatist, 166, 208, 209, 215; fear of vested interests in defense spending, 209-210

Wilson, Charles E.: praised by N. Y. Times before Sputnik, 47; and the policy of the "long pull," 103ff., 108; fear of vested interests in military spending, 104; and the "bomber gap," 105

Wohlstetter, Albert: as a "popularizer," 177-179